ECHOES OF GLORY

TEXAS A&M UNIVERSITY PRESS College Station

ECHOES OF GLORY

HISTORIC MILITARY SITES ACROSS TEXAS

THOMAS E. ALEXANDER and DAN K. UTLEY

First edition

This paper meets the requirements
of ANSI/NISO Z39.48–1992
(Permanence of Paper).
Binding materials have been chosen
for durability. Manufactured in China by
Everbest Printing Co. through FCI Print Group ♾ ♻

Library of Congress
Cataloging-in-Publication Data
Alexander, Thomas E., 1931– author.
Echoes of glory : historic military sites
across Texas / Thomas E. Alexander and
Dan K. Utley.—First edition.
pages cm
Includes bibliographical references and index.
ISBN 978-1-62349-337-0 (flexbound : alk. paper)—
ISBN 978-1-62349-338-7 (e-book)
1. Military bases—Texas. 2. Fortifications—Texas.
3. Battlefields—Texas. 4. Historic sites—Texas.
5. Texas—History, Military. 6. Texas—Antiquities.
I. Utley, Dan K., author. II. Title.
F387.A525 2015
355.009764—dc23
2015013401

Dedicated to CAPY ALEXANDER, *for braving the wilds of remote Texas to take photographs and for keeping Tom from becoming hopelessly lost in the modern-day maze of technologically driven research; and to* DEBBY DAVIS UTLEY, *who, throughout this project and others involving this writing team, never once said, "You can't play with Tom anymore."*

CONTENTS

Superintendent's Residence
Financial Agent's Residence
Outside of Walls West of Penitentiary, Huntsville Texas

ACKNOWLEDGMENTS

It requires the kind and capable assistance of many individuals to make a study as vast as *Echoes of Glory: Historic Military Sites across Texas* a reality. Space limitations and imperfect memories, however, render it impossible to name them all. With apologies but also thanks to anyone we may have inadvertently omitted in this regard, we nevertheless offer here our sincere appreciation to those we recall as particularly helpful to us in our search for little known facts and figures.

Buddy Garza of the Texas Historical Commission (THC) took us on an extensive tour of both the San Sabá Presidio and the site of its doomed mission, and H. Charles Eckart of Mason gave extensive assistance in uncovering esoteric facts about his city's Fort Mason. Maria Watson Pfeiffer provided excellent background material about the former U.S. arsenal at San Antonio, and David Keller of the Center for Big Bend Studies at Alpine enthusiastically shared his knowledge of John Bullis's Camp at Meyers Spring. In addition, Dr. J. Tillapaugh, a founding faculty member at the University of Texas–Permian Basin, provided us with many unknown facts about Camp Marfa/Fort D. A. Russell.

Glenn Williford, of Alpine and Chihuahua, Mexico, is arguably the greatest advocate of Johnson's Ranch. His master's thesis on the subject provided invaluable information on this little known gem. Melleta R. Bell, director of the Archives of the Big Bend at Sul Ross State University, and Jerry Garza, her able assistant, aided us greatly on all things regarding the Big Bend region, just as they have done over the years. THC commissioner Tom Perini, our valued friend and colleague, took time away from his popular Perini Ranch Steak House in Buffalo Gap to conduct a tour of all that is left of Abilene's Camp Barkeley before serving us a delectable lunch. Dale E. Cartee opened Abilene's 12th Division

Museum after hours to provide a balanced view of the city's all but forgotten World War II–era Camp Barkeley. Janis Test at the Abilene Public Library provided reams of material about both Camp Barkeley and Fort Phantom Hill.

Rick Pratt, director of the Port Aransas Museum, shared tales of the coastal area during World War II and opened the museum's warehouse so we could see a model of the gun emplacement that was nestled in the city's Gulf Coast dunes during the war. Jordan Alexander Leggett carried her camera into those dunes so that Grandpa Tom could stay safely on the beach below, keeping a watchful eye on the beer cooler.

Three very special people enthusiastically and selflessly shared their passion for history, especially as it relates to some compelling and complex but generally lesser-known military sites. Those individuals are Larry Sanders, an expert on the Atlas ICBM program in Texas; Mac Woodward, director of the Sam Houston Memorial Museum in Huntsville; and historian and friend Martha Hartzog, who helped provide important access to Daughters of the American Revolution papers related to veterans buried in Texas. Hartzog would be quick to note that she was only part of a DAR team that helped in that regard, so we add our thanks to Pamela Rouse Wright, state regent, Texas Society DAR. The appreciation for the past exhibited by these individuals is contagious, and their generosity to fellow researchers is remarkable.

Equally helpful and generous was Jonathan Gerland of The History Center in Diboll, an esteemed colleague and valued friend who has worked for many years to make all manner of history accessible to the public. He is an inspiration not only in that regard but also because of his personal drive to go where history happened even if it requires him to explore remote stretches of the Neches River by canoe. Also of special note is the assistance of David M. Gaddis of Austin, who suggested the topic of Fort Ewell, a short-lived installation near his hometown of Cotulla. Who knew when author Utley and former banker Gaddis were freshmen roommates at the University of Texas in another century that their friendship would someday be recognized in a book?

Finally, our thanks go to all the helpful folks at the Texas Historical Commission who worked on this project with us for more than three years. Among them, state archeologist Pat Mercado-Allinger and office manager Lillie Thompson deserve special recognition for preserving all of the agency's vast material on our many sites in one easily accessible place, as does Greg Smith, who shared information from the application files of the National Register of Historic Places. With the marker program, special thanks go to Bob Brinkman, the state coordinator, and historian Sarah McCleskey, who provided copies of research files and other documentation for our review. And no recognition of the THC staff would be complete without mention of the agency's military historian, William A. McWhorter, for his enthusiastic assistance and encouragement, and Bratten Thomason, the History Programs Division director, for her capable leadership and also her valued friendship to former colleagues-turned-authors.

Without the assistance of all of these people and of others we have perhaps failed to mention, the stories of the once highly significant Texas military sites included in this book would have likely gone untold, their one-time glory faded into nothingness.

INTRODUCTION

This book is the second in a series of short studies of once important Texas military sites whose glory has faded with the obsolescence of their mission and the inexorable passage of time. The first volume, *Faded Glory: A Century of Forgotten Military Sites in Texas, Then and Now,* was published by Texas A&M University Press in 2012. In this subsequent work, the scope of research has been broadened to include, for example, a historically pivotal, eighteenth-century Spanish presidio, a forlorn frontier fort that should never have been built, and a tiny pre–Civil War cavalry outpost that was the proving ground for an astonishing number of young subalterns who would soon become generals in blue or gray. The book concludes with the bleak saga of a multimillion-dollar Cold War naval station on the Gulf of Mexico that was destined to fail long before it became fully operational.

Historians, both the professional variety and the ardent buffs, have been generous in their praise of our continuing efforts to rekindle public awareness of these now largely forgotten installations and sites. A few readers, however, have good-naturedly (at least for the most part) expressed some dismay that their favorite old military site was not included in the first book. "How in the world could you leave out Fort Spunky?" cried one, and "What about that skirmish at Adam's Hill?" asked another. "Why was that big Marine Corps air base on Eagle Mountain Lake omitted?" queried a crestfallen ex-leatherneck. Why not, indeed! Our measured response to every clearly heartfelt plaint was the simple but valid observation that the military history of Texas, which has spanned five centuries, has served to spawn more than enough raids, skirmishes, battles, presidios, forts, training camps, border incidents, and sprawling air bases to fill thousands of pages and multiple volumes.

One researcher of early U.S. Army fortifications, for example, estimated that at least five hundred such sites had been scattered across the Lone Star State over the years. Records show that, during World War I, nearly thirty military posts were in operation in Texas by the end of the conflict in 1918. Twenty-seven years later, during World War II, at least 110 such installations were operational, as were more than thirty prisoner-of-war camps. Add to that heady mix the countless recorded armed confrontations of varying intensity that flared up over the centuries, and the result is an impressive tally that all but defies comprehensive research. It thus becomes evident that the massive military experience in Texas through the years has shaped and colored the often blood-red rich tapestry that is the history of the state, not solely in terms of actual armed combat but socially, politically, and economically as well.

We are truly pleased that our readers have come forward to demonstrate their recognition of the importance of the military heritage of Texas by making it known that they, too, have favorite sites. As a direct result, some of their suggestions have been incorporated in the pages of this second volume. If only space had permitted, many others would have been covered as well. At any rate, a whole new collection of once vital military sites comes briefly back to life in the chapters that follow. The stories presented here are often of hardship and sacrifice, adventure and boredom, danger and bravery, and sometimes even downright stubbornness and stupidity. Each one is also about honor, love of country, and an unwavering dedication to duty and to flag—whatever flag might have prevailed at the time.

The glory of these now deserted sites is without doubt forever faded, if not completely gone in some cases. Their timeless historic legacy lives on, however, in the imagination of those students of the past who can still hear echoes of ruffling drums and the thrilling calls of long silent bugles.

Map by Molly O'Halloran

1 PRESIDIO DE SAN SABÁ
1752–1772

The Spanish transmitted the horse to Apachería, and through it, to the Comanches, and unhappily created the most fearsome light cavalry—the Plains Indians—the world had ever seen.
— T. R. Fehrenbach

The saga of the ancient Spanish presidio near the West Texas town of Menard holds more than enough dramatic elements to make it worthy of any modern-day screenwriter's attention. Violence, greed, international intrigue, and outright stupidity combine to create a unique tale of eighteenth-century Texas. Marauding Indians, treasure hunters, and even the ghostly presence of the legendary Jim Bowie add even more color to the story of this red stone ruin that was until the early twenty-first century little more than a misshapen and derelict monstrosity in the middle of a golf course. The story began when Spain's fifteenth-century claim to all of the so-called New World was challenged by her traditional enemies in Europe. Fully aware of the quantities of fabulous riches that early Spanish explorers discovered and then shipped across the Atlantic to their mother country, both France and England set about aggressively contesting Spanish rule in the Americas in order to garner for themselves a large share of the still untold treasures of the New World.

The Spanish colony of Texas, while not yet proven to be as rich as Mexico and other mineral-laden regions, was nevertheless ripe with legends and rumors that strongly hinted at immense quantities of gold and silver. Further, it was no secret that the New World teemed with a population of natives who could be forcibly "persuaded" to labor in any precious-metal mines yet to be excavated. Spain itself, understandably agitated by the growing international threat to what had become its major source of wealth, had also been progressively weakened by a series of military setbacks in Europe and by the destruction of its allegedly invincible armada by the English in 1588. Sensing literally a golden opportunity to fill its own coffers with New World riches, France launched an ambitious campaign in and around Texas, hoping to greatly diminish the magnitude of the Spanish presence and, if possible, bring it to an end altogether.

In addition to French incursions into its Texas colony, Spain had another and more immediate problem that cast a dark shadow across its domination of the land north of the Rio Bravo. The indigenous, albeit largely nomadic, people who had seemingly been pacified without difficulty by musket-wielding conquistadors, had suddenly developed new skills in the deadly art of war. By mastering the use of the horse, introduced into the New World by the Spaniards, the native tribesmen transformed themselves from easily subdued foot warriors into hard-riding and highly effective cavalrymen. Further, through the acquisition of captured Spanish armament and French-supplied weaponry, the Indians, fighting on their own familiar turf, soon proved to be more than a match for the now hapless invaders, who only recently had managed to defeat them almost at will. This relatively swift dramatic shift in military advantage might possibly have been eventually reversed by the Spanish had not yet another challenge to their dominance arisen. Newly mounted and effectively armed, other, even more warlike, tribes had migrated into Texas, pushing before them the passive tribes, who had yet to master fully the use of the horse or to abandon Stone Age weaponry completely in favor of the far more deadly guns purloined from their European conquerors.

With dangerously warlike Comanche cavalrymen surging into Texas from the north, apparently well armed by the French, who then openly threatened their claims to a once relatively secure domain, the Spanish appeared hard pressed to find a quick solution to their suddenly multifaceted problem. Unfortunately for the very future of Spanish Texas, the long-deliberated solution proved to be both futile and eventually fatal. Before the combined threat from the invading Comanche, their native allies, and the French came into play, Spain's only regional enemies were the Apache. The tribe, though stealthy and fearless, was by no means an easily conquered adversary, but it was at least less murderous than the totally ruthless Comanche hordes sweeping southward into Texas, bent on annihilating all who stood in their way in a desperate effort to retain their traditional way of life.

Recognizing that their chances for survival seemed limited in this now fiery crucible, which had been their traditional hunting ground for centuries, the Apache turned to the Spanish to protect them from the rampaging Comanche warriors. The Spanish, caught in a somewhat similar dilemma, chose to aid the relatively less vicious Apache in hopes of halting the violence that was crashing toward their domain. Making this decision at least a bit more palatable was that in agreeing to aid the Apache, that tribe might well desist in its long-lasting series of murderous raids against the Spanish town of San Antonio and other burgeoning sites of Western civilization. Coupled with the Spaniards' desires to halt both the Comanche invasion and the unpredictable Apache's predilection for sudden raids against their towns without either warning or mercy was the Europeans' lofty ambition to bring Christianity to the native population of the Americas. The combined stimuli of preservation and conversion put into play an ill-fated plan to expand the Spanish mission system westward to the vast and dangerous territory beyond the existing line of missions along the San Antonio River. Further, a successful new mission, located in that western expanse and well defended by a suitably fortified military installation, might also ensure safe passage for those who needed to travel to the already established missions in what would someday become the city of El Paso.

Thus, all of the important factors that made a new mission west of San Antonio desirable were soon in place. Yet, another alluring and positive aspect made the final decision even more appealing: the likely presence in the region of valuable deposits of silver, which, next to gold and godliness, was one of the principal overall quests of Spanish colonialism. With the discovery of what appeared to be a promising deposit of silver-bearing ore 130 miles northwest of the San Antonio missions, officials launched a search to find an acceptable site for the proposed mission in which to Christianize the Apache and seek the silver, as well as to build a presidio (military fort) to keep the natives' attention focused on their conversion and divert it from their innate tendencies to raid and pillage. The most likely site for this multipurpose endeavor came to be on the banks of the San Saba River close to the present-day city of Menard. Historical records indicate that until the time the Spaniards decided where to place their new outpost, they had made at least relatively logical decisions. The chosen site had good grass for pasturing horses and other livestock, rich earth for planting life-supporting crops, virgin woods filled with game, and a highly reliable source of clear and potable water for man and beast. It was also close enough to San Antonio to be easily supplied, yet distant enough to provide a convenient stepping stone en route to the missions on the Rio Bravo to the west. With the site determined, however, the Spaniards in effect sowed the seeds of destruction for not only the planned mission and presidio but also the empire's presence on the entire Great Plains north and west of the home-base city of San Antonio. These seeds were borne by the age-old chaos that stemmed from dual responsibility and the absence of a clearly defined individual who was in overall command.

In the case of the Spanish endeavor on the banks of the San Saba, the chaotic situation seemed almost comical in its extreme. To begin, the presidio operated under the direction of the New World's viceroy, Conde de Revilla Gigedo, with offices in distant Mexico City. As if to remove any doubt about who was in command, albeit from a quite remote location, the presidio came to bear the viceroy's name. The mission, on the other hand, benefited from private funding by Pedro Romero de Terreros, a member of one of Mexico's wealthiest and most influential families. To ensure that his personally underwritten mission was overseen by a trusted ally, Don Pedro entrusted its oversight to his cousin, Father Alonso Giraldo de Terreros. The viceroy, likewise eager to ensure that his presidio remained in hands both capable and loyal, named Col. Diego Ortiz Parrilla as its commander. Colonel Parrilla, it seems, was a somewhat self-centered senior officer who, unfortunately for the success of the whole undertaking, never envisioned a bright future for the mission he was to protect. As a result, Father Terreros and Colonel Parrilla moved steadily along a course that led to a major and ultimately fatal collision.

After many heated arguments between priest and soldier, the curious decision was reached to place the mission some four miles down the river from the presidio, which had the responsibility of protecting it from any Indian raids. The announced reason for this remarkable bit of illogic was that the soldiers stationed at the presidio might well be a bad influence on any Apache converts who sought both conversion to Christianity and protection from the Comanche, who were determined to drive them from Texas regardless of whether they were newly converted Christians. Every indication is that the Apache, in beseeching the Spanish to bring one of their missions to the natives' turf, had their own preservation much more prominently in mind than any conversion to the white man's religion, which meant little, if anything, to them. If those white men were also willing to distribute food and gifts to them in addition to offering shelter from the marauding Comanche and their allies, so much the better.

The simple fact is that the mission on the San Saba proved unsuccessful in convincing the Apache to accept the Catholic faith. Except for passing by the mission on their way north to hunt buffalo in what was rapidly becoming known as Comanchería, the tribe stopped just long enough to accept some gifts and food before moving on. If they survived their excursion into Comanche land, the hunters might linger for a time on their way back to their traditional winter range. Laden with gifts and full of mission food, the tribe, often numbering in the thousands, would soon move on, leaving behind a disappointed Father Terreros and his two fellow priests, who had thought this time for sure the itinerant Apache had come to stay permanently at the mission. While the padres waited in vain for the wandering Apache to become their permanent guests, the presidio charged with protecting the mission neared completion. Its walls were of jacal construction, utilizing tall vertical poles stuck into the ground and with dried mud used as a form of plaster between them. Roofs were of thatched grass, and floors were of packed earth.

On average, three to four hundred soldiers, some of them with their families, occupied the fortification. Daily life revolved around merely surviving on the harsh and unforgiving frontier. Water from the nearby San Saba River provided the presidio with one necessary aspect of survival, while fish from that same river and game from the woods along the shore supplied another. Infrequent supply trains from San Antonio brought the men and their families the other basic necessities of livelihood. As would be true for countless other soldiers who manned similar outposts in the decades ahead, service at the presidio proved to be essentially a matter of fighting boredom rather than any living human foe. Soldiers within the presidio were not, for the most part, professional warriors in any sense of the term. Most lacked training, and more than a few were conscripts, owing to the belief that a large quantity of raw manpower would likely impress the native warriors more than would a smaller detachment of well-trained professional soldiers, most of whom busied themselves elsewhere fighting Spain's more important wars back on the European continent.

Even though clear evidence continued to show that France had its own colonizing eye firmly on Texas and perhaps even on treasure-laden Mexico itself, the men in the presidio could only continue to wait until the Comanche and their allies, more visible foes, made a move against the Apache, then considered to be at least a friendlier tribe. After more than a year of waiting for the long-anticipated attack to come from the north, the presidio's soldiers' boredom came to an abrupt halt. On March 16, 1758, some fifteen hundred to two thousand Comanche, Tonkawa, and Tejas Indians in war paint surrounded the mission, obviously bent on doing serious mischief. Claiming to be interested in attacking only any Apache that might be around and insisting that they, too, were friendly to the priests inside the mission, the unwelcome intruders bided their time. Spurning the gifts offered by the priests, the raiders finally attacked the mission itself, killing livestock and desecrating religious items, and at the cessation of their ransacking, they set the entire mission complex afire. Of the three priests serving at the mission, only one survived the brutal attack. In total, eight occupants of the mission were killed, and all of the buildings burned to the ground.

As a result of the founding priests' earlier insistence that the presidio, charged with protecting the mission, be placed far from the religious complex, the soldiers had no opportunity to intercede quickly and possibly halt the massacre. After destroying the mission, the raiders launched a half-hearted foray against the presidio itself, although fewer than sixty soldiers manned the flimsy fortification. The timely arrival of Spanish reinforcements with bugles blaring and drums beating discouraged the attackers, who withdrew, their primary goal having been more than satisfactorily attained. The consequences of destruction proved manifold. By befriending the uncooperative Apache, the Spanish reluctantly recognized they had in turn earned the lasting enmity of the Comanche. That enmity eventually extended to all white-skinned usurpers who dared enter Comanchería. The bitter conflict thus created between the two cultures lasted for the next 120 years. In effect, the burning of the mission and the inability of the presidio to prevent it, or even successfully retaliate because of it, marked the beginning of the decline of all Spanish influence in Texas and on the entire Great Plains. There would be no flourishing Spanish cities and no powerfully armed chain of military installations stretching westward from the presidio on the San Saba, and no Spanish trade route would ever connect the settlements on the San Antonio River with the ones on the Rio Bravo.

Colonel Parrilla, of course, could not foresee these dire consequences. Perhaps to mask his failure to save the mission and gain the favor of his commanding officers in Mexico City, he set about forming an expedition to pursue and heavily punish those who had burned the mission. The pursuit part of his plan worked out well, but the punishment phase backfired dramatically. The raiders, minus the Comanche, who had withdrawn to their own domain far to the north, had returned to their base camp on the Red River following their successful attack. When Parrilla's small, untrained army arrived at the camp days later, they found a sturdy fortification facing them rather than the tepees they had expected. The

Indians, armed with up-to-date weapons supplied by the French, quickly and thoroughly trounced the Spanish attackers, who fled back to their presidio, while images of the French flag they believed they had seen in the Indians' encampment continued to flutter in their memories.

The Spanish, outgunned, outridden, and outnumbered by their various enemies, whether domestic or foreign, remained determined to give their presidio one last opportunity to reassert the crown's claim to Texas and its vast frontier. The jacal walls came down in favor of a stone stockade, replete with two impressive observation towers. Workers added fifty rooms inside the stockade, along with a blacksmith shop, a bakery, and an armory. By 1761, the presidio had a distinctly European look as it rose on the banks of the San Saba. It also had a new name that denoted its official endorsement by King Carlos III of Spain—the Real Presidio de San Sabá. The Comanche, likely totally unimpressed by the new royal title, nevertheless remained wary of the artillery that subsequently boomed forth from the towers. Attacks against the new fortification consequently became sporadic, and most of them were mounted instead on incoming supply trains or hunting parties trapped outside its walls.

In 1772, however, the Spanish surrendered to the inevitable. Unable to supply and support their remote outpost, the gates of the presidio swung shut, and the soldiers abandoned the post to await its uncertain fate. As unfounded rumors of the presence of silver in the region continued to swirl, prospectors frequently arrived and set up camp in the ruins of the old fort. Among these were the Bowie brothers, James and Rezin, who visited twice. The name "Bouie," perhaps carved by one of the men, can still be seen inscribed on the presidio's gatepost. The preferred assumption has long been that Jim, destined to die in the Alamo five years later, made the inscription. The different spelling of his name matches the one he had earlier used to sign the church register at San Antonio's San Fernando Cathedral on the day of his marriage there to Ursula Veramendi.

For many years after the Spanish and the Bowie boys had departed, the presidio continued to decay. The establishment of the

In 1936, the ruins of Presidio de San Sabá, shown here in 2007, were somewhat stabilized but incorrectly reconstituted by state and federal agencies. ***The Alexander Collection***

town of Menard in the late nineteenth century was in fact the cause of its most telling destruction. Seeking the already cut stone for their homes and businesses, the newly arrived townspeople carted off tons of the stone blocks that had managed to fend off the Comanche. In 1936, the Works Progress Administration (WPA) undertook an ambitious plan to rebuild at least part of the historic fortification. In a project mandated by the Texas legislature and funded by the federal government, some of the walls and one of the towers rose once again from the prairie. Praised by some and derided by others, the partial and unauthentic reproduction stood untouched for more than seventy years. The town's country club

A 2012 reconstruction of the Presidio de San Sabá did much to establish the integrity of the nearly three-hundred-year-old Spanish colonial site near Menard. ***The Alexander Collection.***

eventually opened just yards away from the rebuilt walls, and golfers occasionally found it necessary to retrieve errant balls sliced or hooked into what remained of the stone ramparts.

Despite the efforts of a local group of preservationists and professional archeologists who recognized the site's historic legacy, the rebuilt walls again began to crack and sometimes crash to the ground. In 2009, however, a combined federal and state effort resulted in the thorough investigation and identification of the presidio's original dimensions. Restoration crews stabilized existing walls, and under the direction of the Texas Historical Commission and Texas Tech University archeologists, researchers recreated an authentic footprint of the historic site. Modern changes to the site included construction of an interpretive center to inform visitors of the significant value of the old ruin.

To be sure, the presidio on the San Saba will never prove to be as popular a tourist attraction as the chapel at the Alamo, although built at nearly the same time. Lacking the touristic lure of San Antonio's Riverwalk and the shrinelike status of the Alamo building, the remote presidio is unlikely to ever attract even a small percentage of the more than 2.5 million visitors who flock to San Antonio each year to view the birthplace of Texas liberty. It is difficult to stand by the walls of the old presidio, however, and not be moved by what once transpired there and what glorious dream of empire died there. The massacre at the mission, on grounds only miles away, set in motion the end of an important era in Texas, which in turn evolved into the state as it is known today. There was, of course, no cataclysmic battle fought there that would inspire countless generations of Texans; nonetheless, the site, now at least partially redefined, stands as a silent monument to the ever-changing tides of Texas history.

LOCATION: The presidio is on US Highway 190 less than two miles northwest of downtown Menard.

ACCESS: The redeveloped site is open to the public and features an interpretive center. The mission site is located approximately four miles east of Menard on FM 2092. It is on private land with no public access, but an official Texas Historical Marker is close to the site on the highway.

SOURCES

Anderson, Eugene R. "The Missing Mine of the Mission San Sabá." Welling, Kent, UK: Author, 1985.

Fehrenbach, T. R. *Lone Star: A History of Texas and the Texans.* New York: Macmillan, 1968.

Hindes, V. Kay, Mark R. Wolf, Grant D. Hall, and Kathleen Gilmore. *The Rediscovery of Santa Cruz de San Sabá: A Mission for the Apache in Spanish Texas.* Austin: Texas Historical Foundation, 1995.

Weddle, Robert S. *The San Sabá Mission: Spanish Pivot in Texas.* College Station: Texas A&M University Press, 1999.

2 FORT TERÁN
1831–1834

Early in 1832 I went to Fort Teran [sic], situated on the Neches in what is now Tyler County. Here Col. Peter Ellis Bean was stationed with a few Mexican soldiers. — George W. Smyth

---

As the Neches River cuts its way south through the Piney Woods of Deep East Texas, primarily through shallow-sided sandy ridges, it is momentarily, but markedly, diverted eastward as it comes up against a landform known as the Kisatchie Wold, a rocky escarpment that reaches from western Louisiana well into Texas. The wold not only redirects the river flow at that point but historically also provided a dependable, high-ridge, east-west route through the dense woods, so Native Americans and later settlers utilized it to avoid nearby swamps and flood-prone bottomlands. Elevations there reach four hundred to five hundred feet above sea level, forming a distinct geological break between the lower coastal plains to the south and the gently rolling hills to the north. At this break of the Neches, where the river flows east, is the juncture of four counties: Angelina, Jasper, Polk, and Tyler. It is in the uppermost and virtually inaccessible reaches of the latter that the exact location of a Mexican fort, in existence for only a brief time, still remains buried, unyielding as yet to archeologists and historians.

One of those historians diligently pursuing the story is Jonathan Gerland, executive director of The History Center in Diboll, Texas. In a 2011 article in the center's publication, *The Pine Bough,* he observed, "Here, at this once strategic river crossing, Fort Terán was built by a government fearful of losing its territory not to an invading army, but to immigrants from America seeking a better life in Texas." Although the story of Fort Terán is short lived, the

A bend of the Neches River, in what may be the general vicinity of Fort Terán, shows the rocky terrain of the Kisatchie Wold.
Photo by Jonathan Gerland, Lufkin.

broader context of its existence goes back much further and includes a mercurial and contested boundary between two great nations—nations, it might be noted, that changed considerably over time. The dispute stems from the colonial claims of Spain and France as they vied to sustain and even increase their influence on the North American continent. Even as France gave way to the United States via the Louisiana Purchase of 1803, and as Mexico replaced Spain through revolution in 1821, the international border remained in dispute, unsettled even by the Adams-Onís Treaty of 1819. As a result, a land without viable governmental authority developed between the Arroyo Hondo (present-day Calcasieu River) to the east and the Sabine River to the west. Principal outposts that flanked the so-called no man's land were Natchitoches, in American Louisiana, and Nacogdoches, in Mexican Texas. The presence of military forces in those two locales, however, failed to check the porosity of the border, and, as Gerland notes, American settlers began moving westward into the East Texas woodlands, traveling along routes such as the Coushatta Trace and the Nacogdoches-Orcoquisac Road, immigration routes that crossed the Neches near the site of Fort Terán.

The true strategic value of the stream crossing came into play soon after the Mexican government commissioned a survey of the area in the late 1820s. The leader of the expedition was José Manuel Rafael Simcón de Mier y Terán. Born in Mexico City in 1789 and educated at the College of Mines, Mier y Terán brought an analytical approach to the military and political endeavors he subsequently pursued. A member of Mexico's first congress, he also became a brigadier general in the army and served as military minister for both war and the navy. His background, coupled with his demonstrated loyalty to the government, made him an ideal choice for the survey of Mexico's northeastern territory. Although Mier y Terán's party formed in part for scientific purposes, utilizing the services of specialists such as a mineralogist, a cartographer, a botanist, and a zoologist, the underlying purpose was to report on the state of affairs in the frontier area too often overlooked by the Mexican government. The timing of the expedition was critical to an analysis of the successes or failures of organized colonial development afforded to Anglo-American empresarios such as Stephen F. Austin only a few years earlier.

Mier y Terán's boundary expedition left Mexico City late in 1827 and arrived in Nacogdoches, via San Felipe, in June the following year. From there, his party made forays into the surrounding territory and compiled information until January 1829, when it began the journey back to the capital. During his time in East Texas, the general grew to appreciate the rugged country despite the heat, heavy rainfall, and ubiquitous swarming insects that dogged his travels. He also came to appreciate the determination and perseverance of those isolated pockets of American settlers who struggled to carve out a sustainable existence against the odds, both political and geographical. These were frontier squatters, backwoods illegal aliens who crossed the border seeking to better their lives, albeit in a wild and untamed land not yet suitable even for marginal development. Even the trails that crossed through the densest parts of the region were little more than narrow paths quickly overgrown by vegetation in the warmer months.

What Mier y Terán discovered during his time in East Texas was that in many ways the land was by then more culturally American than Mexican. American immigrants far outnumbered Mexican citizens and, legally admitted or not, had begun to establish their own institutions, including schools. Such developments were clear indicators to him that the government had to respond quickly to check the transmigration and to assert some governmental authority in the region. Otherwise, the Texas he had grown to love would be lost forever. His findings, however well intentioned, given his commission and his own personal feelings, nevertheless set the stage for what would eventually be a path of no return toward revolution. And along that path was a small isolated outpost on the Neches River that remains largely forgotten to this day. Had circumstances in the course of events that ensued been different, its name might have lingered longer in historical memory.

Mier y Terán's findings quickly fueled his government's concerns over the issue of how to handle the Texas question. As a result, the majority reactions soon outgrew any consideration of a more moderate approach to the colonization experiment and resulted in the Law of April 6, 1830, which became a flashpoint for dissent among the Anglo settlements. Multilayered and focused in its approach, the law limited further immigration into Texas, curtailed the introduction of slaves into the region, and nullified existing colonization contracts. It also called for the establishment of customhouses and an increased military presence, both in existing outposts and in a series of new fortifications that would, in effect, hopefully address the border issue while also surrounding the then current settlements in a frontier line of defense.

Implementation of the new law led to the introduction of additional troops at the existing garrisons of Béxar, La Bahía, and Nacogdoches. The new fortifications, numbering six, were Lipantitlán, on the Nueces River; Tenoxtitlán and Velasco, along the middle and lower Brazos, respectively; Lavaca on same river; Anáhuac, at the mouth of the Trinity River along Galveston Bay; and Terán, on the Neches. There is no evidence that the general, for whom the last outpost was named, ever visited the site, although during his inspection of East Texas he traveled through the Neches valley. The job of establishing Fort Terán fell to Peter Ellis Bean, one of the most colorful and enigmatic pioneers of early Texas. Like Noah Smithwick and other noteworthy Texas characters who seemed to be at key historical locales throughout their lives, Bean had a wanderlust that often placed him in the company of key leaders. Born in 1783 in Tennessee, where his family founded Bean Station southeast of the Cumberland Gap, Peter Bean traveled to Natchez, Mississippi, as a teenager and in 1800 joined Philip Nolan on the mustanger's fourth expedition into Texas. Spanish forces out of Nacogdoches intercepted the party in present-day Hill County in March 1801 and killed Nolan, capturing the surviving members and remanding them to prison in Chihuahua. Released in 1810 during the Mexican War for Independence to fight for the Spanish Loyalist cause, Bean defected and instead joined the Mexican Army. Following the revolution, he became an Indian agent for Texas, rising to become a colonel and commandant of the forces at Nacogdoches. Subsequently, in 1828, he escorted Mier y Terán on his inspection tour of East Texas. Because of such connections, as well as his knowledge of the region, he received an appointment to build and command the new fort on the Neches. Little is known of Bean's time at Fort Terán, although there has been speculation through the years that he used the time and abundant regional resources to better his own financial standing. Regardless, his term there was short lived due to the pressing need for his troops—which probably numbered near fifty—when disturbances farther south at Fort Anáhuac threatened the status quo in 1832. It was around that time, according to most sources, that the government likely abandoned Fort Terán.

The growing friction between Anglo-American settlers and the Mexican government, as well as the coup simultaneously staged by Gen. Antonio López de Santa Anna, presaged overwhelming change for the country. The widespread tension took a heavy toll on General Mier y Terán, as his biographer Ohland Morton has explained, noting the general's personal battles with melancholia and declining health, as well as despondency over what he viewed as the impending loss of the Texas he had desperately hoped to retain. Writing from San Antonio de Padilla, Tamaulipas, on July 2, 1832, he implored of a close friend, "En qué parará Texas? En lo que Dios quiera" (What is to become of Texas? It is up to God). The following day, dressed in full ceremonial uniform, he discreetly made his way to the back of the local church and, propping his sword against the stone wall, fell forward, taking his own life.

Although there are no conclusive records, it is possible Mier y Terán's namesake fort on the Neches may have been in active operation only about ten months and likely consisted of only a few structures of wood and local stone. If remains existed after that time, they were likely destroyed following official orders to that effect in 1834. The abandonment, however, did not mean an end to occupation of the site. During the fort's brief existence, Maryland-born Samuel T. Belt ran a trading post and river ferry nearby. His operations continued on into the 1840s, when he sold out to Frost Thorn, a Nacogdoches land speculator. According to historian Gerland, the deed called out the association by noting the land included the site of "the old camp station or fort known and called by the name Terán." An operation known as Boone's Ferry (later Duncan's Ferry), for which a nearby dispersed rural settlement came to be known, continued at the site into the early twentieth century, eventually giving way to the railroad town of Rockland farther east. In the ensuing years, East Texas experienced a timber boom that lasted into the 1920s, but the second-growth forest, with its tight undergrowth, which eventually reclaimed the site, marked a dramatic environmental change from the high-canopied virgin forests that originally greeted Native Americans and the settlers who followed.

Despite a short life and a military record of questionable significance, Fort Terán has spawned more than its share of legends. As with most, it is uncertain whether any are based in fact. One of the earliest legends regards the Texas Revolution, and it in turn led to another that is perhaps an even more enduring piece of folklore. The background of the first is conjectural but based on speculation about what might have happened if Mexican forces under General Santa Anna had prevailed at the Battle of San Jacinto in April 1836. As the speculation goes, the general may well have turned his army north toward Nacogdoches, which would have put the army on a general course to cross the Neches near Terán. As Gerland relates in his 2011 study of the fort site, Republic of Texas Secretary of State Robert A. Irion, in an 1837 letter to Memecan Hunt, recalled that Indians in service to the Mexican government had been utilized to build rafts at Terán in anticipation of Santa Anna's eventual crossing of the river. Although the letter is intriguing, in no small part because it referenced "a relic of that service" that still remained at the site, there has been no further historical elaboration or corroboration of the claim. However, if such a plan had been considered but rapidly abandoned as a result of the outcome at San Jacinto, such action possibly served as the foundation for a legend of buried treasure, which still haunts the area. In his book *Coronado's Children,* historian J. Frank Dobie recounted a tale of soldiers filling a cannon with gold and rolling it off a cliff into the river, hoping to return and retrieve it another day. With the advent of the Republic of Texas and the governments that followed, that day never came. Instead, treasure hunters have taken up the cause, scouring the hillsides of all of the fort's suspected locations, digging holes, exploring caves formed by boulders, and even trolling the river. If such a discovery has ever been made, it remains unannounced to us, as well as to those who continue to believe in the legend of gold at Terán.

Adding to the mystery of the old fort site is what might be called the case of the misplaced monument. While details at this point might serve only to fuel additional speculation for treasure hunters, the basic information is that the State of Texas, acting through the Texas Centennial Commission, placed a monolithic granite monument in the vicinity of Fort Terán in the 1930s. Records that would indicate conclusively why the state chose that particular site are not known to exist. Access to the remote locale proved problematic through the years, and in the 1960s, when Winnie H. Wilson of Houston generously offered a donation of land to aid in the creation of a Fort Terán park, Tyler County officials gladly accepted. They then petitioned the Texas State Historical Survey Committee (later renamed the Texas Historical Commission) for permission to relocate the marker, which executive director Truett Latimer granted in 1967. The new site was at a point known locally as Money

Hill, although the genesis of the name has been lost over time. And so the speculation and the mystery of Fort Terán continue even to the current day. What many believe to be the fort site may have been compromised years ago by sand and gravel operations, but perhaps remnants of the structures still remain to be found buried deep in the Piney Woods. Until such time as the area can be conclusively ground-truthed by professional archeologists (and no such surveys are planned as of this writing), the story of Fort Terán remains much as it has for more than a century and a half—an interesting sidebar to an important chapter in Texas history.

LOCATION: The actual fort site is undetermined. The badly damaged and relocated centennial monument, according to the Texas Historical Commission Historic Sites Atlas, is accessible only in good weather and utilizing four-wheel-drive vehicles. The monument is located on a dirt road eleven miles northeast of Chester via FM 1745.

ACCESS: Given the remoteness of the site and the potential dangers associated with the dirt road access (more than eight miles long) to the centennial monument, extreme caution is advised. Potential visitors are urged to check with authorities in Woodville or Chester before attempting to travel to the location. The original marker site is now on private property, so access there is prohibited without proper authorization.

SOURCES

Dobie, J. Frank. *Coronado's Children: Tales of Lost Mines and Buried Treasures of the Southwest.* Austin: University of Texas Press, 1984.

Gerland, Jonathan. "Remembering Fort Terán: A Mexican Outpost in the East Texas Pineywoods." *Pine Bough* 16 (December 2011): 2–19.

Jackson, Jack, ed., and John Wheat, trans. *Texas by Terán: The Diary Kept by General Manuel de Mier y Terán on His 1828 Inspection of Texas.* Austin: University of Texas Press, 2000.

Lay, Bennett. *The Lives of Ellis P. Bean.* Austin: University of Texas Press, 1960.

Marler, Don C. *Fort Terán on the Neches River.* Hemphill, TX: Dogwood Press, 2000.
Morton, Ohland. *Terán and Texas: A Chapter in Texas-Mexican Relations.* Austin: Texas State Historical Association, 1948.
Wheat, J. E. "The Story of Fort Teran on the Neches." *It's Dogwood Time in Tyler County.* Tyler County Dogwood Festival program, March 31, 1951.

3 FORT ANÁHUAC 1831–1835

The fact is, he [Juan Davis Bradburn] is incompetent to such a command and is half crazy part of his time. — Stephen F. Austin to Samuel May Williams

---

Visitors to the grand southern entry of the Texas State Capitol in Austin pass through a ceremonial foyer replete with heroic historical reminders of the state's revolutionary era. On prominent view are Elisabet Ney's elaborate Italian marble statues of leaders Sam Houston and Stephen F. Austin. Flanking the foyer on the walls are two large-scale paintings by Virginia-born William Henry Huddle: *David Crockett* (1889) and *The Surrender of Santa Anna* (1886). And imbedded within the elaborate terrazzo floors of the 1930s are the names of key military engagements fought on Texas soil from the revolution forward. Some, such as the Alamo, Goliad, Gonzales, and San Jacinto, are perhaps more familiar to visitors than others, but there are also names from later eras they may not recognize as well, including Palmito and Palo Alto. Among the collection of revered battles is the name Anahuac, perhaps better known today as a coastal city, the seat of Chambers County, than as a flashpoint in the broader story of the Texas Revolution.

Located on a high bluff along the Trinity River where the stream empties into Trinity Bay, the site of Anahuac has long been a strategic point for both commerce and defense. Historically, Atakapan Indians lived nearby, and in 1816 Col. Henry Perry camped in the vicinity during a filibuster expedition, leading early Anglo-American settlers to refer to the general locale as Perry's Point. Organized settlement began in 1830, and almost immediately tensions there between Anglo-American colonists and the Mexican government began to escalate. It was at Anahuac that the tenuous bonds between the two began to unravel, exposing major differences that would soon lead to open revolution.

In order to provide a physical presence for enforcing the Law of April 6, 1830, Gen. Manuel Mier y Terán, commandant of Mexico's Eastern Interior Provinces, called for the establishment of an installation at Perry's Point. Named Fort Anáhuac, after the Aztecan name for Mexico City, it served to check smuggling operations and illegal settlements in the area, while also providing a secure site for the collection of customs. Utilizing convict-soldiers for labor and on-site kilns for the manufacture of bricks, construction began in late 1830 and resulted in a fully functional fortification by the following spring. The initial structure was a large stockaded wooden barracks a short distance north of the bluff within what is now the city of Anahuac. Overseeing the work at the fort was one of the most controversial characters in early Texas, Juan Davis Bradburn, and it was around his actions that colonial systems quickly began to deteriorate.

Born in Virginia in 1787, John (later Juan) Davis Bradburn made his way to Kentucky and then to Natchitoches, Louisiana, by 1814. Some accounts of his life speculate that he may have participated in the Gutiérrez-Magee expedition, an ill-fated filibustering military mission against Spanish Texas that began at the Louisiana outpost in 1812, but to date no conclusive evidence of his involvement has surfaced. What is known, however, is that Bradburn later joined local forces in support of Gen. Andrew Jackson's troops in the Battle of New Orleans in 1815, although their efforts occurred too late to involve them in the fighting. Soon after, Bradburn joined Henry Perry and others in another planned assault on Spanish rule in Texas, this time at La Bahía. As the plan evolved, however, it gave way to a larger, but ultimately doomed, endeavor against Tampico. Although the effort failed, Bradburn gained the trust of Francisco Xavier Mina, the expedition leader, and ultimately chose to cast his lot with the opposition Centralists, a decision that brought him into contact with Anastasio Bustamante and Manuel Mier y Terán, who would play key roles in the ensuing development of an independent Mexico.

Bradburn's connections led to his commission to establish Fort Anáhuac and the town of Anáhuac, but it also put him at odds with José Francisco Madero, the Federalist land commissioner who arrived there in January 1831 to distribute land titles to those settlers outside the existing empresario grants. Almost immediately, the two men clashed over individual interpretations of various provisions of the Law of April 6, 1830, as well as the relative authority of the military versus civil operations. Bradburn, who took a narrow interpretation of the law and had set up the settlement with that frame of reference, moved quickly to assert his power and briefly had Madero arrested. Following his release, however, Madero returned to his work and actively pursued the legal settlement of the lower Trinity River valley, establishing the *ayuntamiento* of Atascosito (eventually the Liberty municipality), which further complicated matters.

The Centralist-Federalist differences represented by Bradburn and Madero were only part of the initial problems at Anáhuac, but they helped fuel other outlying differences, including long-standing disputes between the government and local settlers, who expected quick and definitive solutions to their entangling land problems. Equally incendiary in nature was the work of George Fisher, a Serbian-born Mexican official who arrived at Anáhuac late in 1831 to begin the process of collecting customs at the port city under the 1830 law, which opened sea trade along the Texas coast to foreign carriers. Fisher, like Madero and Bradburn, exerted his own brand of authority, issuing an order that all ships leaving Texas ports had to first secure clearance through Anáhuac. Such a decree needlessly required expensive and exhaustive overland trips to the port city prior to sailings, and that caused more than a few instances of captains trying to elude defensive positions, under fire, hoping their vessels could safely reach open waters. Terán, who understood how such actions could quickly get out of hand, escalating the existing regional tensions, took such actions seriously and soon recalled Fisher from his post. Bradburn, however, remained firmly entrenched as the local symbol of a flawed federal government.

The internal tensions that flared at Anáhuac nevertheless dragged the American settlers into the fray, and with the central government so far distant, the only redress seemed to be against the local military leader, Bradburn, who likely had no more than two hundred to three hundred troops under his command at any one time. Rather than try to placate the concerned citizenry, the commandant only added to their pervasive fears and concerns through his strident actions. One involved the arrest of local attorney Patrick Churchill Jack, named to head a militia company formed ostensibly to provide protection against Indian attacks but in reality an unmistakable symbol of local resolve to stand up to perceived injustices from the Mexican officials. The message of the locals was clear—Bradburn was the central problem, and he had to be dealt with forcibly. Another incident, which proved to be much more complex, also involved Bradburn, Jack, and another local attorney by the name of William Barret Travis, who would later figure more prominently at the Alamo as part of the continuing revolutionary saga.

The incident involving Travis and Jack stemmed from a disagreement over slavery, curtailed in Texas colonies by the Law of April 6, 1830. Soon after Patrick Jack's release, several (two or three) slaves owned by William M. Logan of Louisiana made their way to Anáhuac, where Bradburn gave them safe haven. Logan personally petitioned for the return of his "property," eventually employing Travis's legal services, but his efforts were rebuffed by Bradburn's stalling tactics, including a statement that the men had joined the Mexican army and could therefore not be returned to slavery. Word soon reached the commandant, however, that armed men from the United States were on their way to secure the slaves' release, so Bradburn ordered his soldiers to reconnoiter the land east of the fort, only to discover the rumors were unfounded. Blaming Travis for the ruse, and most likely with good reason, Bradburn had him arrested along with his law partner, Jack. Initially housed in a guardhouse and then later in the brick kilns, when it appeared the two men were planning an escape with local help, they remained under constant guard but without the legal protocol of formal charges. When the word spread that they would either be tried by the military or possibly transferred to Matamoros, the American settlers began planning in earnest to use force to free the captives. A scouting patrol sent out by Bradburn encountered the hastily formed group, which in turn captured the soldiers, hoping to use them in trade for the lawyers. The recalcitrant commandant initially stalled for time, but as the situation grew worse, he retaliated by having soldiers fire on the town, further panicking its citizens.

The armed Americans returned to their camp along Turtle Bayou and drew up a series of resolutions protesting Bradburn's intolerance and confirming their support for the standing government's opposition leader, Gen. Antonio López de Santa Anna. That support would, of course, change quickly as the revolution took hold, but in 1832 the Mexican general was seen as a symbol of positive change for the country. One of the Americans, John Austin, subsequently led a party to Brazoria for the purpose of securing two cannon they felt they could procure for the cause. In the struggle that ensued, fighting along the Brazos River at Velasco between Austin's group and Mexican forces resulted in casualties on both sides, in effect setting the course for revolution.

Back at Anáhuac, circumstances changed dramatically after José de las Piedras arrived with troops from Nacogdoches and Fort Terán in an attempt to quell the disturbance peacefully. He met first with the U.S. troops to get their opinion of the situation and then traveled on to Anáhuac, where on July 1 he met with Bradburn and brokered a deal that allowed for the release of Travis and Jack, with an understanding that they would eventually face a civil trial in Liberty. It never occurred, however. Piedras also agreed to accept the Americans' damage claims and, more importantly to local residents, relieved Bradburn of his command, replacing him with Juan Cortina. With those actions, the 1832 disturbance at Anáhuac came to an end, and in a few days the former commandant, who had been at the center of the local storm, quietly slipped out of town, eventually making his way back to Matamoros by way of New Orleans, albeit with much trepidation along the way. Piedras returned to Nacogdoches, where in August of that year his command fell in a battle that effectively cleared the East Texas area of a military presence.

As the Mexican forces departed the military post in the summer of 1832, they dismantled much of the structure, and local residents in need of building materials scavenged what little remained. A fire at the site later that year also took its toll on the former fort. Despite the loss of the central landmark of the protests, the historical impact of Anáhuac had not yet run its course. In the months immediately following the conflict, life seemed to return to an antebellum pace: local commerce again prospered, and customs went largely uncollected. The rapprochement, however, proved to be tenuous and short lived. In January 1835, the government again sent troops and collection agents to Anáhuac, this time under the command of Capt. Antonio Tenorio, who supervised limited construction of facilities at the former outpost site. When matters escalated that summer over the arrest of local merchant Andrew Briscoe, Anáhuac again became a flashpoint, and Travis, then residing in San Felipe, led a group of settlers to Harrisburg, where they commissioned a vessel, the *Ohio,* and sailed to the beleaguered port city. Caught off guard, the soldiers fled, and Tenorio soon surrendered. Although successful in quickly quelling the second disturbance at Anáhuac, Travis's actions nevertheless threatened to complicate matters even more given the increasingly tenuous political tensions between the government and the Anglo settlers. Stephen F. Austin was then under arrest in Mexico, so the incident at Anáhuac took on even greater significance as part of what appeared to officials as an organized revolt. When Travis learned that his actions thus met with disfavor by both the government and his fellow settlers and threatened to again result in his arrest, he offered his apologies while also working steadily for some public airing of grievances. That and other actions would soon lead to the Consultation of 1835 at Washington-on-the-Brazos and further signs of the growing and irreparable rift.

Following the revolution, the settlement of Anáhuac (now Anahuac) survived despite intense land disputes involving Gen. Thomas Jefferson Chambers and Charles Wilcox. It remained a small but promising town and commercial center, and in 1907 it officially succeeded Wallisville as the seat of Chambers County. Over time, elements of the former fort site along the bluff gave way to exten-

Fort Anáhuac Park at dusk. Past archeological investigations at the site determined the outline of the Mexican fortification, which is now marked by red bumpers for interpretive purposes. ***Photo by Lauren Mercer, Anahuac.***

sive erosion, while other evidence of its existence disappeared in overgrowth or at the hands of vandals and relic hunters. A survey in the late 1930s produced a detailed map of the remaining vestiges, and following World War II the site became part of a county park. Subsequently, a number of careful archeological studies have examined the remaining footprint, and in 1981 the Texas Historical Commission listed it in the National Register of Historic Places.

Fort Anáhuac, although in existence only a short time, played a key role in the events leading up to Texas independence. Confrontations there between the Mexican government and Anglo settlers set in motion actions that reached far beyond the coastal plains. Overshadowed in historical memory by military sites such as the Alamo and San Jacinto, Anahuac nevertheless has earned its place in Texas military history and is worthy of its commemoration alongside the other names found in the terrazzo floors of the Texas Capitol.

LOCATION: Fort Anahuac County Park, 1704 Main Street, Anahuac.
ACCESS: Open to the public during regular park hours. Check locally for additional information.

SOURCES

Henson, Margaret Swett. *Anahuac in 1832: The Cradle of the Texas Revolution.* Anahuac, TX: Fort Anahuac Committee of the Chambers County Historical Commission, 1982.

———. *Juan Davis Bradburn: A Reappraisal of the Mexican Commander of Anahuac.* College Station: Texas A&M University Press, 1982.

McDonald, Archie P. *Travis.* Austin: Jenkins Publishing Company, 1976.

Texas Historical Commission. Chambers County historical marker files.

———. National Register of Historic Places files for Fort Anahuac.

4 GRAVES OF AMERICAN REVOLUTION VETERANS IN TEXAS

Eighteenth and Nineteenth Centuries

*The past is always with us, just around the corner, in a half-remembered world. That is particularly true here in the Texas State Cemetery, a space, a beloved landscape, that has meaning to all Texans. . . . This is a "Library of Stone." — Martha A. Hartzog**

Located on the grounds of the Texas State Cemetery in Austin are numerous monuments to veterans of military conflicts. Most, like those found in the Confederate Field, with its distinctive white headstones precisely aligned, are for individuals who served in the military, but others, like the World War II monument, reflect a particular period of service, while the Purple Heart Monument honors those who exhibited bravery. Regardless the scope of commemoration, all serve as reminders of dedication, sacrifice, and valor.

On the north side of the twenty-two-acre cemetery, adjacent to a walkway that winds along the base of Cenotaph Hill, is a distinctive obelisk of Mountain Red granite cut from a Fredericksburg quarry. Its inscriptions honor a particular element of Texas military history that is largely unknown and undertold. Erected by the Texas Society of the Daughters of the American Revolution (TSDAR at the time; now TXDAR), the monument honors a select group of individuals who participated in the nation's struggle for independence from Britain in the eighteenth century. Some of those individuals served in battles in the original colonies and later made their way to Texas, but others were already here when they worked to support the American army. All are considered "patriots" by members of TXDAR and its parent organization, the National So-

*Hartzog is state historian of the Texas Society of the Daughters of the American Revolution. Her statement in the opening epigraph was made in 2009.

This red granite obelisk in the state cemetery in Austin honors American Revolution veterans who at one time lived in Texas. ***Photo by Dan K. Utley.***

Design detailing of the state cemetery monument placed by the Texas Society of the Daughters of the American Revolution. *Photo by Dan K. Utley.*

ciety Daughters of the American Revolution (NSDAR). The names of thirty-two veterans are incised on the monument, but ongoing research related to others who may qualify for inclusion could result in more names being added over time as the documentation warrants. The monument, therefore, is a work in progress.

One of those dedicated TXDAR members is Martha Hartzog of Austin, who has worked tirelessly and unselfishly to verify the historical records of worthy individuals and potential patriots. A fifth-generation Texan, Hartzog was serving as the organization's state historian when she proposed the monument idea, which received approval during the administration of State Regent Lynn Forney Young in 2006. Recently retired from the University of Texas, Hartzog has a passion for preserving history and has been actively involved with a number of history-minded organizations, including the Travis County Historical Commission, the Austin Historic Landmark Commission, the Austin Civil War Round Table, and Hood's Texas Brigade Association, Reactivated. She currently serves as the national chair for historic preservation for the Daughters of the American Revolution and continues to work with members and patriot descendants to document relevant military service and Texas residency, as well as places of burial. As might be expected, tracking written records from the late eighteenth and early nineteenth centuries can be problematic, but Hartzog and others have persevered, utilizing archival collections from all across the nation. Throughout the process of documenting the names to go on the monument, she maintained extensive files, which she and State Regent Pamela Rouse Wright graciously shared as a basic resource for this chapter.

On Sunday, March 15, 2009, a crowd of about six hundred gathered in the Texas State Cemetery on the near east side of Austin to participate in the dedication of the Patriot Monument. Following an elaborate opening processional of traditional Scottish marches played by the Silver Thistle Pipers, those in attendance heard stirring patriotic remarks by a number of people representing historical organizations and state government. In addition, brief biographical sketches were offered by Nancy Reynolds Tiner, who spoke about the five Spanish patriots noted on the monument, and by Martha

Hartzog, who told of the twenty-seven others who were of Anglo-American and French descent. Four of the individual stories shared that day and explored in more detail here, reflect the diversity of service by Texans associated with the American Revolution.

Of those commemorated by the Patriot Monument, two—Robert Rankin and Stephen Williams—are also buried in the state cemetery. The remains of both veterans were removed from their original graves in East Texas and reinterred in the Republic Hill section of the state cemetery during the Texas Centennial of the 1930s. Although the graves are separated by only a few rows of tombstones, the state-sponsored centennial grave markers for the two veterans ended up hundreds of miles apart.

Born in 1753, Virginia native Robert Rankin enlisted in the Continental Army in 1776, participating in battles at Germantown and along Brandywine Creek in Pennsylvania, as well as at Stony Point in southern New York. Later captured in South Carolina during the siege of Charlestown (which became known as Charleston in the 1780s), he returned to active service following his exchange. After the revolution, Rankin moved his family to the Kentucky territory of Virginia, where he was active in government and was a delegate to the constitutional convention at Danville. A move farther south to present-day Alabama in the early decades of the nineteenth century proved to be economically devastating, and in 1832 he relocated his family to the Mexican state of Coahuila y Tejas as colonists under empresario Joseph Vehlein. He received a league and a labor of land and settled in what is now San Jacinto County, near where the town of Coonskin (present-day Coldspring) would eventually develop as an early commercial center. As Ann Patton Malone has noted in *The New Handbook of Texas,* Rankin developed a friendship with Sam Houston, who depended on the American Revolution veteran's influence to ensure Indian neutrality during the lead-up to what would be the Battle of San Jacinto in April 1836. Later that year, Rankin fell ill, and he and his wife moved to Louisiana, where he died late in 1837. His original burial site was back in San Jacinto County, and reinterment in the state cemetery occurred almost a century later, in 1936.

Stephen Williams, born in the coastal region of North Carolina in 1760, joined the American forces as a teenager and participated in three key battles of the southern theater of the revolution from 1779 to 1781. The first two, at Brier Creek in eastern Georgia and at Camden, South Carolina, were considered devastating losses for the Americans, while the later battle at Eutaw Springs, South Carolina, was viewed as a tactical victory for the British, at best. Like Rankin, Williams drifted from his home country following the revolution and lived in Georgia and Louisiana, where he served in support of the American forces in the latter stages of the War of 1812. Also like Rankin, though, he, too, had experienced economic setbacks by the time he headed to Texas seeking a new start. He arrived as a widower in 1830 and settled on land initially colonized by Lorenzo de Zavala. He lived in present-day Newton County and then what is now Jasper County, both of which were named for veterans of the American Revolution. He lived at Bevil's Settlement (present-day Jasper; not to be confused with the Angelina River town of Bevilport farther to the west in the county). When relations between Anglo-American colonists and the Mexican government began to deteriorate, Williams, even though in his seventies, chose to once again join up for military action, participating in the 1835 Siege of Béxar, serving alongside his grandsons and a son-in-law. He eventually returned to Jasper, where he died and was buried near his homesite. In 1936 the State of Texas erected a centennial marker at his grave there, but when his remains were later moved to the state cemetery, the marker remained behind. It is now located along U.S. 69 south of Jasper near the Zion Hill community. An additional metal marker, placed nearby in 1991, explains the reinterment and provides additional information on Williams, including his death date of 1839. His second and current burial site in Austin is now marked by a slant-topped, ashlar cut, gray granite block erected by the Thankful Hubbard Chapter of the Daughters of the American Revolution, and it bears the death date of ca. 1848. The Austin monument carries the birth date of 1760, as does the 1991 marker, but the 1936 monument in Jasper County shows his date of birth as 1764.

Perhaps the most recognizable name of the American Revolution veterans who later made their home in Texas is that of John

Parker, who was involved in the infamous Indian attack on his family's fort along the Navasota River near present-day Groesbeck, Limestone County, in 1836. Born in Maryland in 1758, Parker later moved to Virginia and from there participated in the revolution. The Parker family subsequently moved to Georgia, Tennessee, and then in 1815 to Illinois, where two grandchildren, Cynthia Ann and John Richard, were born. While in Illinois, the senior John Parker actively participated in Baptist church work and came to be referred to as an "elder," a term of respect for church leaders.

In the early 1830s, John Parker and his son Daniel, also a church elder, made preparations to move the family to Texas, where they planned to establish Predestinarian Baptist congregations. As that got under way, John Parker filed a pension application in Coles County, Illinois, in which he provided a declaration of his American army service, which included two stints:

> Said Parker volunteered under Captain Fields, Colonel Slaughter Commanding the Regiment in General Greene's Brigade. He entered the service of the United States in the year 1777, month of October . . . and was discharged from said service in eleven months afterward.
>
> That again he entered the service as a drafted man under Captain Collier of the Regiment commanded by Colonel Alexander . . . [and] that he marched through Winchester, Virginia, thence through Beisor Town, Pennsylvania[,] and was stationed on a creek called "Ten Mile" in P. State. That he continued in said service . . . for the term of twelve months, making two entire years.
>
> The Declarant was in no engagement with the enemy.

As planned, the Parker family made its lengthy trip to Texas in 1833, with Daniel leading a group to Grimes County and then on to Anderson County near present-day Elkhart. John Parker directed the other members of the contingent to present-day Limestone County. There, the settlers built a family fort in 1834. Two years later, on May 19, 1836, a group of Comanche, Kiowa, and other Indian groups appeared at the fort while many of the settlers were working in nearby fields. A number of the women and children fled the fort before what they believed would be an inevitable assault, heading for the protection of nearby woods, and the fighting that quickly ensued overwhelmed the remaining meager defenses. In all, the attackers killed five settlers, including seventy-seven-year-old John Parker, and captured five, including Cynthia Ann Parker, about nine years of age, and her brother, five-year-old John Richard Parker. What followed was the most celebrated hunt for captors in Texas history. In the case of Cynthia Ann Parker, the search continued until December 1860, when Texas Rangers under the command of Lawrence Sullivan Ross recaptured her following the battle of Pease River. By that time, she had completely acculturated as a Comanche and had three children, one of whom, Quanah Parker, would become the powerful chief of his people. Sadly, despite the best efforts of her birth family, Cynthia Ann Parker never fully adjusted to the ways of her former life and thus led a melancholy existence, dying in 1870 while in her early forties. Originally buried in East Texas, she was subsequently reinterred at Fort Sill, Oklahoma, where Quanah Parker is also buried.

Following the attack on Fort Parker in 1836, the remains of those killed there were interred in a mass grave about a mile away at a site now known as Fort Parker Memorial Park, the burial place of many later family descendants. In the 1930s, during the Texas Centennial, members of the Civilian Conservation Corps constructed a replica of the family fortification, which became a part of Fort Parker State Park, opened to the public in 1941. Following World War II, in August 1946, members of the Col. George Moffett Chapter of the DAR, from Beaumont, dedicated a memorial to Elder John Parker inside the fort.

While the story of American Revolution veterans buried in Texas is not widely known, perhaps even less known is the story of Spaniards in Texas who aided the American cause during the war. Thanks to the focused research of Robert H. Thonhoff, Jesse O. Villarreal, and others, including descendants of the recognized Spanish patriots and members of the TXDAR, that is beginning to change. With regard to Texas, the story of Spanish support for the American Revolution centers largely on the actions of Bernardo de Gálvez. Born in the Málaga province of Spain in 1746, Gálvez first came to New Spain in the 1760s. Named the governor of Spanish

Louisiana in 1777, he began offering his aid to the Americans during their struggle for independence even before his home country formally took similar action, and he did much to provide tactical, strategic, and financial support. Of particular significance was his control of New Orleans, which limited vital Mississippi River access to the Americans, Spanish, and French. Following Spain's declaration of war against Britain in 1779, Gálvez raised military units to move against enemy forces along the river and coastal areas. In order to sustain his actions, which would eventually take him into present-day Florida (Pensacola) and Alabama (Mobile), he sought a steady supply of Texas beef to feed his troops. Consequently, from the assembly point at Presidio la Bahía, Spanish vaqueros and soldiers soon began trailing vast herds of Texas longhorns to Louisiana via Nacogdoches. From 1779 to 1782, it is estimated that more than nine thousand head of cattle rounded up in the interior of Texas made the trip east in support of the Spanish troop movements. It was that effort that led to the inclusion of the Spanish names on the TXDAR monument in the state cemetery.

One of the patriot names is that of Patricio Antonio Rodrigues, born to a family of Canary Islanders who came to New Spain in the eighteenth century and settled in San Fernando de Béxar. Born there in 1748, Rodrigues became a soldier in service to the local presidio. Following his supply missions to Louisiana, he continued to live in the San Antonio area and is believed to have died there, although the site of his grave remains unknown. The exact date of his death is also unknown, but based on available records it was likely before 1817. In 2009, members of the Col. George Dashiell Chapter of the DAR, located in Normangee and serving both Leon and Madison counties, placed a monument to Rodrigues in the San Fernando Cemetery Number 1, near downtown San Antonio. Because of the chapter's efforts and the support of TXDAR, the story of Rodrigues and those who served with him on behalf of an emerging American republic continues to intrigue those who learn about it through the monuments.

Much has been done to record the history of the Texas connection to the American Revolution, but more research is needed, particularly with regard to the military service of individuals. In some cases, burial sites are unknown, and gaps exist in the biographical records of most of the veterans, but those are challenges that compel dedicated local historians and genealogists to continue their pursuit of documentation. They are greatly aided in that endeavor by technological advancements that make available new and possibly significant resources not yet tapped. The story goes on.

LOCATION: The Texas State Cemetery is located at 909 Navasota Street in Austin.

ACCESS: The visitor center is open from Monday through Friday, 8:00 a.m. to 5:00 p.m. The cemetery grounds are accessible seven days a week from 8:00 a.m. to 5:00 p.m.

SOURCES

Brakebill, Clovis H. *American Revolutionary Soldiers Buried in Texas.* Wolfe City, TX: Texas Society, Sons of the American Revolution, 1998.

Caughey, John Walton. *Bernardo de Gálvez in Louisiana, 1776–1783.* Gretna, LA: Pelican Publishing Company, 1972.

Patriot Monument application files. An active collection maintained by the Texas Society of the Daughters of the American Revolution. Accessed by permission from TXDAR.

Texas Historical Commission. Official Texas Historical Marker files, Austin.

Thonhoff, Robert H. *The Texas Connection with the American Revolution.* Burnet, TX: Eakin, 1981.

TSDAR Patriot Monument Dedication booklet, written by Martha Hartzog and privately printed by the Texas Society of the Daughters of the American Revolution.

Tyler, Ron, ed. *The New Handbook of Texas.* 6 vols. Austin: Texas State Historical Association, 1996.

Villarreal, Jesse O., Sr. *Tejano Patriots of the American Revolution, 1776–1783.* Privately published, 2011.

5 THE RIVER FORTS 1848–1947

For eons upon eons, the Rio Grande was simply a river. Since 1848, it is now an international border, an instant dark dividing line between two vastly conflicting cultures and rife with violence.
— Maj. William W. Chapman, December 18, 1859

Having lost its bitter war with the United States in 1848, Mexico could hardly expect the provisions of the Treaty of Guadalupe Hidalgo, which officially ended the war, to be favorable. Indeed, the conflict had caused Mexico to cede roughly a third of its original prewar land to the victorious "colossus of the north." Further, the long-contested international boundary issue between the two battling nations had at last been determined: The Rio Grande was legally established as the bordering river rather than the Nueces, which Mexico had so fervently demanded. One provision of the treaty, however, did offer some solace to the defeated Republic of Mexico. Under the terms of Article XI, the parties "solemnly agreed" that all incursions by the "savage tribes" of the United States were to be forcibly restrained by the victorious nation. The wording of the article specifically called for the government of the United States to consider any Indian raids into Mexico to be just as serious as any such incursions "against its own territory, against its own citizens." The treaty was signed on February 2, 1848, ratified by President James K. Polk on March 16 of the same year and proclaimed on the Fourth of July almost four months later. In an apparent show of good faith and in stunningly swift adherence to Article XI, the United States immediately established a chain of military outposts on the Texas side of the Rio Grande. The declared primary mission of these so-called river forts was to restrain any Indian incursions on both sides of the newly decreed U.S.-Mexico border. History proved, however, that the noble-sounding mission would be all but impossible to accomplish during the rest of the nineteenth century.

Fort Brown, located at present-day Brownsville, Texas, played a key role in the recently concluded war and was subsequently enlarged in order to provide an eastern anchor to the long line of U.S. Army fortifications, which soon stood as sentinels along the river. From these forts, troopers could ride out to intercept and deter any North American warriors from doing their malicious mischief across the Rio Grande. Using the reinforced Fort Brown as its base near the mouth of the river, at the Gulf of Mexico, the army quickly established a more modest outpost some eighty miles upriver at Rio Grande City in October 1848. Called Ringgold Barracks for a time, the installation later became known as Fort Ringgold. On March 3, 1849, a little more than a year after the ratification of the Guadalupe Hidalgo treaty, the United States established a more significant military installation at Laredo, ninety-five miles up the river beyond the Ringgold site. Known as Fort McIntosh, the post remained active, more or less, for nearly one hundred years. Just two weeks following the opening of McIntosh, Fort Duncan was established 102 miles even farther upriver at present-day Eagle Pass. Far to the west, where the Rio Grande begins its more than twelve-hundred-mile course, which defines the U.S. and Mexican border in Texas, a series of forts had already been established at what is today known as El Paso. Each named Fort Bliss, the successive sites anchored the western end of the army's chain of Texas river forts in 1849. Modern-day Fort Bliss is one of the largest military installations in the world, and its glory still bright, whereas every one of the other early river forts has now faded away with the passage of time, but not before serving in ways that could never have been imagined by the signers of the Treaty of Guadalupe Hidalgo.

The alacrity with which the U.S. government established its new line of fortifications along the river suggests the existence of motives other than just halting Indian raids. Though defeated, Mexico was far from crushed. Diminished and weakened, however, the Republic of Mexico nevertheless remained proud and largely resentful of the manner in which its war with the United States had evolved; moreover, it was dissatisfied with the structure of the nominal peace at its conclusion. Although fifteen million dollars richer in gold from the monies paid by the United States for the vast territory it acquired, Mexico set out on a tragic path of social upheaval that would involve the river forts for decades. Perhaps fully aware that victory in the Mexican War was unlikely to ensure a peaceable border for long, the United States could very well have expedited construction of its postwar forts along the river to be in a position to deal with whatever might eventually evolve on the opposite banks. History would unfortunately prove any such forethought to be valid.

FORT RINGGOLD

For much of the nineteenth century, the Rio Grande was both wide and deep enough to permit regular steamship traffic, at least along its lower reaches, as it made its way to the Gulf of Mexico. In 1847, a riverboat landing sprang up at a site on what is now the Texas side of the river. Because of its easy accessibility via steamship, the U.S. Army identified the tiny village that grew up there as a likely spot for one of its post–Mexican War installations. On October 26, 1848, Capt. J. H. LaMotte of the 1st U.S. Infantry established what was at first called the Post at Davis Landing. The small outpost initially consisted of a series of poorly constructed buildings hastily erected on an unusually high riverside bluff that afforded a clear view of the important port city of Camargo across the Rio Grande. Shortly after its creation, the post became known as Camp Ringgold and then later as Ringgold Barracks in honor of Samuel Ringgold, the creator of the "flying artillery" concept, which proved so effective early in the Mexican War. Ringgold died as the result of losing both his legs during the battle of Palo Alto, near present-day Brownsville, the first pitched clash of arms in the war. The naming of military installations in honor of the heroes of the 1846–1848 conflict became a widely used practice in the years immediately afterward. Forts Martin Scott, Mason, McKavett, and Lancaster, among others, each bore the name of a victim of that war.

Although the announced mission of the new installation had to do with quelling Indian incursions into Mexico, there were few reports of actual contacts with any warlike tribes. The soldiers' duties consisted of perfunctory drilling and sentinel maintenance, all the while keeping a watchful eye on political activities across the river at Camargo. In 1850, the War Department declared the fort a permanent installation. This reassuring but frequently fleeting designation served to generate a new building effort. In time, the shoddy early huts and sheds gave way to handsome, gleaming-white stone buildings featuring long sun-blocking arcades and tile roofing that reflected the Hispanic heritage of the region. The two-story barracks for enlisted personnel featured mess halls and dayrooms on the first floor and at least relatively cool sleeping accommodations upstairs. Eventually four such multipurpose barracks were erected at the fort. Officers below the rank of major shared eight rooms, while captains lived in four of the rooms, and two lieutenants had a room each. By nearly any army standard at the time, the living accommodations appeared superior. The problem, however, was that given all of this relative luxury, Fort Ringgold's personnel had little to do to warrant the stronghold's existence after the possibility of Indian activities diminished and the lingering fears of a resurgence of Mexican military action all but disappeared, at least temporarily. The presence of Mexican bandits did offer some relief to the monotony, but soon even that often frustrating activity lessened, only to reignite in 1860 with the appearance in the region of the elusive bandit Juan Nepomuceno Cortino, a violently anti-American former soldier in the Mexican War.

In 1856, an event took place at the fort that gave local historians a fascinating topic to speak of in later years. An army officer then of little if any renown rode into the fort to conduct court martial proceedings. He billeted in the commanding officer's quarters, a small white clapboard building perched high on the bluff that towered over the Rio Grande immediately below. Although he stayed at the house for only a few days, it is proudly known today as the Robert E. Lee House. Lee in fact returned to Ringgold on two more occasions before he rose to fame as the iconic symbol of the Confederate States of America. While it is now a widespread belief that Lee seemingly visited every former nineteenth-century mili-

This building, known today as Robert E. Lee House, was actually the post commandant's home at Rio Grande City's Fort Ringgold for years after the Mexican War. ***The Alexander Collection.***

tary installation in Texas, he actually did stay at Fort Ringgold, if only briefly.

Three years after the future Confederate general's first visit and one year before his final one, the army abandoned Fort Ringgold despite its earlier status as a permanent installation. A year later, it reversed the decision and once again declared the fort had permanent status. The outbreak of Cortina's most violent activities on the border made necessary the reopening of the fort, along with the other installations in Brownsville and Laredo, which had also only recently been closed. Lee again came to the region to assess the situation. According to some accounts, he was once more invited to stay in the commanding officers' home but declined, preferring to sleep in a tent pitched next to the house. Perhaps he had previously found it difficult to sleep soundly in the home, which had every one of its walls covered with detailed military maps of the region. Those maps, incidentally, remained affixed to the walls until they were unfortunately painted over in 1919.

In 1861, a year after Lee's last visit, the Civil War began, and troops at all U.S. Army outposts in Texas surrendered to Confederate forces, usually volunteer militiamen. During that war, the entire Rio Grande borderland continued to be of special interest to North and South alike. Occasionally, Mexicans became involved in the skirmishing, which continued throughout the war as both sides competed to control the river and the ports on the nearby Gulf of Mexico. Not until after the war did Ringgold Barracks officially become Fort Ringgold. With the return of U.S. troops in 1865 came a major building program at an installation that still had little to do in terms of a specific mission. During the violent decade of the Mexican Revolution, however, the fort served as a center for border patrols and as a guardian against armed incidents that often spilled across the river from 1910 through 1920.

As World War II approached in 1940, the 12th Cavalry, stationed at Ringgold, received reassignment to Fort Bliss, effectively terminating Ringgold's usefulness. As a result, the army deactivated it in 1944, even before World War II ended. This time, the deactivation and closure were truly permanent. The base once declared the most attractive in the entire state would never again become home to the nation's soldiers. The site, however, did survive fairly intact, unlike most other shuttered facilities in the post–World War II period. The elegant buildings that served decades of officers and men now serve as offices for the Rio Grande City Independent School District. The Robert E. Lee House has been restored, without the maps on its walls, following a determined campaign by the Starr County Historical Commission. Other buildings, long glistening in the hot sun of South Texas, however, now show the evidence of many years of deferred maintenance.

Despite all of its setbacks over the years, the old fort still somehow manages to hint at its one-time martial existence. The Rio Grande, now usually nothing more than a pale reflection of its steamboat-bearing years, still meanders by just below the sandy ridge where the so-called Lee House stands, the only true hint of the glory that once was Fort Ringgold.

FORT MCINTOSH

There is no known written history that indicates for just how many decades Indians living in the present state of Texas had splashed across the Rio Grande in the vicinity of Laredo to ride into what is now the Republic of Mexico. To those nomadic tribes, the crossing had no international significance, of course, and no political implications. They simply wanted to get to the other side as easily and as safely as possible. The best way to accomplish that was to cross at El Paso de los Indios, later sometimes known as El Paso de Jacinto. The usually shallow, rocky fording place on the Rio Grande likely had no name at all in any Native American tongue, but its location remained known from one generation to the next. When the Spanish came into that area of northern Mexico, they simply followed the trail worn smooth by the nomadic natives and crossed the Rio Grande at the same ford used for hundreds of years by those constantly migrating tribes. The newcomers honored the traditional crossing point by referring to it as the Pass of the Indians.

Despite the ever-increasing presence of Spanish settlers on the river, Indian tribes continued to use the traditional ford as they had for countless years. With the founding of the village of Laredo and the establishment of numerous ranches in the region, open conflict between the native and European cultures erupted, while the ford still served as the principal avenue for Indian raiders. At the end of the war with Mexico, the decision to place a U.S. Army outpost overlooking the ford appeared compatible with Article XI of the Treaty of Guadalupe Hidalgo. Having given Mexico its solemn pledge to halt Indian incursions across the Rio Grande, the United States could have found no better spot for that purpose than along the river at Laredo—at the very site of the Indians' traditional crossing for their numerous raids.

The post on the ridge was founded on March 3, 1849, although no significant construction took place until 1850. Initially called Camp Crawford for the secretary of war at the time, the name was changed to Fort McIntosh in early 1850. The new name honored Col. James Simmons McIntosh, who died on September 26, 1847, from wounds he suffered at the battle of Molino del Rey. The men of the 1st Infantry, who were the first to occupy the site, faced an unusual social situation stemming from the American victory in the Mexican War. Many citizens of Laredo, until then longtime citizens of Mexico, faced the occupation of their nearly one-hundred-year-old village by U.S. soldiers with considerable concern. Taking advantage of another provision in the Treaty of Guadalupe Hidalgo, those

Fort McIntosh, deactivated as an army post in 1946, is now the site of Laredo Community College. Many of the former military buildings are still being used. *The Alexander Collection.*

who had serious concerns simply crossed the newly declared international boundary to remain Mexican citizens in the hurriedly created village of Nuevo Laredo, located immediately across the Rio Grande.

At first, what passed for serious construction at the fort was the building of a so-called star fort similar to the one constructed earlier by Gen. Zachary Taylor at Fort Brown at the beginning of the Mexican War. While laboring to build what most army engineers then realized was essentially of little defensive value, the troopers lived in tents and suffered from the heat, humidity, and frigid conditions that sometimes occur in South Texas. When not working on their earthen fort, the men found time to take to the field. It proved difficult to break the Comanche warriors of their long-established practice of raiding villages and ranches in what was then Mexican territory across the river. The Indians, still oblivious to which nation they were raiding, found no allies on either side of the boundary river but continued their attacks until 1858. Then, likely realizing that the odds of both superior manpower and firepower ran strongly against them, the warlike tribes moved out to the western frontier of Texas to continue their marauding practices. With no Indian attacks to quell, the original mission of Fort McIntosh came to an end within ten years of its establishment. Accordingly, the army abandoned the fort in early 1859. When it closed, only twenty-six men were stationed there.

Satisfied that the Indians had left the area, and likely almost as pleased that the U.S. Army had also departed, the town of Laredo laid claim to the property, and some of the few permanent buildings were sold at auction. Renewed activities of Mexican bandits and insurrectionists, however, caused the army to reactivate the fort in 1860, but only for a year. Federal officers again closed it in March 1861, just prior to the Civil War. Reopened as a Confederate installation days later, it remained in operation by civilian volunteers during the war. The outpost's vantage point overlooking the Rio Grande made it possible for the garrison to ensure that matériel vital to the Confederate cause could be safely transported to Mexican ports, thus thwarting the Union blockade of Texas shipping points on the Gulf of Mexico. When the Civil War ended in 1865, Fort McIntosh was once again occupied by U.S. Army troops. A rapid building program soon transformed the installation into a major military facility.

With the coming of the Mexican Revolution in 1910, violence increased all along the border. Nuevo Laredo frequently saw violence during often-heated activity by various military, or quasi-military, units on both sides of the conflict. The garrison at Fort McIntosh substantially increased during this time as Laredoans attempted to dodge bullets that often flew across the river and struck downtown buildings.

During World War I, some thirty thousand troops were trained at the fort. Despite the presence of such a large army contingent, Mexican banditry and militia-like activities kept the citizens of Laredo apprehensive. Just before the war, a fire set by counterrevolutionaries destroyed most of Nuevo Laredo. At the end of its limited service during World War II, Fort McIntosh finally closed for the last time. Its many buildings, some dating back to the 1880s, became the property of Laredo Community College. Today, each of the old buildings is clearly marked with a sign telling of its original use and its history. Through breaks in the line of shrubbery that masks the school's western boundary fence, it is easy to see the smoky sprawl of Nuevo Laredo across the river. It is also easy to imagine the bitter days of a century ago, when the waters of the Rio Grande ran red.

FORT DUNCAN

Located roughly one hundred miles up the Rio Grande from the site of Fort McIntosh, Fort Duncan was established on March 27, 1849. Built on borrowed land neither purchased nor leased, it served the army's purposes because of its strategic site, which was close to a long-established river crossing point. In addition to its primary mission of preventing Indian incursions into Mexico, the fort also protected the flood of American settlers surging westward in the course of their nation's expansion at the end of the Mexican War. Although the military installation reflected a well-chosen site, its early garrison often proved to be too small to be effective against any large-scale attack by raiding Indian tribesmen. Cora Cazeneau, a pioneer in the region, noted that the Indians seemed impressed enough with the obvious fact that the army had set up a small fort in the region to forego attempts to undertake any significant raiding. Instead, most of such raids occurred across the river in Mexico, beyond the reach of the tiny U.S. force stationed at the fort.

Soon after the army established the military outpost, the small village of Eagle Pass began to take shape adjacent to it. A year after the opening of the fort and the emergence of its supporting town on the Texas side of the Rio Grande, the village of Piedras Negras came into being on the Mexican shore directly opposite. By 1851, a stagecoach route was running from San Antonio to Eagle Pass and beyond, reportedly created, at least in part, in the belief that the presence of Fort Duncan would ensure safe passage for its traveling clientele. The fort, the American town of Eagle Pass, and its Mexican neighbor, Piedras Negras, soon developed something of a symbiotic relationship. Fort Duncan at least supposedly protected the town, while it in turn supplied the military garrison with the many necessities that the government failed to provide. The Mexican town grew to be an additional marketplace for both the fort and its adjacent community.

Despite this symbiosis, however, the growth of the unofficial partnership was, by the mid-1850s, less than robust. Not quite five hundred officers and men garrisoned the fort, while Eagle Pass could claim only six hundred full-time residents. Piedras Negras reportedly had fewer than three hundred residents.

The fourth in the chain of forts along the Rio Grande was Fort Duncan at today's Eagle Pass. It, too, has a dwelling said to have been briefly occupied by then Lt. Col. Robert E. Lee before the Civil War. Few official records remain to substantiate that claim. *The Alexander Collection.*

During the years immediately preceding the Civil War, several officers whose exploits in that conflict soon made them famous passed through the fort. Among them was Philip H. Sheridan, a small-statured second lieutenant whose temper proved to be even shorter than his height. Eastern born and raised, Sheridan did not relish his service on the wild Texas and Mexico border. His overall lackluster performance caused him to continue at the lowest grade in the army's hierarchy until the rapid promotions stemming from the Civil War allowed him to move upward at an accelerated clip. His performance as a master cavalryman eventually propelled him to the top levels of Union army command.

Another soon-to-be-famous future general visited the fort on at least two occasions. He was none other than Bvt. Lt. Col. Robert E. Lee, mentioned earlier, whose travels along the border and indeed throughout all of Texas before the Civil War can be described as at least mildly extensive. There is definite proof that the future Confederate general traveled to Fort Duncan in 1854 and then again just before he resigned his U.S. Army commission in order to lend his inestimable support to the Confederate cause. On March 20, 1860, the visiting Lee wrote letters from the fort to Texas governor Sam Houston and to the army's adjutant general in Washington. Both letters survived the Civil War, and each bears the inscription "From Fort Duncan, Tx," as well as Lee's signature.

In later years, champions of the fort saw fit to embellish the Lee legend by bestowing the name Lee Memorial House on a small stone hut that remained on the abandoned site. They contended that Lee, then a lieutenant colonel, had slept in the tiny structure during one of his two visits. According to an Eagle Pass historian, the army eventually grew weary of politely denying the claim and issued a statement that the hut did not even exist when Lee came to visit, making all of the tales that he had lived within its limestone walls obviously invalid. Undismayed by the army's flat denial of their "Robert E. Lee Slept Here" legend, the local group refused to accept the army's statement. The building still stands on the site of old Fort Duncan with a prominent sign proudly proclaiming it to be the Lee Memorial House.

When the Civil War came, Bvt. Maj. Gen. David Twiggs ordered the abandonment of Fort Duncan on March 20, 1861. Soon thereafter, volunteers sympathetic to the Confederacy occupied the fort. The town of Eagle Pass quickly proved to be a vital shipping point for all manner of commodities flowing in and out of Texas, bypassing the Union blockade, which all but closed ports on the Gulf of Mexico. Freighters moved Texas goods across the river, where they were exported to Europe from ports in neutral Mexico. In this way, Texas cotton ended up in England, for example, in exchange for the importation of guns, ammunition, and other vital war supplies. Clashes between Confederate soldiers and Union sympathizers seeking to halt the trade across the river were frequent. When the war ended in 1865, Eagle Pass became something of an outlaw city and a center for banditry and cattle rustling, but the reopened fort was scarcely capable of effectively suppressing the lawlessness. With the coming of the railroad and an enhanced military presence in the region, the town eventually became a vital center for international trade. By 1910, Eagle Pass had a population of approximately thirty-five hundred, while Fort Duncan claimed a garrison of more than 750 men.

The year 1910 marked the beginning of the Mexican Revolution, and Fort Duncan, because of its strategic location, assumed its most important role since its founding. By 1916, more or less the midpoint of the revolution, the station comprised more than sixteen thousand officers and men. Fortunately for the thousands of new arrivals at the fort, the U.S. Army had earlier launched a major expansion and improvement after its reoccupation following the Civil War. Most of the new buildings were of substantial stone construction, replacing the wood-sided buildings built many years before. The rebuilt Fort Duncan had thirty-five buildings, including five quarters for married officers, an elegant officers' club, and suitable housing for other commissioned and noncommissioned officers, as well as a large mess hall. The sprawling five-thousand-acre facility also included a commissary and another smaller mess hall. Of that vast space, however, only 155 acres accommodated buildings and the drill field; the balance was devoted to practice ranges and field training areas.

Several factors explain why Fort Duncan took on such importance during the Mexican Revolution. Already well established and only recently enlarged and improved, it was near the Texas and Mexico Railway line, which crossed the Rio Grande at Eagle Pass to reach Piedras Negras, the gateway to the interior of the beleaguered nation. Mexican president Porfirio Díaz, the initial reason for the revolution, saw fit to change the name of Piedras Negras long before the fighting commenced. He named it in honor of his favorite Mexican president of all time, namely, himself. Combatants on both sides during the conflict then seemed determined to either keep the new name or go back to the old one, apparently willing to die to accomplish their objective.

Fort Duncan, across the river, stood guard throughout the violence that tortured Mexico for a decade. Always alert to the real possibility the fighting might quickly spill over into Texas, U.S. Army and National Guard commanders remained cautious. Soldiers from as far away as New York, Maryland, and Tennessee crowded into the fort. By 1917, many of those soldiers had left Texas to fight in the Great War (World War I). Although the threat of any large-scale Mexican incursions across the river abated, a reduced force remained to maintain a vigil on the American side of the river. Bandit raids did occur from time to time, and troops from the fort occasionally crossed the river to recover livestock stolen by Mexican rustlers. With its mission substantially diminished at the war's end, the fort officially became Camp Eagle Pass to reflect its decreased importance. By the end of the war, the camp's twenty-five-hundred-man garrison redeployed, and in 1919 the army abandoned the site. In 1938, the entire property was conveyed to the city of Eagle Pass for use first as a recreation area and then as the site of a sizable hospital located not far from the old fort's medical facility.

Several of the buildings erected by the army and used extensively during the Mexican Revolution era and World War I still stand. Most feature signs that describe their utilization nearly a century ago. On one corner of two intersecting and easily identified former military streets stands the little limestone hut where, as the locals still insist, the great Robert E. Lee spent one night, poised on the threshold of immortality.

Fort Ringgold

LOCATION: On the eastern edge of Rio Grande City.

ACCESS: Public property.

Fort McIntosh

LOCATION: On the western edge of Laredo.

ACCESS: Now part of a college campus, with easy public access.

Fort Duncan

LOCATION: On the western edge of Eagle Pass.

ACCESS: Public park with easy access.

SOURCES

Briggs, Alton K. "Archeological Investigation of an Area Proposed for Vegetation Management at Fort McIntosh, U.S.A. (1849), Laredo, Webb County, Texas." Laredo: Laredo Junior College District, 1982.

Cazeneau, Cora Montgomery. *Eagle Pass or Life on the Border.* Austin: Pemberton Press (reprint), 1966.

Frazier, Robert W. *Forts of the West: Military Forts and Presidios and Posts Commonly Called Forts West of the Mississippi River to 1898.* Norman: University of Oklahoma Press, 1965.

Greene, Shirley Brooks. *When Rio Grande City Was Young.* Edinburg, TX: Pan American University Press, 1987.

Horgan, Paul. *Great River: The Rio Grande in North American History.* New York: Holt, Rinehart and Winston, 1954.

Kinsall, A. Ray. *Fort Duncan: Frontier Outpost on the Rio Grande.* Eagle Pass, TX: Maverick County Historical Commission, 1999.

Robinson, Charles M., III. *Frontier Forts of Texas.* Houston: Lone Star Books, 1986.

Timanus, Rod. *An Illustrated History of Texas Forts.* Plano, TX: Republic of Texas Free Press, 2001.

Warren, James E. "Historic Archeology at Fort McIntosh in Laredo, Webb County." Laredo: Laredo Junior College, 1988.

6 FORT EWELL 1852–1854

I fear a summer in Texas, especially this part of Texas.
— ***Bvt. Maj. John S. Simonson***

It is the nature of military preparedness that some installations outlive others, whether that is due to redefined missions, the cessation of immediate threat or conflict, or difficulties arising from an inappropriate location. With regard to the latter, specifically as it related to the establishment of army fortifications along the Texas frontier, it often fell to topographical engineers to reconnoiter the landscape to select sites they considered strategically viable and defensible, as well as partially sustainable. Regardless of who initially selected a fort site, the location had to be vetted through the chain of command and assessed for maximum effectiveness. Even with such planning and scrutiny, however, the ultimate decision sometimes proved to be ill conceived and unmanageable. Such was the case with a short-lived installation in present-day La Salle County known as Fort Ewell.

Established in 1852 on the south side of the Nueces River, where the stream intersected the eighteenth-century route known as the San Antonio to Laredo Road, Fort Ewell provided protection for both settlers and supplies moving along the important corridor. At the time, the so-called Nueces Strip remained an uneasy and untamed area fraught with raids by Native Americans and outlaws and subject to political uncertainty at the end of the Mexican War only four years earlier. Additionally, it presented a harsh environment that challenged and frustrated soldiers and would-be settlers alike. An area prone to not only drought but also the frequent flooding of the shallow-sided stream, the strip remained only sparsely settled in the years prior to the Civil War. Yet, it was an area that needed a military presence to ensure at least a modicum of security.

Final approval of the site of Fort Ewell came from Bvt. Lt. Col. William Wing Loring, a North Carolina native reared in Florida and who served with distinction in the Mexican War at Cerro Gordo and Churubusco, where he was wounded in action. Again injured during the fighting around Chapultepec, resulting in the loss of his left arm, Loring received two brevets for his exemplary combat service. He remained with the army following the war, later serving as commandant of the Oregon Territory. Shortly after, he received command of the Rio Grande frontier in Texas, and it was during that assignment that he approved the selection of the sites for Fort Ewell and other installations in South Texas.

As part of Loring's effort to secure the area, the location where the San Antonio to Laredo Road crossed the Nueces seemed a logical choice for a fortification. The name of the new installation there honored Lt. Thomas Ewell, of the Mounted Rifles, who was mortally wounded early in the Mexican War during the fighting at Cerro Gordo on April 18, 1847. A native of Virginia then serving from Tennessee, Lieutenant Ewell was the brother of Capt. Richard Stoddert Ewell, a somewhat eccentric and enigmatic leader in the Southern command during the Civil War whom some sources credit as the namesake of the Texas fort along the Nueces.

The commanding officer at Fort Ewell was Bvt. Maj. John Smith Simonson, a Pennsylvania native and War of 1812 veteran who later served in the Indiana legislature, where he became speaker of the house. In 1846, Simonson became a captain with the U.S. Army Regiment of Mounted Riflemen and saw service in the Mexican War. In 1852, he received the orders that resulted in his new command along the Rio Grande frontier. Almost from the beginning of that command, the conditions at Fort Ewell proved to be unwieldy primarily due to environmental conditions, including periodic flooding, inadequate building materials, and a relentless summer heat that withered crops, but also as the result of an unsupported mission and internal military conflicts. Formally established on May 18, 1852, by Capt. Andrew Jackson Lindsay, the outpost was

Although nothing remains at the remote site of Fort Ewell, which is inaccessible to the public and on private land, these photos of the general region of the South Texas brush country along the Nueces River are evocative of the nearly impenetrable vegetation and harsh conditions soldiers had to contend with as they established the short-lived outpost in the years before the Civil War. *Photo 1 by William A. McWhorter, courtesy of the Texas Historical Commission. Photo 2 by Patrick Cox, Austin.*

garrisoned by companies E, G, and I of the Mounted Riflemen. Troops patrolled the immediate vicinity of the main route and also participated in longer expeditions in conjunction with military posts along the Rio Grande and the coast. By the fall, Simonson clearly seemed disillusioned, as he noted in a November 4 letter to his wife, Betsy (Elizabeth). Preserved in the Simonson papers in the Briscoe Center for American History at the University of Texas, the letter notes the marginal conditions of the site. "I have nothing new," Simonson wrote, "except that I have a chimney built to my tent and am much more comfortable with my little fire inside, then [*sic*] outside the tent. I have also a table and wash stand and will have andirons soon, and having a floor in my tent and four additional blankets hope to keep warm during the winter." Providing further detail of living conditions at the fort, he added, "I had a treat yesterday—old Ellen (Lieut Jones Negro woman) [*sic*]sent me a pitcher of Butter Milk, but our potatoes have given out and we need that article much—I have sent to Corpus Christi for another barrel. There is several cases of scurvy in the hospital and the Doct thinks potatoes the best preventative for that horrible disease."

Simonson wrote of skirmishes in the area and of "trouble with the Mexican population in this area" but also spoke fondly of his colleagues in the headquarters command at Corpus Christi, some of whom decided to buy town lots and settle in the area permanently. As for his own condition, though, he noted, "My ankle mends slowly—I fear sometimes it will never be straight or well—the Doct speaks encouragingly however." Although the exact nature of the injury remains unknown, he noted that it required regular treatments of iodine and liniment, as well as changed bandages twice a day. Simonson's condition may not be the only factor, however, that caused him to add, "It seems to me impossible to remain much longer in the Army. I must retire soon." Despite that melancholy prediction, he remained in active service until 1861, when he retired as a colonel with the 3rd U.S. Cavalry.

Simonson was thus still stationed at Fort Ewell in June 1853, when Bvt. Lt. Col. William Grigsby Freeman arrived for his personal inspection of installations under the command of the Eighth Military Department (Texas). A Virginia native who entered the U.S.

Military Academy at the age of fifteen, Freeman served as an assistant adjutant general during the 1850s. His report provided detailed accounts of activities in the various Texas forts, where a sizable number of the U.S. Army then served. The opening part of his report on Fort Ewell gives the clearest record of conditions there only a year after its establishment:

> The river at the ford is about 75 feet wide and 4½ feet in depth, but it frequently overflows its banks covering the bottoms and salt marshes on either side to the extent of a mile. The site of the post is somewhat elevated, but the surrounding country is a low salt marsh. Suitable timber or stone for building cannot be obtained within less distance than ten or fifteen miles, good grazing for animals cannot be found in the vicinity, and every attempt thus far to make a kitchen garden has been unsuccessful. Indeed a less inviting spot for occupation by troops cannot well be conceived.

Freeman also wrote of other conditions affecting the long-term viability of the site: "The title of the land around Fort Ewell is not in the Government, but is claimed by a resident of San Antonio, who has notified the post Quartermaster that he intends to present a bill for timber destroyed and for occupancy." He added, "The buildings standing at the post (and which were all put up by the labour of the troops) consist of one commissary storehouse, one blacksmith's shop, and two sets of company quarters—each built of adobes." Freeman went on to describe the marginal condition of the structures, some with canvas roofs: "If the post is to be maintained, it is important that suitable buildings should be provided as soon as possible."

Freeman's inspection turned up a number of internal command concerns, one of which involved Capt. Noah Newton, then under arrest and being held at Fort Ringgold. "This officer," Freeman observed, "was arrested August 13, 1852, and he informed me that up to the period of my visit—ten months afterward—he was ignorant of the charges against him, or the steps, if any, taken to bring him to trial." Sadly, the inspector noted further, "Capt. Newton is since dead, but as his case came under my observation officially, I have not felt at liberty to pass it over in silence." With regard to the enforcement of military regulations and uniform standards, Freeman reported onsite training modifications relative to the *Manual of Arms* and observed that although the soldiers wore standard uniforms, they disliked the army caps, which were "complained of as not being suited in any particular to the climate of Texas." He also observed problems with the army-issued rifle, which he determined was an "inconvenient weapon for a horseman" that "cannot be loaded without dismounting, nor fired with accuracy from the saddle." He called instead for the use of Sharp's carbines rather than the standard "cumbrous arm."

In a positive vein, Freeman gave high marks to the soldiers, whom he described as "young and active." He added, "Their officers represent them to be generally temperate and subordinate, and judging by appearance I do not think I have ever met with finer material in the ranks of the Army." However, he further noted, "Many desertions have occurred since the regiment arrived in Texas, the men sometimes taking their horses and arms and escaping into Mexico." Regardless, he explained, "The utmost harmony prevails among the officers of Fort Ewell."

Echoing the earlier letter from Simonson, Freeman reported on the spread of disease at the outpost brought on by the trying environmental conditions. periodic flooding and stagnant water, coupled with extremes of heat and cold throughout the year. Speaking specifically of scurvy, he wrote, "The scorbutic condition was also observable in influencing other diseases; and there is at all times such a tendency to this disease as to make a constant supply of potatoes extremely desirable, as it is impossible to cultivate a garden, on account of the excessive heat, and the want of rain, dew and even moist winds."

In large part due to Freeman's report, army officials reconsidered the purpose of Fort Ewell, and in December 1853 they formally ordered its systematic abandonment. The remaining officers and soldiers departed by October 1854, leaving behind only ruined elements of the short-lived fort. Although the outpost closed, the influence of Fort Ewell continued for a few years under the name some of the residents gave to a nearby community, also known as

Guajoco. When the legislature moved to create La Salle County in 1858, naming it in honor of the French explorer René Robert Cavelier, sieur de la Salle, the dispersed community was one of the few pockets of settlement in the area. Formal establishment of the county came in 1880, but early communities such as Fort Ewell eventually gave way to the development of commercial centers along the railroad routes. One of those, Cotulla, became the county seat in 1883.

Although the military operations at Fort Ewell were short lived, they represented the federal government's intent to bring security and stability to the land along the formerly untamed area known as the Nueces Strip and in the process put the U.S. stamp on the region for good. Fort Ewell provided a necessary military presence in the region following the close of the Mexican War and served to enforce the tenets of the Treaty of Guadalupe Hidalgo. As a result, within a few years the area opened to organized political settlement that grew steadily with great promise and purpose.

LOCATION: The fort site is twenty-five miles southeast of Cotulla, where the old San Antonio to Laredo Road crossed the Nueces River.

ACCESS: The fort site is on private property and not accessible to the public.

SOURCES

Crimmins, M. L., ed. "W. G. Freeman's Report on the Eighth Military Department." *Southwestern Historical Quarterly* 51(1) (July 1947): 54–58.

———. "W. G. Freeman's Report on the Eighth Military Department." *Southwestern Historical Quarterly* 51(3) (January 1948): 252–58.

Fort Ewell Records. Briscoe Center for American History, the University of Texas at Austin.

Hughes, Jeremiah, ed. *Niles' National Register: Political, Historical, Geographical, Scientifical, Statistical, Economical and Biographical Documents, Essays and Facts Together with Notices of the Arts and Manufactures, and Records of Events of the*

Times, vol. 72, March 1847–September 1847. Baltimore: Editor, 1847.
Simonson, John S., Papers. Briscoe Center for American History, the University of Texas at Austin.
Texas Historical Commission marker files, La Salle County.
Wessels, William L. *Born to Be a Soldier: The Military Career of William Wing Loring of St. Augustine, Florida.* Fort Worth: Texas Christian University Press, 1971.

7 FORT MASON
1851–1869

I am determined to defend Fort Mason at all costs.
— Lt. Col. Robert E. Lee, January 21, 1861

It is hardly a secret that some well-intentioned if overly zealous promoters of small towns occasionally distort their community's history. As a result, a listing of names of one-time residents might include individuals of considerable renown, who in fact never came near the city being highly touted as an ideal place to dwell. Mason, on the northern edge of the Texas Hill Country, however, has every right to its claim of once being the home of, and the proving ground for, many well-known Civil War generals. Included on that list of twenty flag-rank senior officers are men of magnitude such as Albert Sidney Johnston, John Bell Hood, James Longstreet, and Robert E. Lee, the most renowned Southern commander of all. Lee and nineteen other eventual Confederate generals served at the town's Fort Mason in the years just before the war, along with eight soon-to-be generals who continued to wear their uniforms of Union blue after the war commenced in April 1861. Earlier, all had been officers of either the 2nd Dragoons or the U.S. Army's elite 2nd Cavalry, each handpicked to serve by the U.S. Secretary of War and future president of the Confederacy, Jefferson Davis.

In 1985, an enterprising journalist suggested that yet another former Union general had been at the post. George Armstrong Custer, the writer claimed, rode out of Fort Mason immediately before leading his men to their doom in the valley of the Little Big Horn in present-day Montana. As the Texas fort permanently closed eight years before Custer's legendary last battle in 1876, though, little credence can be given to the reporter's colorful story.

The U.S. Army established the fort on July 6, 1851, in response to a plea by Texas governor Peter Hansborough Bell to Gen. George M. Brooke, commander of the military Department of Texas. The governor's concern stemmed from a letter he received from Hill Country settlers, who complained of increasing Indian raids in the region. The site of the new fort was on a high ridge not far from the Llano River and a little more than one hundred miles from San Antonio. Who actually selected the site and for whom the fort was named are not clear. Some sources credit Bvt. Maj. H. W. Merrill as the officer who recommended the location, whereas others claim that Lt. William H. C. (Little Billy) Whiting was the first to suggest building the fort at the vantage point afforded by its hilltop location. Whiting had previously noted that the "old Spanish presidio on [the] San Saba River" would be an ideal location for a new fort charged with the mission of protecting settlers and travelers heading west during the post–Mexican War gold rush. Most sources, however, name Bvt. Col. William J. Hardee, a future Confederate lieutenant general, as the person who actually selected the site. Hardee survived the first skirmish of the Mexican War, in which his friend Lt. George T. Mason died after refusing to surrender. It is generally believed that Hardee named the new fort in honor of his fallen friend and comrade-in-arms.

In July 1851 Bvt. Maj. H. W. Merrill commanded the 1st Dragoons when the unit arrived at the chosen site. With orders to construct an installation substantial enough to anchor what would become the army's second line of frontier forts in Texas, Major Merrill quickly set his men to work creating a fort on the rocky ridge. The first building constructed was a log hospital, followed by officers' quarters of the traditional dog-run design. The installation, constructed on the privately owned thirteen-hundred-acre site, soon took on the appearance of a better-than-average frontier fort. A garden and bakery augmented the supplies delivered by pack train from San Antonio. Military officials purchased meats and produce from the increasing number of ranchers and farmers who began streaming into the region following the army's arrival. A strong spring located on the property proved more than adequate for the 150 men and ninety-one horses who were quartered at the fort during its early years.

In August 1853 Col. W. G. Freeman inspected the post and proclaimed it to be in finer order than any cavalry station he had visited, "second to none in the Department except Ringgold Barracks." Colonel Freeman went on to declare the fort's stables to be excellent, although his discovery that nearly a third of the horses were "non-effective" meant that in his view only a portion of the garrison could "suitably appear as Cavalry." Among the early commanding officers of Fort Mason during its short existence as the home of the 1st Dragoons was the flamboyant Col. Charles A. May, a hero of the Mexican War. Despite his previous fame and colorful reputation and at the age of only forty-three, he resigned from the army a week after the beginning of the Civil War. May's second-in-command was Maj. Philip St. George Cooke, who became a Union general in the Civil War. He also had the challenging distinction of being father-in-law to the legendary Confederate Gen. J. E. B. Stuart, an officer likely even more colorful than Colonel May. Despite Colonel Freeman's relatively glowing inspection report of August 1853, orders to abandon Fort Mason arrived just five months later. It took opportunistic Kiowa, Lipan Apache, and Comanche warriors little time to rekindle their vigorous efforts to drive the unprotected settlers out of the region. Once again, the endangered pioneer ranchers and farmers appealed to the governor of Texas, now Elisha M. Pease, who in turn pleaded with army officials to rescind the order abandoning the post. Finally, a year after the fort closed, the welcome news came that a newly created cavalry unit was on its way back to Fort Mason.

The outfit was the creation of Secretary of War Jefferson Davis, himself a hero of the Mexican War and by all accounts a good judge of some of the men with whom he served in that conflict. With Albert Sidney Johnston as its commanding officer, Robert E. Lee as second-in-command, and future Civil War legends such as William J. Hardee and George H. Thomas as majors, the U.S. Army's 2nd Cavalry marched out of Jefferson Barracks, Missouri, en route to Fort Mason on October 25, 1855. Colonel Johnston and his command reached the reopened installation on January 19, 1856. It had taken them nearly ninety days to travel the roughly 750 miles to their new Texas post. The route of march followed a trace that is now US Highway 69 to modern-day Denison, Texas, then to Fort Phantom Hill (north of today's Abilene), and finally along what is now US Highway 283 to their destination.

Without doubt, the best record of the progress of the 2nd Cavalry en route to Texas comes from the diary of Eliza Griffin Johnston, second wife of the widowed commander, Albert Sidney Johnston. Her journal begins on October 27, 1855, the day she and other family members, along with slaves and servants, began the long trek to Texas. As one writer later observed, the retinue departing from Jefferson Barracks probably looked more like an emigrant train bound for the goldfields of California than a cavalry unit riding off to quell Indian raids in Texas. A talented artist with a trained eye for the beauty of nature, Mrs. Johnston wrote more about the rivers and trees she saw on her way south to Texas than about the six-inch sheets of ice that often covered their wagon tops each night. Colonel Lee was not with the unit when it arrived at Fort Mason. His years as superintendent of the U.S. Military Academy, plus his own innate sense of both duty and fairness, gave him the gravitas necessary to function as president of many army court martial proceedings. As a result, he had gone directly to Camp Cooper, located near Fort Griffin in present-day Throckmorton County, rather than to Fort Mason. From there he traveled throughout Texas to preside at the trials.

The seven hundred men of Colonel Johnston's command, along with their remuda of eight hundred horses, survived three months of unusually cold and wet weather only to find upon their arrival a dilapidated and totally abandoned installation. The six companies of troopers, some with their families in tow, hurriedly began restoring and rebuilding Fort Mason. With six times more men to be accommodated, the installation needed to be expanded even as it was being made basically habitable. In time, the fort would boast twenty-five buildings, some made of wood, but more constructed from stone quarried nearby. The garrison also included a hospital and a kitchen, along with an adequate mess hall to serve all of the cavalrymen on a staggered schedule. Eventually there were six buildings just to house the regimental officers. When the Johnstons arrived at the fort in January 1856, however, they found only one two-room building suitable for the regimental commander, his wife, and children. Rather than claim the two small rooms for their own exclusive use, the Johnstons decided to share the cramped quarters with a junior officer, Capt Richard W. Johnson, his wife, Rachel, and their three children. Although some observers noted that this arrangement reflected the warm and generous nature of Mrs. Johnston, her diary indicates she was not all that pleased to have her family living in such proximity to another. On January 16, 1856, she wrote that her neighbors used her room "as if it were their own." She further lamented that she "might just as well have 6 children of my own for they [the neighbor's offspring] are almost as much trouble."

In early March 1856, Mrs. Johnston had an opportunity to observe Colonel Lee in his role as the presiding officer in a court martial at Fort Mason. On trial was a Lieutenant Woods, an officer apparently not at all well respected by Mrs. Johnston. After Colonel Lee had been called on to testify about the lieutenant's character, Mrs. Johnston made a scathing entry in her diary, decrying how Lee handled the matter. Noting that the future Confederate icon had "hemmed and hawed" and failed to comment one way or the other, she found the colonel's decision to suddenly depart the post "a mean act," claiming Lee knew quite well of Woods's less than sterling character. This observation is among the few negative views of Robert E. Lee to survive in history's otherwise glowing portrait of the great man.

Fortunately, Mrs. Johnston did not have to suffer the overcrowded situation for long. On March 24, 1856, Colonel Lee arrived at the fort on his way to take full command of the 2nd Cavalry's post at Camp Cooper. In addition, Maj. William Hardee, then at Cooper, would soon return to Fort Mason to take command. Colonel Johnston received orders to leave on April 1, 1856, to assume command of the entire Department of Texas in San Antonio. On April 5 Mrs. Johnston and their two sons left their crowded quarters to join her husband at his new headquarters, having been at Fort Mason less than ninety days.

Soon Hardee was on his way to a new assignment as commandant of the U.S. Military Academy at West Point. Upon Hardee's departure for New York, Capt. E. Kirby Smith, eventually to become a general in the Confederate army, assumed command of the fort. In time, Maj. George H. Thomas assumed command of the garrison. During the Civil War, which would erupt in three short years, the Southern-born Thomas become a Union general and rose to fame as the "Rock of Chickamauga."

Despite another favorable report by an army inspector, the fort closed early in 1859. Nine months later, it reopened, however, in response to the pleas of local settlers, who had once again been subjected to Indian raids while the fort remained unmanned. In December 1860, Colonel Lee reappeared at the fort, this time as its commanding officer. Two months later, he received orders to leave at once for Washington, DC. He did so on February 13, 1861, relinquishing command to Capt. Richard Johnson, the man whose noisy family had given so much grief to Mrs. Albert Sidney Johnston some six years earlier. After encouraging his replacement to ensure the security of Fort Mason in the war, which nearly all of the officers sensed was imminent, Lee left the installation on his way east and into posterity. The fort on the high ridge was to be his last command as an officer in the United States Army, which would soon be his adversary.

Unlike his predecessor, Captain Johnson chose to remain in the Union army. When he and his troopers left the fort under a flag of truce granted by occupying Confederate soldiers on March 29, 1861, the installation soon fell into disuse once again. It is interesting to note that because of Bvt. Maj. Gen. David Twiggs's eagerness to surrender all federal installations in Texas to the Confederate forces, Fort Mason was transferred more than two weeks before the Civil War actually began at Fort Sumter, South Carolina. By December 4, 1866, when Fort Mason was reoccupied by Union troops, the war was over, and Fort Mason was once again occupied by now victorious Union troops. During the war, the fort deteriorated badly even though it housed some two hundred German settlers held as prisoners of war because of their professed Union allegiance.

Despite a major renovation effort at the fort on the faulty assumption that it would soon become a permanent installation, an order resulted in closure on April 15, 1868. Local settlers, correctly

Reproduced Commanding Officers House sits atop a hill overlooking Mason. General Albert Sidney Johnston's wife proclaimed the view to be one of the "grandest and most extensive" she had ever seen. Many officers on both sides of the Civil War earlier served at this fort. *The Alexander Collection.*

guessing that this time the fort would never reopen, began a long process of carrying away quantities of the stones soldiers had quarried over the years. Soon little remained of what had once been the military home of heroes in both blue and gray. The landowners of the site tried in vain to halt the vandalizing of the fort, but eventually it was to no avail. One of those landowners had a name well known to supporters of both sides during the Civil War. He was James Longstreet, the Confederate lieutenant general whom General Lee called his "Old War Horse." Tax records indicate that Longstreet originally owned three hundred acres of the land that included the fort site. By the time he sold the property in 1867, his holdings had fallen to two hundred acres. The future general originally purchased the property from Richard A. Howard for $50 on March 26, 1860,. He apparently retained ownership throughout the Civil War before selling it. As paymaster of the 2nd Cavalry prior to the war, Longstreet, during one of his official visits, appeared sufficiently impressed with the fort to purchase some of its acreage.

In 1870, the Texas Rangers utilized some of the few buildings still serviceable in an effort to control the civil violence that continued long after the war was over. After the removal of most of the Indians from the region, the fort permanently closed in 1871. A hundred years later, a group of preservation-minded citizens of the town of Mason set about recreating at least one building of the fort that had spawned their community and given it its name. The result was a fairly accurate replica of one of the officers' quarters, similar to the tiny building in which the Johnstons once shared space with the Johnsons.

Time has erased nearly every other features of the fort's presence. A good historical museum in town recounts the history of the installation and displays artifacts collected at the site over the years. Some of the artifacts were unearthed by fourth-, fifth-, and sixth-grade students from Mason schools in 1987 and 1988. Although scientific archeological studies have been contemplated from time to time, only the reproduction of the one building and the legends about the many great Civil War commanders who served there in the 1850s remain. The ridge itself is without doubt the most enduring part of the Fort Mason story. The view to the south is, as Mrs. Albert Sidney Johnston recorded nearly 160 years ago, "one of the grandest and most extensive ever to be seen anywhere."

LOCATION: On a ridge east of downtown Mason.
ACCESS: Open to the public. Replica of officers' quarters on site.

SOURCES

Bierschwale, Margaret. *A History of Mason County: Fort Mason, Texas.* Mason: Mason County Historical Commission, 1980.

"Fort Mason: A Texas Frontier Fort. Mason, Texas, 1851–1869." Mason: Mason County Historical Society, n.d.

Johnston, Eliza Griffin. "The Diary of Eliza (Mrs. Albert Sidney) Johnston." *Southwestern Historical Quarterly* 60 (April 1957): 101–108.

Mason County Tax Records, Deed Book B.
Simpson, Harold B. *Frontier Forts of Texas*. Waco: Texian Press, 1966.
Smith, Thomas T. *The US Army & the Texas Frontier Economy, 1845–1900*. College Station: Texas A&M University Press, 1997.
Swenson, Ed, ed. "Fort Mason Guarded Hills." *Kerrville Hill Country* 16(4) (1957): 358–77.

8 FORT PHANTOM HILL 1851–1875

I cannot believe that God ever intended white man to occupy such a barren waste. — Lt. Clinton Lear, Fort Phantom Hill, 1852

Unlike nearly all U.S. Army installations constructed along Texas' progressively expanding western frontier after America's 1846–1848 war with Mexico, Fort Phantom Hill was obviously not named for a fallen hero of that conflict. How the short-lived and relatively unimportant outpost did get its colorful name has, however, been the subject of conjecture for many years.

Established on November 14, 1851, the post was part of the second line of army fortifications created to protect settlers who flooded onto the Texas prairies after the defeat of Mexico in 1848. Officially known as the "Post on the Clear Fork of the Brazos," the installation joined other new outposts such as forts Belknap, Mason, McKavett, and Chadbourne along the frontier. The surge of white civilization pushed back the stubborn and often violent resistance of Native American tribes who believed themselves rightful stewards of the hills and prairies of Texas. Earlier fortifications once located on what had been the frontier just a few years earlier had been closed as the white man advanced inexorably westward and the buffalo herd receded.

General Order no. 91, issued by Bvt. Maj. Gen. Persifor Smith on November 3, 1851, designated that a post be established "on the Clear Fork [of the Brazos River] at or in the vicinity of a point known as Phantom Hill." Although that directive should be sufficient explanation of how the outpost got its name, other versions have circulated in the region for years. One claims the name came from the sighting of a lone Indian on horseback, completely wrapped in a long white robe. From a distance at least, this apparition ap-

Ghostlike chimneys are nearly all that remain of the ill-fated Fort Phantom Hill, north of Abilene. *The Alexander Collection.*

parently appeared to a viewer as a phantom rather than a solitary horseman. Another version has the name stemming from a miragelike effect that some say causes the slight hill of the outpost to appear relatively large from a distance, only to shrink in magnitude upon approach. Others attribute the ghostly effect created by the sight of the chimneys that tower, ethereally in the moonlight, above the now ruined fort as the source of the name. "Phantom Hill" appears in an army general order well before the construction of the chimneys, however, thus significantly diminishing that theory.

Perhaps the colorful if somewhat eerie name Phantom Hill itself has served to generate all sorts of other legends about the old post.

One tale claims that none other than Sam Houston built the fort. In an article written in 1923, Ray Rector, a local newspaperman, discredited that notion. In the same piece, he also debunked another story that Lt. Col. Robert E. Lee had built the fort and in fact lived there for a considerable time. An additional part of the Lee legend had the mild-mannered future Confederate leader killing a Comanche chief in hand-to-hand combat near the fort at the exact time Lee was serving as commandant of the U.S. Military Academy in New York, far removed from Texas and any Comanche chiefs eager to do battle with him. In a final bit of Lee legend rebuttal, Rector set straight a pervasive local tale that a small grave at Fort Phantom Hill contained the remains of Lee's first son, born at the fort, only to die there. Clearly a journalist with a determination of steel, Rector wrote to Gen. George Washington Custis Lee, Robert E. Lee's eldest son, in 1911 to either nullify or verify this claim. In his 1923 article, Rector stated that the general replied by mail and stated unequivocally that "Gen. R. E. Lee has no child buried in Texas."

In addition to its abundance of folklore, Fort Phantom Hill's checkered past also includes misfortune but little in the way of heroic military accomplishment. For one thing, it was not a fort at all but instead a cantonment, a place for officers and men of the 5th Cavalry to live between their various duties: riding patrol, escorting settlers, and protecting the frontier from Indian marauders. At one point, the post had a single fieldpiece, but otherwise it did not possess the heavy artillery usually found at most frontier fortifications. Another curious aspect of the installation's record is that it was allegedly not built at the site originally designated for it. A newly assigned general officer determined that his choice of location was far superior to the one initially specified by his predecessor. That unwise change in plans became one of the major factors in the eventual decision to abandon the post at an early date.

From the fort's first day of occupation, it was apparent that the absence of a reliable source of water would become a serious problem. The Clear Fork of the Brazos soon proved frequently to be less than clear enough to be consistently potable. The rotting buffalo carcasses upstream as well as the ever present silt made the water all but useless to people and just slightly more useful to horses. A spring that briefly flourished on the hillside near the fort stopped flowing in the stifling heat of every Texas summer. An eighty-five-foot well produced at first mud and then only silt as the summer wore on without measurable rainfall. Shortly after the fort opened, its only reliable source of water was a well located nearly five miles distant. Heavy wagons loaded with barrels carted the water to the fort many times each day.

The location of the cantonment also failed to have an adequate supply of wood, essential for cooking, warmth, and building purposes. Construction-quality wood could be found only at a distance of more than six miles, while soldiers quickly exhausted the original local supply needed for other daily functions. Game proved to be scarce on the treeless prairie that surrounded the fort. Most food supplies were therefore delivered by wagon trains from the army's supply depot in Austin, some 250 miles to the east. Bands of Indians, also suffering from the absence of game and the once mighty herds of buffalo, often preyed upon the wagons as they creaked westward toward the fort. As a result of both the distance and the frequent attacks on the trains, the incoming flow of food supplies proved unreliable.

Records indicate that the soldiers at the fort made a genuine effort to replenish their often insufficient food supplies. They created a thirty-acre garden in the hope that it would provide enough vegetables to satisfy the garrison of more than one hundred men. The harsh chemical composition of the soil and the lack of adequate rainfall, however, soon turned the garden into an incinerated tangle of dried vines and brittle leaves.

Without the products envisioned from the garden and with the unpredictable receipt of enough fruit and vegetables arriving on supply wagons, sickness and disease frequently weakened the men of Phantom Hill. Scurvy, dysentery, and other ailments were magnified in their severity and duration by the extreme heat and equally debilitating cold. At first, housing accommodations consisted of nothing more than jacals. Constructed of vertical wooden poles daubed with dried mud, the simple huts offered little protection from the elements for the officers and their men, who inhabited them until sturdier buildings could be erected.

None of these unfortunate shortcomings came as a surprise to the army's senior officers, who inspected the site when it first received occupants. The outpost's first commanding officer, Bvt. Lt. Col. J. J. Abercrombie, reported his accurate assessment of the site's many drawbacks to his superiors, but to no avail. In the narrow view of army headquarters in San Antonio, construction had to be completed despite the colonel's "very serious objections," if for no other shortsighted reason than that elements of his immediate command were already living at the site, and more were on the way. By the end of November 1853, five companies were in residence at the soon-to-be-built cantonment, consisting of eleven commissioned officers, 153 noncommissioned officers, a small band of musicians, and a quantity of privates. Colonel Abercrombie's wife was also present, as were the wives of several other officers.

Within a month's time, the arrival of even more troops swelled the population of the garrison to nearly three hundred men. The increased number predictably put even more demand on the food supply and on the relative trickle of available water. Despite the hardships Abercrombie so frequently and so clearly identified, his superiors remained resolute, if not downright stubborn, in their insistence that Fort Phantom Hill stay exactly where it was, without further discussion. Its officers were under orders to solve any problems that made the location unpleasant. In time, the army found a good source of building stone not too distant from the garrison. Motivated by the pressing need to improve their lot in life, the men worked together to build at least some acceptable structures in which to live and go about their daily duties.

By the time Bvt. Lt. Col. W. G. Freeman arrived to inspect the facility in early 1853, conditions had only slightly improved. There were a few stone buildings, and soldiers identified local purveyors of basic foodstuffs, reducing to some degree the outpost's almost total reliance on supply trains. At the time of his inspection, Colonel Freeman noted that 219 men were posted at the fort but that 123 of them were raw recruits. This inordinate proportion of untrained personnel likely reflected the unusually large number of deserters who frequently stole away from the installation, believing they had suffered long enough from the army's obvious insensitivity in ordering them to live in such a godforsaken outpost plagued by disease and starvation.

Although the only significant military rationale for the existence of the fort was the anticipated trouble with the local Indian tribes and nomadic bands such as the Comanche, few warlike Native Americans were ever to be found anywhere near the fort. On one rare occasion, however, a band of Comanche estimated by an eyewitness to be around twenty-five hundred in number did approach the installation. Forewarned, the soldiers came out "in battle array" to confront them. After glaring at the army men for several minutes, the tribe's chief, Buffalo Hump, uttered a command, and the band "passed on with scowls and angry looks, going in a westerly direction."

In keeping with standing orders, small patrols of infantrymen routinely marched out of the fort to discourage Indian raiders from attacking ranches in the region. Previous experience, however, should have prompted the army to frown on the use of plodding foot soldiers in combating the fast-moving, highly capable cavalry that tribes such as the Comanche and the Kiowa had become with the arrival of the horse. Fortunately for the men of Fort Phantom Hill, the main threat the Indians usually posed was only the petty theft of supplies and livestock. While duty at the post was clearly not hazardous, it proved to be both boring and isolated. Communication with more civilized points remained limited, and the absence of water, the poor quality of the food, and frequent sickness made Fort Phantom Hill a singularly unpopular assignment.

On April 27, 1852, Colonel Abercrombie passed command of the fort to Lt. Col. Carlos A. Waite, who was in turn succeeded by Maj. Henry Hopkins Sibley on September 24, 1853. According to his biographer, Sibley was not at all pleased with his new assignment, apparently with good reason. Although army personnel erected several more permanent buildings, the new commanding officer's quarters remained in one of the infamous, hastily built, pole-sided jacal huts from when the post had first opened. Sibley's headquarters did have a reading room equipped with a small number of books shipped in from the Austin supply depot. The building that housed it was among the few made of stone and thus provided at least an acceptable place for common frontier post activities such as card playing and the drinking of whiskey. The latter pursuit, when later taken to an excessive level by Major and later Brig. Gen. Sibley of the Confederate army, contributed to his ultimate disgrace as an officer. His botched command of the Confederacy's invasion of the New Mexico Territory in 1862 reportedly stemmed from his frequent intemperance.

In March 1854, Sibley departed from the fort, with 1st Lt. Newton C. Givens assuming command. The progressively lower grade of commanding officers from lieutenant colonel to major to lieutenant indicated the diminution of the fort's importance. On April 6, 1854, the army officially abandoned the post. Shortly after the soldiers had left, the fort went up in flames. Those blamed for the arson over time included Indians, the irate wife of an officer, Lieutenant Givens's slave, or the departing soldiers themselves. Supporters of the latter theory suggest that the departing men might have torched the despised outpost if only to ensure they would never again be assigned there. When Lt. Gen. William T. Sherman stopped at the ruins a few years after the Civil War, however, Randolph Marcy, who accompanied him, told him the fort had been destroyed by federal sympathizers at the beginning of the Civil War. The accounts of when the fort burned and who caused the damage clearly differ, and no definitive answer has as yet been found. At any rate, reduced to ashes or at least only partially standing, the site served as a mail station for a time after its abandonment. During the Civil War, Confederate sympathizers occupied the site, using it as a base for dealing with Indian warriors who returned to their marauding ways when the army left to fight in the war back east.

In General Order no. 115, issued on June 5, 1871, the army's Department of Texas designated Fort Phantom Hill as a subpost of Fort Griffin, some forty miles to the north. The new lease on active-duty life, however, continued for only a short time. In 1874, a detachment from Fort Griffin bivouacked at Phantom Hill before clashing with seventy-five Indians nearby in one of the last relatively large-scale battles in this section of the Texas frontier. Six Indians died in the ninety-minute battle.

Even with the fort again officially abandoned in 1875, the village of Phantom Hill, which had sprung up around the installation, survived for a number of years, with merchants availing themselves of the still-standing buildings on the fort grounds. When the oncoming rail line bypassed the town, however, it also quickly withered. By 1900, the village had all but disappeared, and agriculture replaced mercantile activities as the main source of income. Until the late 1930s, even the land where the fort once stood gave way to the plow. A farmer also lived in one of the old buildings and used several others as barns and pig sties for his livestock.

In 1971, a new owner of the fort property set about studying, stabilizing, and hopefully restoring some of the shells of the old buildings that had survived the fire, the plow, and the often unkind climate. Under the new ownership, the public benefited from free access to the site once hazards to personal safety had been corrected. The Texas Historical Commission and other agencies soon uncovered a sizable inventory of artifacts that told a fascinating tale of life on a frontier fort in the 1850s, albeit not necessarily a happy one. In 2012, the Texas Department of Transportation constructed a sizable rest stop immediately adjacent to the southern boundary line of the old fort. Interpretive panels in the new building explain the history of the outpost. An official state marker states that the site is listed in the National Register of Historic Places, an honor its troubled past so richly deserves.

For those in too much of a hurry to stop and read such markers, there is much clear evidence of what at one time occupied this lonely piece of Texas. Tall chimneys, towering more than twenty feet above their foundations, dominate the site. The walls of most of the old buildings have given way to decay and gravity over the decades, yet the chimneys remain, standing stark and in an orderly file as they trail off to the middle distance. One of the great puzzles encountered by early and later students of the site is that those chimneys have somehow remained standing tall and unyielding despite the cumulative forces of more than 160 years of hard-blowing Texas "blue northers" and the mindless efforts of generations of vandals dedicated to toppling them. Perhaps it is the eerie sight of the chimneys that has indeed given the old fort its enduring spectral name. In the late nineteenth century, a correspondent for the *New York Herald* passed by the abandoned post and recorded what he saw. “Most of the chimneys are still standing,” he wrote, “and as they reflected the light of the full moon as we drove up, it was clear that these were the true ghosts of Phantom Hill.”

LOCATION: Site is thirteen miles north of Abilene on FM 600.
ACCESS: Privately owned, but the public is welcome. Ruins of buildings are open twenty-four hours daily.

SOURCES

Abilene Reporter News. February 15, 1966; January 16, 1970.

Freeman, Martha Doty. *A History of Fort Phantom Hill: A Post on the Clear Fork of the Brazos River, Jones County Texas*. Abilene: Fort Phantom Hill Foundation, 1999.

Freeman, W. G. “Report of Inspection of Eighth Military Department.” Washington, DC: Adjutant General’s Office, November 4, 1853.

Rector, Ray. “General Robert E. Lee in Texas.” *Stamford (TX) Leader*, January 16, 1970.

Rister, C. C. “The Border Post of Phantom Hill.” *West Texas Historical Association Year Book*, vol. 14, 1938.

———. “Ft. Phantom Hill and Its Military History.” *Frontier Times* 3(3) (December, 1925).

Thompson, Jerry. *Confederate General of the West*. College Station: Texas A&M University Press, 1996.

Western Weekly. San Antonio, Texas, October 4, 1925.

9 UNITED STATES SAN ANTONIO ARSENAL 1859–1976

The institution is well worthy of a visit by a stranger and is one of the numerous attractions of this city. — Stephen Gould, San Antonio, 1882

By the time the war with Mexico ended in 1848, the South Texas city of San Antonio was serving as a major military center. Its location at the confluence of many roads and its reliable availability of water and grazing land combined to make the growing city the hub of the western expansion, which had been triggered by the defeat of Mexico. In April 1849, nearly a year after the costly war ended, the United States Army determined that San Antonio would become the headquarters of its Department of Texas. To ensure its new headquarters could satisfactorily marshal the supplies and ordnance required to support its rapidly expanding network of military installations on the western frontier, the army took steps to locate suitable warehouses and arsenals to house its vast quantities of provisions. The first site of the army's several logistical centers was at what remained of the not yet world-renowned Alamo. The army rented the derelict buildings from the Catholic Church for $150 per month. A curved roof had been added to the chapel to make it weatherproof and capable of securely holding military supplies. The curvature of the roof made it necessary to add a new facade to the western front of the building. Its bell-like shape gave the more than one-hundred-year-old chapel the distinctive appearance by which it would in time become recognized worldwide.

While giving the Alamo's old church a new look, the army also leased other properties in order to expand its warehousing capabilities. It rented a twenty-acre site adjacent to the Alamo complex from Samuel A. Maverick and purchased another sixteen-acre plot on the San Antonio River northwest of the Alamo to provide a government-owned parcel of land on which to erect a permanent arsenal complex. Until such a facility could be built in San Antonio, the army met its growing ammunition and weaponry needs by availing itself of the government's arsenal in Baton Rouge, Louisiana. The shipment of the often urgently needed ordnance involved a costly and time-consuming transportation routine. First, steamboats shipped the matériel down the Mississippi River to New Orleans. From there the goods traveled by ship to Indianola, Texas, and then on slow-moving wagon trains to San Antonio's rented warehouses. The total distance exceeded eight hundred miles, and the time required varied widely depending on flood conditions on the river, storms on the Gulf, and muddy roads between Indianola and San Antonio.

The army paid a relatively exorbitant $1,000 per acre for the site for its new arsenal on the San Antonio River. The richly rewarded sellers of the property were former Texas governor Peter Hansborough Bell and Gregory Devine. The Bell parcel had only recently been owned by Gregory's brother, Dr. James M. Devine, whose stately home had been acquired by Governor Bell in the transaction. Thomas, another Devine brother, owned an adjacent parcel of land also purchased by the army for the arsenal site. James Devine's former home eventually served as the commander's quarters, on what would become officially known as the United States San Antonio Arsenal. While the construction of the installation took place, Capt. R. H. K. Whitley, the army's initial overseer of the project, lived in the Devine house. Some preliminary site work on the arsenal began in November 1859, but the actual construction did not commence until mid-March 1860. A newspaper account claimed that all six of the buildings were of the "very best quality of material" to be found. As if to allay any concerns that the government might decide to discontinue the project, the paper went on to note that "Uncle Sam has a long purse, and there is no danger of the arsenal plan being scrapped."

Work on the arsenal did indeed continue, but on February 28, 1861, it came under new management in anticipation of a pending conflict between the states. The Southern-born U.S. Army Bvt. Maj. Gen. David E. Twiggs met with Col. Ben McCullough in the Devine house to transfer ownership of the arsenal to Southern sympathizers, along with all of the other federal military facilities in Texas. Although General Twiggs agreed to turn over the federal properties in his negotiations with McCullough, the actual transfer of the deed was made to none other than Thomas Jefferson Devine, one of the civilian owners of the property when the army bought it. Devine was to play a major role in the Civil War, declared some sixty days after Twiggs surrendered all Texas military properties. As a senior Confederate diplomat, Devine managed to arouse the ire of U.S. officials to the extent of becoming one of the three Confederates indicted for treason after the war. Only former president Jefferson Davis and Confederate stalwart C. C. Clay shared this inglorious distinction. Never convicted, however, Devine had his U.S. citizenship restored in 1867. The Texas town of Devine was named in his honor in 1881.

The victorious U.S. Army returned to the arsenal following the Civil War to find it in deplorable condition. Nearly every building had suffered from neglect during the Confederate occupation. The commanding officer's house, for example, showed marked deterioration from the five years of occupation by Confederate officers. The floors were in ruin, its long balcony had all but collapsed, and every window had broken panes. Government officials denied several requests for federal monies to fund the repairs, but in time the entire site was returned to good condition, and new construction was soon under way. By 1882, there were five buildings being used at the arsenal. A year later, Mr. Devine's old 1859 home had been replaced, even though part of the original house had been retained in the process. By the end of 1883, nearly forty new buildings had been constructed at the installation, bringing its appraised value to nearly $900,000, compared to only $100,000 two years earlier. It was estimated at the time that the arsenal had some two million dollars worth of ordnance stored in its magazine, which comprised 235,000 square feet of available space.

Additional land adjacent to the original site had also been acquired in anticipation of the ever-increasing need to provide all of the ordnance required by Texas' frontier forts and camps. The army purchased four acres south of the initial site from Toutant Beauregard, brother of Confederate general Pierre Gustave Toutant Beauregard, for $11,000, thus proving that Uncle Sam did have the long purse mentioned in the 1860 newspaper article. So controversial was the purchase price that it prompted a congressional investigation. After eight years of hearings in Washington, however, the acquisition finally won approval.

One of the arsenal's natural assets was the San Pedro acequia, which coursed through the center of the property. Originally constructed in the 1730s to provide irrigation water to the then tiny community of San Antonio, the canal had been lined with large stones in the mid-1850s to minimize erosion. Still in wide use as late as 1911, the acequia's constant flow of water was utilized to ensure a lush, semitropical landscape effect at the arsenal. Although the acequia was shut down in 1912, workmen uncovered remains of the canal some seventy-five years later.

When demands for ordnance from frontier forts ceased altogether in the late 1800s, the San Antonio Arsenal supplied ammunition, guns, and saddles to the U.S. Army during the Spanish-American War of 1898. A short time later, starting in 1917, the arsenal provided ordnance for more than two-thirds of all U.S. Army flying fields during the First World War. The number of employees working at the arsenal increased twentyfold during the war years.

In between the two world wars, the army continued to expand the arsenal's warehousing capacity. By 1922, the government had completed an additional $500,000 of new construction. That same year, matériel stored at the facility included some ten million rounds of ammunition and 150,000 rounds of high-explosive artillery shells. During the late 1930s, the army determined that the presence of such highly volatile material in magazines adjacent to San Antonio's prestigious King William District posed too great a risk. As a result, officials ordered artillery rounds transported to the Camp Stanley, several miles northwest of the city. During World War II, however, the arsenal remained active despite the absence of the heavy artillery ordnance. Reportedly the facility held 337 million rounds of small-arms ammunition prior to shipment to army units serving throughout the world.

Constructed in 1883, the commanding officers' quarters at the 1849 U.S. San Antonio Arsenal incorporates materials from the original building. It is now a senior citizens center. *The Alexander Collection.*

More than a year after World War II ended, government officials announced plans to close the arsenal after nearly ninety years of service. Protests by city leaders proved to be ineffective in reversing the federal decision, as is frequently the case. On June 30, 1947, the *San Antonio Light* featured a front-page photograph showing a watchman padlocking the facility's main gate. The staged locking episode was in fact largely symbolic. Even though the arsenal no longer received, stored, or shipped immense quantities of military ordnance, it proved too valuable to be totally abandoned. In time, various government agencies, including the Department of Agriculture, the Department of Labor, the Treasury Department, the U.S. Navy, and the U.S. Marine Corps maintained offices on the site.

Government officials considered a number of alternative uses for the entire property in the years following the war. They included an international trade headquarters, a junior college campus, a civic center, a police academy, and a branch campus for the University of Texas Medical School. When none of these prospects materialized, the National Guard moved onto the property in 1950 and used the site once again as an armory until 1976. When the government finally put its portion of the property up for sale, the City of San Antonio acquired the venerable commanding officer's house for use as a senior citizens' center. It was still in use as such in 2013.

The dramatic transformation of the property, which would make it a masterpiece of historic preservation, began in 1981, when San Antonio's successful H-E-B Grocery Company purchased much of the remaining land. Rather than destroying many of the still standing military buildings, the firm set about painstakingly rehabilitating them for use as its company headquarters. Working with state and local historians and archeologists, H-E-B ensured the integrity of the site but still made maximum use of the attractive riverside property. Although modern-day security concerns have made it necessary to enclose all of the company buildings within a well-guarded fence, it is easy to view and then appreciate how old buildings from another era and with very different original usages can be preserved and spared the seemingly inevitable wrecking ball that mindlessly destroys so much of lasting value.

LOCATION: On the San Antonio River just west of downtown San Antonio.

ACCESS: Most of the site is privately owned, but the former commander's quarters are now an activity center for senior citizens.

SOURCES

San Antonio Evening News. November 8, 1946.

San Antonio Express. January 5, 1947; January 14, 1947; February 13, 1947; March 31, 1972; May 19, 1976.

San Antonio Light. November 14, 1946; November 22, 1946;

December 16, 1946; December 27, 1946; October 10, 1948; January 3, 1954.
Smith, Thomas T. *The U.S. Army & the Texas Frontier Economy, 1845–1900*. College Station: Texas A&M University Press, 1999.
Texas Historical Commission. The United States San Antonio Arsenal National Register Nomination, 1969.
University of Texas–San Antonio Institute of Texan Cultures. Vertical files.

10 THE "BATTLE" OF ADAMS HILL

May 9, 1861

I have taken all the US troops in Texas prisoners of war, and now lean back in my chair and smoke my pipe in peace, so far as campaigning is concerned, for the present. — Gen. Earl Van Dorn, May 10, 1861

Although the general story of how Texas formally seceded from the United States on February 1, 1861, to become the so-called seventh star of the Confederacy is well documented, relatively little has been written of how the actual transfer of military power played itself out on the Texas landscape. While bits and pieces of a larger story can be found in official records, some surviving letters, and other archives, they are most commonly overshadowed by the dramatic and uncontested surrender of U.S. forces and installations in the state by Maj. Gen. David E. Twiggs on February 16, 1861. Regardless of how controversial his actions were at the time, the results were not immediate and without some measure of risk and uncertainty. To appreciate how the Confederacy came to secure its claim on Texas with relative ease early in 1861, it is important to understand events associated with the federal evacuation process, and one of the landmarks along the way is a small promontory above San Lucas Springs, west of San Antonio, known as Adams Hill (shown in some accounts as Adam's Hill and Allen's Hill).

As the political situation deteriorated following the presidential election in 1860, rushing the nation toward regional division and ultimately war, the commanders of federal forces in the Southern states most likely to secede faced the likelihood of confrontation without adequate direction from either military or political leaders. In the opening days of the conflict, the central command authority structure at the national level failed to coalesce, and so there was no clear direction for dealing with the unfolding crisis. Complicating the situation was the fact that as federal leaders sorted through their options, so, too, did the individual military leaders. If there was to be widespread secession, where would their loyalties lie? One of those facing such a dilemma and feeling particularly vulnerable was Maj. Gen. David Emmanuel Twiggs, commander of the federal forces in Texas. Although he would ultimately be labeled a traitor in the North, Twiggs had few viable options open to him in late 1860, when he resumed his command following a lengthy illness, during which time Robert E. Lee had briefly taken his place. A Southerner by birth, Twiggs distinguished himself in service to the U.S. Army during the Mexican War in the two opening battles on Texas soil—Palo Alto and Resaca de la Palma—and afterward through departmental commands. He, like many others in similar situations, hoped there would be some speedy resolution to the mounting tension in the antebellum era, but as 1860 drew to a close he began earnestly seeking the advice of others, including Gov. Sam Houston. Ultimately, he realized that he was in an untenable situation: he would be condemned if he chose to relinquish his troops following the inevitable secession of Texas, but he would be betraying his heritage to do otherwise. Adding to the pressure he faced was the fact that by February 1861, no spark had yet set off a civil war; the firing on Fort Sumter in Charleston harbor was still several months in the future. Significant, too, was Twiggs's assertion that he could not in good conscience open fire on American citizens, not even those who acted to split the United States. Seemingly without hope, he asked to be relieved of his command, but the news of his replacement came too late. Even after Texas seceded on February 1, he stalled for time, hoping to delay the inevitable until March, when hopefully his replacement would have reached San Antonio. Facing sustained pressure from the commissioners appointed by the Secession Convention and from the threat of military action under the leadership of Benjamin McCulloch, though, and lacking orders to the contrary, Twiggs prepared for the end of his command. When it unraveled, it did so quickly. The Texas militia under McCulloch moved to secure the federal posts on February 15, the same day Col. Carlos A. Waite replaced Twiggs as commander. The change came too late, however, and on the following day, Texas forces captured Twiggs en route to his headquarters, and in short order he capitulated, offering up all of the soldiers and fortifications under his command. (Waite soon surrendered as well.) Twiggs's single request, which the commissioners granted in order to hasten the departure of troops from the state, was that as the forces made their way to the coast, where they would be loaded on transports heading north, they be permitted to retain their firearms. With the surrender thus formalized, the mass evacuation—including the removal of troops from as far west as El Paso—began immediately. It would be several months, however, before those on the frontier could make their way to port cities such as Galveston and Indianola. Formally dismissed from federal service by Pres. James Buchanan following the surrender, Twiggs joined the Confederate Army in May 1861, assuming command of the Department of Louisiana. In ill health, however, he saw no action and died in July 1862.

As the surrendered federal troops from the western forts slowly made their way to the Texas coast, the replacement Confederate command structure began to take shape. A central figure in the transition for Texas was Col. Earl Van Dorn, a Mississippian who went by the moniker "Buck." In one of those coincidences that marked many of the personal relationships among soldiers throughout the war, Van Dorn and Twiggs were close friends following their earlier U.S. military service together. Initially directed to Texas as the war unfolded in order to recruit Confederate soldiers from within the departing federal ranks, Van Dorn met with little success. He soon left to accept a new command, which would have sent him to New Orleans, but along the way he received orders to return to Texas under a new plan of action that would drastically change the orderly exodus of enemy forces. Acting under the authority of the secretary of war, Adjutant and Inspector General Samuel Cooper wrote the following on April 11, 1861 (as recorded in the *War of the Rebellion's Official Records of the Union and Confederate Armies,* or *Official Records,* series II, vol. 1):

> You are charged with the important duty of making the necessary arrangements to intercept and prevent the movement of

the US troops from the State of Texas. . . . The whole of the US force, both officers and men, must be regarded as prisoners of war. Such of the men as may be disposed to join the C.S. Army you are authorized to take into service; those not so inclined must be held as prisoners of war, at such place as may be judged to be most safe. The commissioned officers may be released on parole, and in special cases, of which you must judge, the men may be released on oath not to serve against the Confederate States.

> The above instructions are given under the circumstances that hostility exists between the United States and Confederate States.

Cooper was an enigmatic figure in the Confederate command structure. A native of New York, he nonetheless joined the Southern forces shortly after one of his last official acts under federal service—the dismissal of Twiggs. Early on the morning following Cooper's orders to Van Dorn, Confederate forces began firing on Fort Sumter to disrupt its resupply, and the U.S. Civil War was undeniably under way. It was a point of no return for the Confederate states, and the implications for Texas were far graver than they had been just a couple of months before.

One day later, on April 13, even as the fighting continued at Charleston, Cooper addressed another communiqué to Van Dorn, this time informing him of intelligence related to ongoing evacuations on the Matagorda Island community of Saluria. He followed that information with a clarification of his earlier order: "You are hereby instructed to give the orders heretofore received by you a liberal construction, and to arrest and seize all troops and stores of the United States *in transitu* or otherwise, wherever found in the State of Texas, and to use for that purpose all the means of this Government which you can make available in said State." With his charge thus clearly laid out, Van Dorn moved first to capture U.S. troops at Saluria and Indianola, using considerable trickery to take the steamship transport *The Star of the West,* which had, only in January, been turned away by hostile fire as it endeavored to resupply Fort Sumter. With a large number of Union forces now officially prisoners of war in Texas, Van Dorn turned his attention to the units moving overland from the western forts to the coast. Thus the stage was set for an encounter at Adams Hill, thirteen miles west of San Antonio.

Leading the combined federal forces from forts Bliss, Quitman, and Davis—a group that numbered 320 as it departed the latter and included, in addition to regular forces, "ten officers, two hospital stewards, and twelve musicians"—was Bvt. Lt. Col. Isaac Van Duzer Reeve. By the time the contingent reached Castroville, the number had dwindled to 270 due to sickness, desertion, and, as Reeve reported, "drunkenness or other causes." A native of New York and a graduate of the U.S. Military Academy, Reeve was a seasoned officer who had served in the Seminole Wars, the military occupation of Texas following annexation, and the Mexican War, participating in fighting at Palo Alto, Resaca de la Palma, Vera Cruz, and Churubusco. He was stationed at Fort Bliss at the time of Twiggs's surrender. Considered a highly disciplined officer, he always strove to follow regulations to the letter, a trait that would be a defining factor in his subsequent wartime service.

Among the best primary sources of the events that took place on the prairie west of San Antonio on May 9, 1861, are reports and correspondence found in the *Official Records*. In his May 12 report to U.S. Adjutant General Lorenzo Thomas, Reeve provided a detailed account of the eastward exodus, including the fact that he had heard a rumor upon reaching Fort Clark, at Brackettville, that those who had surrendered at San Antonio under a formal understanding of orderly evacuation had subsequently been taken as prisoners of war and stripped of their weapons. Rumors of a possible confrontation with rebel forces ahead persisted and became more credible as the troops neared Fort Inge, at Uvalde, and there Reeve had to make a decision. Faced with limited rations for the men and even more meager provisions for the animals, he realized a return to the west was not an option, especially given the regarrisoned Texas forces at Fort Clark. Escape to the south into Mexico was also not an option for the commander, as he reasoned that "it was yet uncertain whether we should not only break the treaty with Texas, but also compromise the United States with Mexico by crossing troops into her soil." As he received better intelligence of the disarming of federal forces along the coast, he decided, "We then had no course open to us but to proceed, and, unless overpowered by numbers, to endeavor to fight our way to the coast, with the hope that some way of escape would be opened to us." Reeve thus ordered his men forward to San Antonio, where he had reason to believe the number of enemy forces would be substantial but not necessarily overwhelming.

The general plan of action that followed came from Lt. Zenas Randall Bliss. A Rhode Islander by birth and a longtime veteran of federal military operations in Texas, Bliss had extensive knowledge of the terrain west of San Antonio. As he later wrote:

> I knew an old road that had not been used in some years that ran to the south of the usually travelled road to San Antonio, and I suggested that we should make large camp fires and do all we could to make the people of the town [Castroville] believe that we were to remain all night and then move out and try and pass the Rebel Army, and get into San Antonio behind them, and there attempt to make a fight. If we could at least reach Adams Hill, where there was a large stone ranch with corral walls, and a fine spring of water, and where we could make a better fight than at any other place on the road, . . . we would be in a stronger position there.

More detailed intelligence of an advancing army began to reach Reeve. Thus, near midnight on the evening of May 8, he moved his men forward through the darkness to a place called San Lucas Spring, in the vicinity of what he called Allen's Hill. There, approximately eight miles from the camp of the Texas forces, he decided to await the impending encounter, ordering the wagons to be grouped together for defensive purposes. All was in place by the early morning of the next day. What followed speaks not only to the gravity of the situation but also to the formality of war in the mid-nineteenth century.

The sun had risen above the horizon only a few hours earlier on the morning of May 9, when two of Van Dorn's officers, bearing a white flag of truce, approached the federal camp and demanded unconditional surrender to what was, they indicated, a vastly superior force in numbers. Rightfully cautious, given the vegetation and hillside terrain that blocked his view of the enemy troops, Reeve declined and told the officers he would not surrender to a force he could not see. Subsequently, Van Dorn ordered his approximately seventeen hundred men to move into view along the hill, removing any doubt about their strength. Still, Reeve hesitated and then agreed to Van Dorn's invitation for a closer inspection. He thus instructed Lieutenant Bliss to move forward under Confederate escort for that purpose. As Reeve continued in his report to Thomas, "Lieutenant Bliss rode the whole length of the enemy's line with thirty yards, estimating the numbers and examining the character of his armament. He reported to me that the cavalry were armed with rifles and revolvers, the infantry with muskets (some rifles) and revolvers; that there were four pieces of artillery, with from ten to twelve men each; that he estimated the force at 1,200 at least, and there might be 1,500 (since ascertained to be 1,400)." Justifying his subsequent actions, Reeve added: "With this force before me, and odds of about five to one, being short of provisions, having no hope of re-enforcements, no means of leaving the coast, even should any portion of the command succeed in reaching it, and with every probability of utter annihilation in making the attempt, without any prospect of good to be attained, I deemed that stubborn resistance and consequent bloodshed and sacrifice of life would be inexcusable and criminal, and I therefore surrendered." Thus ended what has come to be known as the battle of Adams Hill. Van Dorn allowed the federal troops to proceed unchecked to the coast, where on May 11 they gave up their weapons to their Confederate captors. In closing his report from the following day, Reeve wrote, "I will state here that we have been treated, in the circumstances of our capture, with generosity and delicacy; and harrowed and wounded as our feelings are we have not had to bear personal contumely and insult."

With the capture of sizable units along the coast and at Adams Hill so early in the war, Van Dorn was among the first Confederate commanders who had to deal with the matter of prisoners of war. He ordered many of those captured at Adams Hill and at Twiggs's headquarters into temporary facilities at Camp Van Dorn, about seven miles east of San Antonio. Following his earlier orders from Cooper, he remanded most of the captives into camps in Texas, but he also planned to offer paroles to many in return for their pledge not to take up arms against the Confederacy. With regard to the parole plan, just to be sure, he sent a messenger to the Confederate capital at Montgomery, Alabama, for official confirmation. One of those to whom he made the initial offer of parole was I. V. D. Reeve. Writing to Colonel Thomas from Kankakee, Illinois, on June 18, 1861, Reeve offered his version of what had occurred several days earlier: "I received the sad, crushing intelligence of the death of my oldest daughter, and Colonel Van Dorn at once offered me the privilege of coming home." He continued: "I availed myself of his generosity both with the view to make arrangements for the care of my remaining children and to communicate with the War Department, in the hope of being of some service to the prisoners of war in Texas by representing their true state and condition." He added more details of those conditions, providing what is certainly among the earliest official accounts of POWs in the Civil War.

Although such conditions would grow harsher and more desperate on both sides as the war continued, in June of 1861, Reeve nonetheless observed, "In all this they have been as well if not much better treated than is the usual fate of prisoners of war." Regardless, their time in Texas would not end soon, and it was not until February 1863 that the last exchanges took place in Baton Rouge, Louisiana, resulting in the final disposition of the captives taken under Van Dorn's command in 1861. Reeve himself continued to honor the terms of his parole even after returning to New York. Ordered into service at Scarsdale, following a trip to New Haven, Connecticut, where he placed his son in school, Reeve protested the situation, pleading the terms of his parole as justification for his actions. Clearly reflecting a heightened sense of personal integrity, he wrote in September 1861, "It most positively forbids me from doing the duties to which I am ordered, and I do not see how it is possible to enter upon them or any other duties which will either directly or indirectly operate to the prejudice of the Confederate States or the rebel cause without a violation of my honor. I most earnestly hope that no such duties will be insisted upon. It would be bad indeed," he went on, "under all the trying circumstances of my position to add to them the necessity of breaking my parole or being driven from the service."

Threatened with dire consequences for his action, Reeve sought redress directly from President Lincoln, who essentially backed the commander's viewpoint, albeit with some interpretation of limited service that could be considered allowable under the terms of the parole. Regardless, Reeve prevailed until he was formally exchanged in August 1862, more than a year after his capture outside San Antonio. Subsequently, Reeve worked in recruiting offices and related services until war's end, attaining the rank of colonel and receiving a brevet promotion to brigadier general in 1865. He died in December 1890, and a eulogistic article written by George W. Cullum in association with a West Point reunion the following summer addressed the paradox of Reeve's distinguished career. "It was a hard fate," Cullum wrote, "for a gallant officer to be kept from the field, and, instead of fighting the open enemy, to be continually battling with disreputable politicians, substitute brokers, bounty jumpers, scoundrelly contractors, and rogues of every grade seeking their own villainous ends." But, the article concluded, despite the ignominious end of what had been a promising career, Reeve remained at all times a man of "fine soldierly bearing."

Earl Van Dorn, whose forces prevailed at Adams Hill, had a checkered career throughout the remainder of the war, serving less than gloriously at Pea Ridge, Arkansas, and with questionable actions at Corinth, Mississippi, but prevailing against U.S. Grant's forces at Holly Springs, Mississippi. Considered by many military historians as a tragic figure in the Confederate command, the general met his demise on May 7, 1863, at Pleasant Hill, Tennessee, where he was murdered by a local doctor. Whether the result of an affair involving the doctor's wife, complications of an intense political nature, or other reasons, the incident remains shrouded in mystery and conjecture.

In 1965, the Bexar County Historical Commission placed a state marker in the vicinity of the confrontation at Adams Hill on the north side of US Highway 90 and west of FM 1604 near San Lucas

Texas historical marker at the site of Adams Hill. Despite its proximity to the San Antonio metropolitan area, the hill still provides a sense of history with its westward view, the direction from which the Union soldiers would have approached. ***Photo by Dan K. Utley.***

Creek and the Medina County line. The title of the marker was "The 'Battle' of Adams Hill." Later road construction at the site led to the marker's displacement and eventual loss. By the time efforts were under way in 2006 to secure a replacement marker, both the roadway and the cultural landscape had changed considerably, and a retirement village occupied the site of the confrontation. The new property owners worked with the county commission to provide a more secure site, leading to the placement of a new marker, this time titled "The So-Called Battle of Adams Hill." Although no battle per se took place at the site, in the earliest days of the Civil War there was considerable doubt on both sides as to whether an armed confrontation could be avoided. That it was speaks to both the general confusion and the military protocols of the time, and the story remains one ripe for speculation about what might have been.

LOCATION: Montgomery Road, 0.3 mile north of US 90 and 2.3 miles west of Loop 1604, San Antonio.

ACCESS: Access to the marker is open; the surrounding land, however, is privately owned.

SOURCES

Bowden, J. J. *The Exodus of Federal Forces from Texas, 1861.* Austin: Eakin, 1986.

Carter, Arthur B. *The Tarnished Cavalier: Major General Earl Van Dorn, C.S.A.* Knoxville: University of Tennessee Press, 1999.

Cullum, George W. Article on I. V. D. Reeve. In *Twenty-First Annual Reunion of the Association of Graduates of the United State Military Academy at West Point, New York, June 12, 1891.* Saginaw, MI: Evening News Printing and Binding House, 1891.

Davis, Maj. George B., Leslie J. Perry, and Joseph W. Kirkley, Board of Publication. *The War of the Rebellion: A Compilation of the Official Records of the Union and Confederate Armies,* series II, vol. 1. Washington, DC: Government Printing Office, 1894.

Hartje, Robert G. *Van Dorn: The Life and Times of a Confederate General.* Nashville: Vanderbilt University Press, 1967.

Official Texas Historical Commission. Marker files. Texas Historical Commission, Austin.

Smith, Thomas, Jerry Thompson, Robert Wooster, and Ben E. Pingenot, eds. *The Reminiscences of Major General Zenas R. Bliss, 1854–1876: From the Texas Frontier to the Civil War and Back Again.* Austin: Texas State Historical Association, 2008.

11 WARTIME CLOTH MANUFACTURING, TEXAS PENITENTIARY, HUNTSVILLE 1861–1865

As any wartime veteran can attest, an engaged and supportive home front is vital to an effective military campaign, both individually and strategically. Whether that involvement comes in the form of civil defense preparedness, the production of ample matériel, the role of diplomacy, or the moral support of soldiers and sailors, it can make a significant impact on the overall war effort. In recent memory, one needs only to compare and contrast the home fronts associated with World War II and the Vietnam War to understand the complexities involved. Home fronts are societal reflections of their eras, resulting in myriad uncertainties, fears, hopes, and results. As integral extensions of war, they are also necessarily a part of any broadened interpretation of military sites. With regard to the built environment, they can range from scrap-metal drive collection points and USO canteens to coastal aircraft spotting stations and wartime industrial facilities.

During the Civil War, the Texas home front dealt with the general concerns shared by all of the states, North and South. There were the wartime production shortages, the personal sacrifices, the fears of invasion, and the daily assortment of news reports and rumors from the battlefronts. Additionally, however, Texans faced unique concerns that grew out of a vast, inadequately protected coastline, an even larger and perhaps more vulnerable frontier line, the proximity to federal fortifications north of the Red River, and the political instability to the south of the Rio Grande. There were also the issues of how to deal domestically with wartime captives and deserters and what to do with the waves of refugees who entered East Texas as they fled from the fighting, particularly in Arkansas and Louisiana. Equally of concern were how to maintain agricultural production to sustain the economy and contribute to the war effort and how to convert limited industrial output to respond to the increasing military needs of the Confederacy.

At the onset of the Civil War, Texas, like the other states of the South, had an agrarian-based economy—a distinction that would hold well into the twentieth century. In the early days of statehood, the state's ample agricultural productivity provided it with the necessary trading power to supply the manufactured goods its citizens needed. In many ways, particularly with regard to industry-related transportation and large-scale manufacturing, Texas lagged significantly behind the others during the antebellum era, and the impact of a federal blockade during the war further thwarted development. Despite this, numerous industrial operations made viable contributions to the Confederate war effort. A survey of the *Historic Sites Atlas* of the Texas Historical Commission reveals documented sites more diversified in scope of output and geography than might commonly be expected. For example, mines in Archer County produced copper ore used in the production of gun caps. Around Daingerfield, in northeast Texas, local iron ores supplied foundries, and tanyards utilized cattle hides to make shoes. Moreover, in Anderson County, ironworks produced guns and bayonets and, in Cherokee County, manufactured pots and skillets in addition to armaments. Not far away in Marshall, an operation employed up to forty workers in the manufacture of military hats and blankets. In the latter stages of the war, when gunpowder stores from beyond the Mississippi River and in Arkansas were beginning to dry up, Marshall also became a center for the production of both powder and small arms to aid Confederate troops. At Gilmer, in Upshur County, a shoe factory produced footwear and horse tack—saddles, harnesses, halters, and reins.

Across the state in New Braunfels, industrial workers produced, among other things, cotton and wool cloth and writing paper, and in Hearne, the Brazos Manufacturing Company also turned out cloth, utilizing a multilayered procurement system that even included the subscription and donation of local crops. Near Tyler was the sizable Neches Saline operation, now beneath the waters of Lake Palestine, which supplied hundreds of bushels of salt monthly to the Confederacy. In the capital city of Austin, the General Land Office building provided space for the production of ammunition, and even a basement area of the capitol became a sewing room. Among the towns aiding in the production of firearms were East Columbia, Lancaster, Houston, Bastrop, Corpus Christi, Fredericksburg, and San Antonio. In many cases, such wartime production came as a result of private enterprise, but on occasion the state government also subsidized the operations, particularly with supplies deemed to be in critical need.

Most of the sites associated with manufacturing and production during the Civil War years in Texas, however, remained small in scope and short lived, leaving at best severely limited historical resources to track their existence or effectiveness. As a result, most have faded from collective memory and from the visible cultural landscape, although there are likely to be archeological remains that may be uncovered or in other ways documented in the future. Regardless, relatively little is known about the details of wartime production in the state or about its impact on the Confederate war effort. One important exception to the norm, however, is the story of how government and military leaders worked to utilize prison labor at the state penitentiary for the manufacture of cloth.

With the phenomenal growth of the Texas penal system in recent years, with units constructed in all regions of the state, it is difficult to imagine a time when there was no centralized statewide program of incarceration. Yet, such was the case in Texas until the middle of the nineteenth century. In the Republic of Texas era and later in the early days of statehood, municipal and county jails provided space for convicted criminals to do their time, and the levels of punishment varied as much as the accommodations. That changed in 1848, when, following earlier efforts, the Texas legislature finally approved sweeping revisions to the state penal code and authorized the establishment of a state penitentiary. The changes grew out of national penal reform efforts and prevailing state models from New York and Pennsylvania, which focused on incentivized personal improvement. Additionally, the reforms allowed for a profitable labor system to offset state expenses. Duly appointed commissioners moved quickly to select Huntsville as the site of the state penitentiary. At the time, the Walker County seat was a small settlement of only a few hundred citizens, but they had grand plans for the young town, including possible consideration as a new state capital. Construction on the prison got under way immediately, and in 1849 the institution accepted its first prisoner.

Within a few years, convict laborers, under the direction of Pennsylvania native and former Walker County jailer John Slater Besser, started construction on the first phase of a textile mill that would be the basis for funding the penitentiary over the ensuing years. Initially, the prison looms produced course cotton and wool cloth, much of it used to clothe slaves. As Robert Perkinson notes in *Texas Tough: The Rise of America's Prison Empire,* the practice created an "economic circuit" whereby "slaves produced the raw materials, which convicts then converted to textiles, which then ingloriously covered those same slaves toiling in the fields." As the quality of the cloth improved and the demand expanded to other markets, the financial experiment paid off for the state, with revenues far outweighing expenses, as promised. By the advent of secession and the commencement of war, the systems were in place for the mill to begin providing cloth to the Confederacy or at least for Texas troops serving with the Confederacy. Clarification of that important distinction would be central to state leaders' production concerns in the early part of the conflict.

As Paul Michael Lucko noted, the penitentiary's textile mill enjoyed the status of being the state's leading industry, "employing 130 of the state's approximately 200 convicts on one hundred looms, seven hundred cotton spindles, and two sets of woolen machines," producing four thousand yards of cloth per day. The output was one-fourth twilled wool and three-fourths osnaburg, a coarse, muslinlike fabric that was durable and utilitarian. These were not finished goods per se, but in the early days of the war the Confederate supply officers were not picky. Demand far outstripped supply, and west of the Mississippi River, the Texas prison mill was the primary provider of material for tents, uniforms, and other essentials. In October 1861, the managers of the penitentiary entered into a contract with Capt. Irby Morgan, quartermaster,

This early view from inside the Texas Penitentiary at Huntsville includes ancillary buildings associated with the institution.
Photo courtesy of the Texas State Library and Archives Commission.

to provide half of the mill's output to the Army of the West over a six-month period. Although the contract initially proved lucrative, it quickly came under intense criticism from those who feared it would lead to increased domestic costs and fail to address the needs of the Texas forces. As a result, Gov. Francis Lubbock had little choice but to cancel the agreement. As Herman Lee Crow has pointed out, the incident led to a new set of priorities for the mill, "first to supply the needs of the Texas soldiers, then their families and last the civilian consumer, but under no circumstances was a yard of cloth to be sold to retailers or speculators." Legislators reinforced the system by providing severe penalties, including time in the Huntsville prison, for those who would otherwise try to take advantage of preferential rates for personal gain. Despite some inconsistencies and minor scandals along the way, the priorities remained in place for the duration of the war. Even with the lower rates, the revenues were substantial, representing the latter years of the war: "thirty-eight percent of the state's revenue, an amount exceeded only by the state property tax," as Lucko documented. In 1864 alone, he added, "the factory was the state's leading source of income." By aiding the war effort, even at reduced prices, the state also realized phenomenal profits while other states faced unprecedented economic decline. The factory-for-hire system and the purchases of local cotton, on which the system relied, were two of the various reasons that Texas emerged from the war on a relatively sound financial footing.

Despite the overall success of the arrangement, it was not without inherent limitations, especially in the latter years of the war. One vexing problem once military recruitment, training, and a mobilization program were under way was that the number of convicts sent to Huntsville decreased. Fewer convicts meant fewer laborers at a time when orders for cloth were on the rise. Initially, there were calls for increased work hours and the utilization of Union prisoners of war to offset the decline in numbers, but such proposals failed to garner sufficient support from state officials. Efforts were also made to utilize captured African American combatants and freedmen, whom the South considered runaway slaves and therefore not formally prisoners of war, and house them in the state prison. Additionally, a few court martialed Confederate prisoners, as well as prisoners from neighboring states under immediate Union threat, faced shipment to Huntsville. Nonetheless, such combined efforts produced insignificant numbers of workers. Much more promising was the use of hired labor, treating the mill as a true business operation. As historian Michael R. Moore observes, the legislature approved such a plan. Beginning in 1864, it provided for the hiring of whites, who worked for wages, and slaves, whose masters received the slaves' compensation.

Moore also points out that the prison mill system eventually suffered from an overall lack of replacement parts, tools, dyes, and maintenance materials, such as industrial-strength lubricants, especially as Union forces disrupted supply routes, overtook manufacturing plants farther east, and tightened the coastal blockade. Alternative supply routes through Mexico, which seemed to many a viable option, often proved to be inefficient, time consuming, and unduly costly. They also failed to address what became an increasing obstacle in the process: the shipment of finished goods to the front lines, where they were desperately needed. Despite such setbacks, by 1864 there were calls for further expansion of the Huntsville operation, but such plans remained unrealized at the cessation of the war the following year.

The conclusion of the four-year conflict did not mark the end of problems for the prison mill, however. As the military system broke apart and near anarchy prevailed in some areas, bands of mutineers and discharged soldiers, unsure of their futures, sought some measure of retaliation to assuage their fears and personal losses. One particular group of a hundred or more attacked the facilities at Huntsville and laid siege to the operations, threatening to release the prisoners and plunder the storehouses if their demands for redress, financial and otherwise, went unanswered. As they began to arm themselves for further action, prison officials had no other recourse but to bring in a special police force to secure the area, quelling the brief riot. As Michael Moore describes the scene, "Only an [*sic*] heroic defense saved the penitentiary from destruction in the anarchy of the Confederacy's collapse. The Texas prison entered the Reconstruction era battered but with the textile machinery, the source of its earlier successes, still intact."

Overall, the penitentiary textile operations in Huntsville proved to be an integral part of the state's home front, producing an estimated seven million yards of cloth from millions of pounds of locally produced cotton and wool, thereby clothing and sheltering countless soldiers in the process. It also became the largest source of revenue for the state during the war, far exceeding tax revenues, and provided a foundation for some measure of economic recovery during Reconstruction. The end of the war, however, brought new related issues to the forefront, such as the creation of "a penal system in the image of slavery," as Perkinson describes it. The social fallout of the war, including what to do with a "penology for profit" mindset in the public arena, would be tremendous and remain unresolved for generations.

ACCESS to the Walls Unit of the Texas Penitentiary, which housed the textile mill during the Civil War, is restricted, but those interested in learning more about the wartime industrial operations in Huntsville, as well as other aspects of the state's penal history, may visit the Texas Prison Museum at 491 State Highway 75 North in Huntsville.

SOURCES

Crow, Herman Lee. "A Political History of the Texas Penal System, 1829–1951." PhD diss., University of Texas, 1964, 59.

Historic Sites Atlas. Texas Historical Commission.

Lucko, Paul Michael. "Prison Farms, Walls, and Society: Punishment and Politics in Texas, 1848–1910." PhD diss., University of Texas at Austin, 1999, 107, 110.

Moore, Michael Rugeley. "The Texas Penitentiary and Textile Production in the Civil War Era." Honors paper, University of Texas at Austin, 1984, 148.

Perkinson, Robert. *Texas Tough: The Rise of America's Prison Empire*. New York: Holt, 2010, 78, 101.

Walker, Donald R. *Penology for Profit: A History of the Texas Prison System, 1867–1912*. College Station: Texas A&M University Press, 1988.

12 FORT MAGRUDER 1863–1864

People stared at us very curiously and our arrival caused a great deal of anxiety. — Confederate Engineer Getulius Kellersberger

---

Street names can sometimes be indicators of long-forgotten military sites, even when the historic names are misspelled. Such is the case with Fort McGruder Lane, which runs roughly east to west just north of Ben White Boulevard between South First Street and South Congress Avenue, south of downtown Austin. It crosses through an area that was, during the latter years of the Civil War, the location of a hastily constructed and quickly abandoned earthen installation known as Fort Magruder. Although remnants of the fort were discernible on the land surface into the twentieth century, its history did not fare as well. What was once the location of a defensive stronghold designed to protect the capital city from a Union invasion from the Texas coast, which never materialized, gave way to modern development as Austin grew and prospered after World War II. In the 1990s, however, when the Texas Department of Transportation began planning for expansion of the Ben White thoroughfare, a major artery also known as US 71, archeologists found both archival and physical evidence clearly indicating the fort site. Despite its ties to the Civil War, the spot lacked both historical and archeological integrity, so the field investigations proved sufficient to allow the road construction to proceed. As a result, cars along the westbound frontage road now travel where once were trenches cut by slaves, and nearby commercial development covers the remains of a fort named for one of the more colorful military characters ever to pass through Texas.

The story of Fort Magruder has its roots in the defensive predicament confronting Texas during the war. The reality that both

Urban development in Austin along South Congress near Ben White Boulevard has obliterated any visible remains of the Civil War–era defensive installation known as Fort Magruder, which was hastily built to defend the capital city against an anticipated attack from the south. Given incidents at Galveston, though, the attack never occurred. This street sign, which references the fort, does not bear the correct spelling. *Photo by Dan K. Utley.*

state and Confederate leaders faced was that Texas' sheer size and frontier setting made it vulnerable to attack, particularly from the coast, which extends roughly 367 miles, anchored on the east by Sabine Pass and to the south by Brownsville. Although such an extensive and minimally defended line posed immense problems, however, it also made the area advantageous to Southern blockade runners. As a result, Texas represented an important link in the commercial chain for the Confederacy, not just along the coast but farther inland as well, where wagons laden with cotton regularly plied roads leading to lucrative markets in northern Mexico. Keeping those trade routes open and viable was a key concern for Southern military leaders.

Adding to the complexity of this situation was a porous, lightly guarded frontier line stretching from the Rio Grande north to the Red River and beyond, which remained subject to both Union and Native American attacks. North of the Red River was the Indian Territory, which included a Union presence at key installations, another possible threat. To the east was Louisiana, already controlled in part in 1863 by federal forces, and the problem of what to do with refugees moving into East Texas seeking its relative isolation. What few rail lines the state had in the 1860s crossed sections of Southeast Texas but failed to connect to major centers farther inland, making the movement of both military personnel and matériel difficult.

This was the vexing situation facing Confederate Brig. Gen. John Bankhead Magruder when he assumed command of the District of Texas, New Mexico, and Arizona in 1862. The new assignment reflected the disfavor Gen. Robert E. Lee felt for Magruder stemming from actions related to the Seven Days' battles in Virginia, particularly the Battle of Malvern Hill on July 1, 1862. There, Magruder's confusion on the battlefield led to significant casualties for the South. Although the Virginia-born Magruder had shown great promise in the Mexican War, most notably as commander of a "flying artillery" unit at Cerro Gordo, and in the early days of the Peninsular Campaign of the Civil War, where he thwarted the objectives of Union forces under Maj. Gen. George B. McClellan, Lee viewed him as inept and therefore relegated him to command in Texas. There, drawing on the depth of his military training and prior battlefield successes, Magruder quickly demonstrated his renewed worth by focusing on defenses at Galveston, leading a multistaged attack against occupying Union forces that resulted in the recapture of the vital port city for the South on January 1, 1863. Although the battle of Galveston brought some measure of relief to Texas, it was understandably viewed as only a stopgap measure against what would likely be continued attempts to cut the Lone Star State off from the rest of the Confederacy. As a result, Magruder made plans to defend the capital city from an anticipated coastal invasion. Regardless of where such an attack might occur next, Austin would no doubt be a prime objective for the invaders.

In an effort to provide some measure of broader security, Magruder called on two of his most trusted engineers, Polish-born Valery Sulakowski and Swiss-born Getulius Kellersberger (later Julius Kellersberg). Among their first actions were the hurried construction and the reinforcement of military installations at Galveston following the battle. With those improvements in place, Kellersberger received orders to proceed east to the settlement of Sabine Pass, where he helped establish a battery that would prove critical to the fighting that ensued there in September 1863. With the Confederate victory in the battle of Sabine Pass, which successfully brought an end to Gen. Nathaniel P. Banks's plan to invade Texas, planning began in earnest on defensive measures for the capital. As a result, with little time for rest or reflection, the weary Kellersberger received new orders to proceed immediately to Austin, where he was to use slave labor to construct a series of earthworks that would come into play should Union forces eventually pierce the coastal defenses. Even then there were growing rumors that enemy forces were again massing for such an assault.

In his memoirs published years later, Kellersberger revealed his deep-seated skepticism for his new assignment and his distrust of his immediate command, as well as a secondary motive for their actions. Calling Magruder and Sulakowski "trigger-happy" and noting that their plan would make him their "scapegoat," Kellersberger wrote, "They wanted to take advantage of the opportunity to strike a blow at the population in the city where there were a great number of Union sympathizers." To be sure, in certain areas of Texas, most notably the German Hill Country and counties farther north along the Red River, Union support remained strong, or at least troublesome to the South, but several counties in Central Texas, including Travis, with Austin as the county seat, were also among those opposed to secession in 1861. A Confederate presence in the area, then, would serve the dual purpose of providing necessary defenses and also checking possible internal resistance.

Despite his personal concerns and his open disgust at being called again to action, especially during the Christmas season, when he wanted to be with his family, Kellersberger followed orders and proceeded to Austin from Sabine Pass, via headquarters in Galveston. Along the way, he later wrote, he hooked up with the first of his construction crews, slaves impressed into service to the Confederacy. "I met the 500 negroes in La Grange," he wrote. "They were half-frozen since the winters of 1863 and 1864 were very cold ones. We had 11 to 12 degrees weather and naturally no winter clothing and because of such cold we had to bind the stirrups of our saddle in straw." Slowly making the trek west, Kellersberger remembered that, on reaching Austin, "People stared at us very curiously and our arrival caused a great deal of anxiety."

Although the engineer recorded few details of his construction efforts in the weeks ahead, his memoirs provide important personal perspectives on life in the wartime capital city. One of those is a lengthy account of the problems associated with quartering slaves, which was the duty of the local quartermaster, who chose a reportedly abandoned church south of the Colorado River for that purpose. Many of the local populace viewed this action as a sacrilegious affront, and Kellersberger soon faced the immediate concern of what to do with his workers, while also respecting the townspeople's concerns. "I had immediately sent word to the quartermaster, who could not be located," he wrote, "so I took a crate from our magazine and had packed all the sacred articles in it, covered the altar and roped off the approach thereto, and ordered the guard not to permit any negroes to come near it—more I could not do." And, as a final note on the incident, he added, "Four years later when I passed through the city the church had been converted into a livery stable."

Utilizing the slaves gathered at La Grange and from plantations closer to Austin, Kellersberger soon began to oversee the work at three fortification sites. They included a position to the southeast, along the road to Houston in the vicinity of what is now Webberville Road, and a high elevation of ground at "college hill," not the site of what would decades later become the central campus of the University of Texas, as some have since believed, but a proposed school site along what is now West Avenue near the intersection with 15th Street. The third and most ambitious of the sites was immediately south of town along the San Antonio road, which was in effect an extension of South Congress Avenue. Should an invasion come, Fort Magruder, as the site became known, would likely be the focal point for the Confederates' last stand to protect the Texas capital.

Almost as soon as the work at Fort Magruder got under way, circumstances combined to bring an end to the operation. By January, slave owners began recalling their slaves for work associated with the upcoming planting season, and their ranks at the fort site dwindled. Equally significant, though, was a shift in Union tactics from a coastal assault on Texas to a more substantial invasion via the Red River and into East Texas from Louisiana. As a result, work on the Austin entrenchments ended, and all available Confederate forces remained on alert to deployment farther east. It is likely, therefore, that the site along South Congress was never garrisoned. Certainly, the fortification itself was never completed.

As anticipated, fighting associated with the Union's Red River Campaign—with Banks making another ill-fated attempt to cut Texas off from the Confederacy—proved to be intense. Ultimately, key battles at places such as Mansfield and Pleasant Hill, Louisiana, helped turn the tide for the South, albeit regionally, once again protecting the Lone Star State from invasion. Soon after, however, the war played to its inevitable conclusion, and life in the capital city, as elsewhere in the former Confederate states, became focused on Reconstruction and a hopeful return to normalcy. In the process, the former fort site south of town remained abandoned, eventually targeted for residential and commercial development as the city continued to grow in the late nineteenth and early twentieth centuries. As part of that development, new thoroughfares crossed the landscape to provide access for the increased population. Only occasionally did Fort Magruder enter the collective memory of Austin residents. Although there were reports that historical markers once denoted the site, they eventually disappeared, but the scar on the land remained. As noted in a 1930s chamber of commerce publication, "These trenches and the dug-out are still plainly visible." With further development on the site, though, even those passed from view.

By the late 1980s, with the Antiquities Code of Texas in full effect for the systematic review of cultural resource management issues, such as the impact of a state-funded highway project on a short-lived Civil War installation, the story of Fort Magruder once again surfaced. Archeological investigations under the purview of the Texas Department of Transportation, in review consultation with the Texas Antiquities Committee of the Texas Historical Commission, produced evidence of the fort imprint and led to further archival research. According to the findings, compiled in a detailed formal report by John W. Clark Jr. and David Romo and published following the road construction, "The area in which Fort Magruder was found was covered with structures, including private residences and commercial buildings dating to the 1950s." The homes were part of a development platted as the Fortview Addition to the city. According to the archeological report, "The most interesting feature was the L-shaped fortification trench. This feature was cross-sectioned at one point and overburden stripped off at several points so the orientation of the trench could be mapped.... No Civil War period artifacts were found."

With Fort Magruder once again a remembered part of Austin history, the United Daughters of the Confederacy, the Austin Civil War Round Table, and other interested parties called for the placement of a state historical marker to commemorate and interpret the defensive installation. After several efforts to provide the requisite documentation, success came in 2003 with state approval for the marker. For reasons of security and public access, it went up nearby at a post office in the 3900 block of South Congress. As the historical narrative accompanying the application noted, the site of Fort Magruder, as well as those of the two other outposts planned for the defense of Austin, serve as "testament to the very real threat by the Union forces in early 1864 and to the importance of Texas during the Civil War."

And what about the namesake of Fort Magruder? An enigmatic character known by some as "Prince John" for his flamboyance and penchant for concerts, songwriting, and amateur theatrical performances, John Bankhead Magruder managed, through his actions in Texas, to restore some of the luster of his earlier career, and he was beloved in Galveston for rescuing the port city against incredible odds. Toward the end of the Civil War, he temporarily assumed command of the Department of Arkansas but then returned to his former command in Texas, where he was in 1865 when Gen. E. Kirby Smith surrendered the Trans-Mississippi Department. Eventually fleeing the United States, he offered himself for service, as other former Confederates did, to Emperor Maximilian I of Mexico. When the effort to establish French rule in Mexico eventually failed, Magruder returned to Texas and lived in Houston. He died there in 1871 and was buried in Galveston, where a state historical marker now stands adjacent to his final resting place in the Episcopal Cemetery. In addition to the unfinished Austin fortification that bore his name, there were two other Fort Magruders during the war—one at Williamsburg, Virginia, and another, fittingly, on Galveston Island.

LOCATION: The Fort Magruder marker is located in the 3900 block of South Congress in Austin on the east side of the road. There is no vehicle pull-off for reading the marker, however, so access is via the sidewalk.

ACCESS: There are no visible remains of the fort site, which is now privately held or within the right-of-way of Ben White Boulevard. There is public access, however, for the state marker.

SOURCES

Barnes, Michael. Column, *Austin American Statesman,* August 15, 2012.

Casdorph, Paul D. *Prince John Magruder: His Life and Campaigns.* New York: Wiley, 1996.

Clark, John W., Jr., and David Romo. "Archeological and Archival Investigations at Fort Magruder (41TV1380), a Civil War Period Fortification in Austin, Travis County, Texas." Report filed in compliance with the Texas Antiquities Committee. Austin: Texas Department of Transportation, 1995.

Eskenazl, Stuart. "Austin's Forgotten Fort: Road Workers Unearth 130-Year-Old Confederate Redoubt." *Austin American Statesman,* March 12, 1992, B-1 and 7.

"Fort Magruder." *Austin Chronicle,* July 4, 2003, 36.

Kellersberger, Getulius. *Memoirs of an Engineer in the Confederate Army in Texas.* Privately published 1957. Translated from German by Helen S. Sundstrom. The photocopied version of the publication used in this research came from the holdings of the Perry-Castañeda Library at the University of Texas.

Settles, Thomas M. *John Bankhead Magruder: A Military Reappraisal.* Baton Rouge: Louisiana State University Press, 2009.

Texas Historical Commission. Marker files. Austin, Texas.

13 CUSTER'S MARCH THROUGH TEXAS 1865–1866

Land wretchedly poor and the people too poor to be wretched.
— 1st Lt. Thomas S. Cogley, 7th Indiana Cavalry Volunteers

Contrary to a widely held public misconception, the Civil War did not end when Gen. Robert E. Lee surrendered his troops to Gen. Ulysses S. Grant at Appomattox Court House, Virginia, on April 9, 1865. Although that certainly signaled the inevitability of the end, it was only part of what would become a ragged edge to the story of the conflict. More events were still to be played out, and much of what centered on the eventual culmination shifted toward the southwestern part of the crumbling and short-lived confederacy. With the South in almost total disarray and suffering from a lack of central leadership, both political and military, following Appomattox, rumors that the war might continue in some altered state began to emerge. Stories abounded, for example, that Confederate president Jefferson Davis himself was in full flight to Texas, where he hoped to regroup remnants of his military units to fight on, perhaps with some assistance from the French forces then in control in Mexico. Indeed, Gen. Joe Shelby and others made their way to the Rio Grande for the same purpose.

To be sure, unrepentant and active rebel forces were still in the southwestern confederacy, most notably along the Mexican border, where Confederate troops under the command of John S. "RIP" Ford managed to secure one final, albeit meaningless, victory for the South at the battle of Palmito Hill near Brownsville on May 13, 1865. More significant, perhaps, was the eventual surrender of troops under the command of Gen. Edmund Kirby Smith at Galveston on June 2, 1865. By that time, however, plans were already in place to move federal forces into strategic positions within Texas to stabilize the postwar situation, to implement the presidential plan for reconstruction, and to provide a semblance of order for the vast state. Texas had fared far better economically than the other states of the South and had largely managed to avoid any devastating military engagements on its soil, and so at least to some there was the appearance of a relatively easy return to status quo antebellum. However, beneath that deceptively calm appearance were the same disquieting concerns faced by all states of the failed confederacy and indeed by the nation as a whole as it struggled with a reconsideration of purpose, unity, and direction.

In Grant's view, so significant was the Southwest to national reconstruction efforts that he ordered his trusted friend and battlefield colleague Gen. Philip H. Sheridan to personally oversee the detailed operations that would be required to bring about lasting peace. Sheridan was by no means unaware of the task ahead, noting in a letter to Grant in late May, "Texas has not yet suffered from the war and will require some intimidation." To broker that intimidation, he called upon the services of several field-tested military leaders to move as quickly as possible to position themselves in key areas of the state, including the capital, Austin, to ensure the optimum chances for quick success. Even as the Union forces moved on the state, however, lawlessness spread unchecked. As William L. Richter has noted in his book, *The Army in Texas during Reconstruction, 1865–1870,* "The state was swept by chaos and anarchy." And, he added, "dejected Texas troops roamed the countryside," degenerating into "disorganized mobs that broke into arsenals and took arms and ammunition, in violation of the surrender terms. . . . Those who disagreed or suffered losses were too few to halt the raging mobs."

The chaotic conditions in Texas, although violent and focused, soon dissipated at least in part as Union forces moved on the state from multiple positions, both along the coast and from East Texas via Louisiana. A pivotal wing of that multifront occupational move would be led by Bvt. Maj. Gen. George Armstrong Custer, who had assumed command of the forces assembled at Alexandria, Louisiana. There he had control of several cavalry units, including the 7th Indiana, 1st Iowa, 5th Illinois, 12th Illinois, and 2nd Wisconsin.

Even though the troops he began working with in late June were for the most part seasoned and ready for service, substantial vexing undercurrents of unrest roiled within the ranks. War had taken its toll on the soldiers, and most were more than ready to leave the service and return home. The prospects of pursuing peace in a hostile land—both politically and climatically—failed to rally their resolve for the monumental task ahead. As a result, Custer had to move quickly and deliberately to enforce discipline, issuing orders that called for severe disciplinary measures—even courts martial and death—for violators of his directives. General Orders no. 2, issued on June 24, provided this overarching admonition: "Now that the war is virtually ended, the rebellion put down, and peace about to be restored to our entire country, let not the lustre of the last four years be dimmed by a single act of misconduct towards the persons or property of those with whom we may be brought in contact." Regardless of the warnings, the commander faced strident opposition from the ranks and so moved deliberately toward enforcement, even calling for arrests, floggings, and executions. As a result, he was severely criticized by those above and below him in rank, but he persevered and by August, despite some delays, had his men prepared for the overland march to Austin.

Emmet C. West, of the 2nd Wisconsin, and Thomas S. Cogley, of the 7th Indiana, provided detailed accounts of the march, and excerpts of their reports are noted in John M. Carroll's book *Custer in Texas: An Interrupted Narrative.* According to their reports, the units left Alexandria on the morning of August 8 and crossed the Sabine River five days later. They passed through the town of Jasper, where they temporarily bivouacked, and then proceeded westward, fording the Angelina River, likely in the general vicinity of Bevilport, and then crossed the Neches, which West recorded as the Natchez, on a pontoon bridge. From there, they passed through Tyler County and Polk County, with Cogley wryly observing, "Marched out of the woods, into the woods, and through the woods, and camped, God only knows where." On August 20, they reached the Trinity River ferry crossing at Swartwout and camped on the west bank of the stream at a place they dubbed Camp Rattlesnake, for obvious reasons.

In the ensuing days, the troops passed through Cold Springs (Coldspring) and Waverly, causing Cogley to observe that although the villages were small, they "showed both thrift and taste" and included the first churches and schools he had seen in the state to that point. On August 22, they passed through the "flourishing" Montgomery County village of Danville, which later declined when bypassed by transportation routes, and then proceeded on to the county seat of Montgomery. Soon after, word came for the contingent to bypass Houston to the west through the settlement of Cypress City (present-day Cypress).

Accompanying the soldiers on the arduous trip through East Texas was the general's wife, Elizabeth ("Libbie") Bacon Custer, who wrote of her experiences in a multivolume work titled *Tenting on the Plains: General Custer in Kansas and Texas*. She traveled in a specially outfitted ambulance that afforded her some modicum of comfort, although she suffered greatly from the heat, humidity, bugs, snakes, and the continual jarring and pounding of the wagon, which resulted in what she noted as "break-bone fever," a malady that affected everyone on the trip, including the commander himself. "No one knowing about it can read these words and not feel a shudder," she wrote. "I believe it is not dangerous, but the patient is introduced, in the most painful manner, to every bone in his body." The only treatments, it seemed, were to try to take short naps at every break, although the lack of suitable deep shade and the presence of relentless heat made that problematic at best, and to take large doses of quinine, which she did.

Moving west from Cypress toward Hempstead, Custer's army reached the expansive Liendo Plantation of Leonard Waller Groce, on whose land the Confederates had operated a recruiting center and prisoner-of-war camp during the war. Despite his support of the rebel cause, Groce accommodated the soldiers, who camped there until December 1, and he and his family displayed the best hospitality they could under the circumstances. In particular, Libbie Custer and Courtney Ann Fulton Groce had pleasant encounters during that time, in part because of Mrs. Groce's attentive care of the ailing Mrs. Custer. The kindness of the former was not lost in the memory of the latter, who wrote as follows of her experiences at Liendo: "Our own relatives (aside from the home ones) would not do so much for us as some of these Texans who were prominent and active rebels. We shall never forget their kindness to us. No country in the world can equal the South for hospitality." When the orders came in November to move on to Austin, Libbie Custer recalled the final days at Liendo with sadness. "It was with real regret," she remembered, "that I saw our traps packed, the tents of our pretty encampment taken down, the arbors thrown over, and our faces turned toward the interior of the State."

Regardless of the misgivings, all members of the Union contingent knew the capital city represented the true mission, and the command had earlier made its way to Austin, passing by way of Brenham, Union Hill (precursor to present-day Burton), La Grange, Winchester, and Bastrop in the process. As the main party followed later, divided in part along regimental lines, it took roughly the same route, although as they neared the city, rather than antagonize the populace, they camped some distance away—some along Walnut Creek and the Colorado River, and others at Seiders Springs (near present-day 38th Street), only a few miles from the city center. Texas governor A. J. Hamilton, appointed by Pres. Andrew Johnson to oversee the state's transition, offered the Asylum for the Blind for use as the command headquarters. The central structure of the asylum campus, which still stands as part of the Heman Sweatt (also known as Little Campus) complex of the University of Texas at the southwest corner of Interstate 35 and Martin Luther King Jr. Boulevard, afforded the Custers their first true experience with comfort since their departure from Louisiana several months earlier. Designed by Abner Cook, the city's preeminent builder and the architect of local landmarks such as the Governor's Mansion, Woodlawn (Pease Mansion), and the Neil-Cochran House, the commodious limestone Greek Revival structure provided upstairs space for the Custer entourage and room downstairs for their servants. A photo of the Custers, joined by family and staff on the front porch of the building, is one of the iconic images of Reconstruction Texas.

In general, the headquarters staff experienced kind treatment from the local residents. Although they received numerous invitations to public receptions, headquarters staff members frequently

A building from the Asylum for the Blind, now on the campus of the University of Texas, served as Custer's headquarters during his time in Texas. Here he is shown with members of his staff, as well as his wife, Libbie. ***Courtesy of the Austin History Center.***

provided their own entertainment with music, dancing, and elaborate suppers, to which they invited members of the citizenry, as well as military wives. As Libbie Custer recalled, on such occasions the staff helped her with the preparations. "We dressed the long parlors in evergreens, made canopies of flags, arranged wax-lights in impromptu wooden sconces, and with the waxed floor it was tempting enough to those who cared for dancing. The soldiers soon organized a string band, and a sergeant called off the quadrilles." On one notable occasion, a contingent made its way northwest of the city to the top of Mount Bonnell (which Libbie incorrectly identified as Mount Brunell). As the soldiers and their guests picnicked on the promontory high above the Colorado River valley, the band played the "Anvil Chorus" ("Coro di zingari") from Giuseppe Verdi's 1853 opera, *Il trovatore* (*The Troubadour*).

Libbie Custer also warmly remembered how her husband allowed himself one special escape from the pressures of his command when he would visit the Deaf and Dumb Asylum south of the Colorado. Housing children from the ages of ten to sixteen, the asylum provided classes that the general found particularly compelling. "My husband riveted his gaze on their speaking eyes," she wrote, "and as their instructor spelt the passions of love, hatred, remorse, and reverence on his fingers, one little girl represented them by singularly graceful gestures, charming him, and filling his eyes with tears, which he did not seek to hide."

Despite such memorable and moving diversions, General Custer remained busy with his oversight of Reconstruction Texas, receiving reports on conditions and requests for military assistance on a regular basis. He also remained largely unpopular with his men, who regarded his disciplinary measures, which had abated only slightly since he took command in Louisiana, to be heavy handed and unduly severe. Even so, the occupation of Austin remained relatively uneventful, and the transition to change made steady progress, although clear differences existed between military command and the emerging civilian leadership over issues such as loyalty, social order, and the rights of freedmen. Many changes remained to be addressed even a year after the war ended and would continue to be in doubt all the way through Reconstruction and beyond. However, by early 1866, signs of the new direction were becoming clear with the assembly of a constitutional convention, the effective role of the Freedmen's Bureau, and the election of a new governor, James Webb Throckmorton, who had opposed secession but nonetheless remained loyal to Texas, serving as an officer during the war. Although much remained to be done, in effect the role of the occupying forces seemed to be largely achieved by 1866, and in January came orders for the officers to stand down and report back to their respective commands. At the same time, Custer and other officers received notice they had been formally mustered out of service, and within days the general was hastily on his way to the rail connection at Brenham amid a great deal of secrecy and protective cover to ensure his safety, both from the citizenry and the soldiers of his former command who seemed determined to do him harm.

As he made his way to the Texas coast and subsequent transportation north, Custer faced an uncertain future, one that would eventually bring him far more fame—or infamy—than his brief stint in Texas. His service to the United States in the earliest days of Reconstruction remained mired in controversy long after he left the state. However, although he certainly had his detractors, others had admired him for his sensitivities to the plight of the people and for the dignity he bestowed on them. Such warm feelings prevailed only a decade later after Custer's death in the Battle of the Little Bighorn, in June 1876, when the Texas legislature issued a resolution of condolence:

> Whereas General G. A. Custer has endeared himself to the people of the frontier of Texas and elsewhere by his bold and dashing operations against the Indians; and whereas the news of his late sudden death, while in discharge of his dangerous duties is received: Therefore,
>
> Be it resolved by the legislature of the State of Texas, That we tender our sincere condolence to the family of the deceased and to the people of our suffering frontier; and that the governor be requested to forward a copy of this joint resolution to our Senators and members of Congress, with the request that the same be spread upon the journals of Congress and a copy of the same be forwarded to the family of the deceased.
>
> Approved July 28, 1876.

Custer's actions in Montana have long overshadowed his time in Texas, and today his role in helping Texas reenter the republic of states is largely forgotten. Certainly many of the vestiges of his service have faded from memory. Yet reminders remain of an era of military occupation in the Blind Asylum Building (now the Arno Nowotny Building) in Austin, Mount Bonnell, and privately owned Liendo Plantation near Hempstead in Waller County. Also available are the diary of Libbie Custer and the written reminiscences of those who served with the general in Texas. Gone with little discernible trace to date are the various campsites and stream crossings his large army employed en route from Louisiana to Texas, even as the outcome of the Civil War remained in doubt to many. In Texas, as in Montana, he remains largely an enigmatic figure whose story is still being explored almost a century and a half after his death, with no end in sight.

LOCATION: The site of Custer's Texas headquarters is on the southwest corner of Martin Luther King Jr. Boulevard and Interstate 35 in central Austin. The property belongs to the University of Texas at Austin and is open to visitors during normal business hours.

ACCESS: None of the sites associated with Custer's march through Texas, including the extended campsite at Liendo Plantation, have been conclusively ground-truthed through professional archeological investigations, and so they remain the subject of conjecture.

SOURCES

Carroll, John M. *Custer in Texas: An Interrupted Narrative.* New York: Sol Lewis and Liveright, 1975.

Custer, Elizabeth Bacon. *Tenting on the Plains, or General Custer in Kansas and Texas,* vols. 1 and 2. Norman: University of Oklahoma Press, 1971.

Ramsdell, Charles William. *Reconstruction in Texas.* Austin: University of Texas Press, 1970.

Richter, William L. *The Army in Texas during Reconstruction, 1865–1870.* College Station: Texas A&M University Press, 1987.

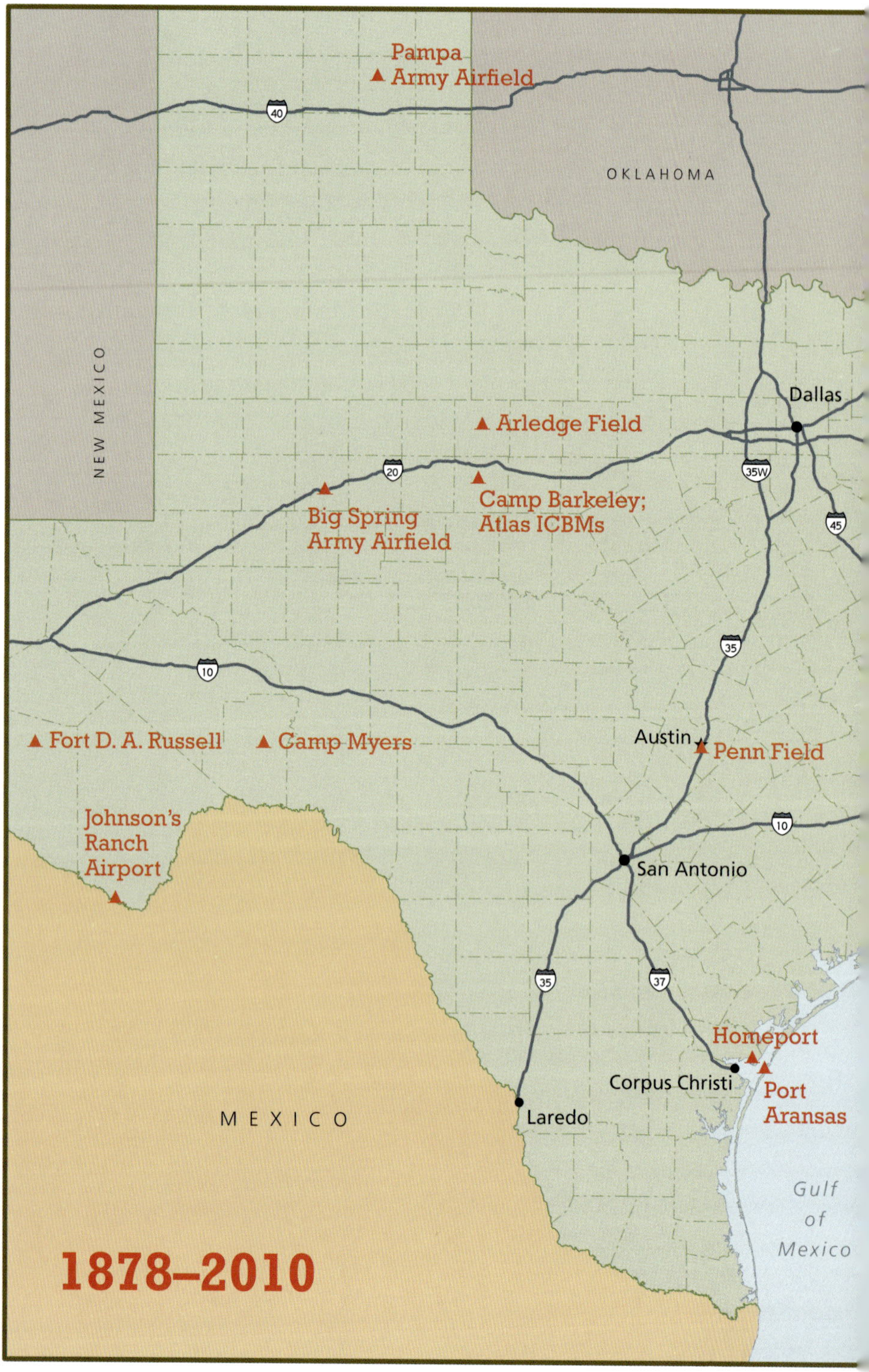

Map by Molly O'Hallora

14 CAMP MEYERS 1880–1884

He protected our homes, our homes are open to him. — Inscription on a sword presented to John L. Bullis by citizens of West Texas, 1881

When the brilliant spectacle of the setting West Texas sun washes across one of the remaining buildings at Camp Meyers, the effect is breathtaking enough to make it difficult to concentrate on the harsh but important role the site played in Texas history. Here, men from a different culture used their native wiles to help bring to an end the Native American domination of the entire region. Commanded by John Bullis, one of the U.S. Army's more resourceful Indian fighters, the Black Seminole Scouts based at this remote subpost fought on the Texas frontier with distinction, only to eventually fade almost entirely from the pages of history. The tiny site has had many names over the years, including the fanciful Fort Bullis, the more descriptive Bullis's Camp at Meyers Spring, and the commonly used Camp Meyers. The men stationed there have also been known by several names, ranging at first from Seminole Negro Scouts and Seminole Maroons, to the Seminole Scouts and the Black Watch, and, more recently, simply the Black Seminole Scouts. The confusion about which name is appropriate arose from many questions about the true ethnicity of this small group of fighting men who served at Camp Meyers, as well as at Fort Duncan and Fort Clark during the late nineteenth century. Those questions were to haunt the men for years and eventually led to their disappearance from most annals of Texas history.

Their story began in the mid-1700s in the Spanish colony of Florida. Their ancestors were runaway black slaves who fled their harsh overlords on plantations in Georgia and the Carolinas and sought a better life in Florida. Under Spanish law, all foreign slaves

This ruin is virtually all that remains standing at Lt. John L. Bullis's camp at Meyers Spring, north of Dryden. The site was home to a unit of the Black Seminole Scouts, ca. 1873. ***Courtesy of the Center for Big Bend Studies, Sul Ross State University, Alpine, Texas. Photograph by David Keller.***

who came to the colony would be granted their freedom. Once in Florida, the newly arrived black immigrants eventually managed to become integrated into communities earlier established by Indians who had long before emigrated to escape the intertribal violence created by British expansion into their original homelands. The confederation formed by the emigrant Indians in Florida became known as Seminole, derived from a Spanish word meaning "runaway." The black runaways were welcomed into the Seminole confederation, but as a separate community. Their relationship with the Indians was one of relatively benevolent slavery, to the extent that such an institution can be considered to be benevolent in any way. The newcomers had their own leaders and were allowed to flourish in a system that closely resembled a sharecropper-landowner arrangement rather than the traditional slave and master institution from which they had successfully fled.

Efforts to put an end to the unique Seminole way of life, which was attracting an ever-increasing flow of runaway black slaves, eventually led to two memorable armed clashes. The First Seminole War (1817) led directly to the annexation of Florida by the United States in 1824, and the Second Seminole War (1835–1843) brought about the end of Seminole resistance in Florida. The successful waging of this second war proved costly to the U.S. army, involving the expenditure of more than twenty million dollars and the loss of nearly fifteen hundred men in clashes with the Seminoles, who were abetted by the runaway slaves and their descendants. The cost to the Seminoles would prove to be even dearer. The very reason for the second war had been the planned removal of all residents within the Seminole confederation of Florida. As victors in that war, the United States promptly began the relocation of the composite Seminole population, both the Indians and their black neighbors, to the Indian Territory, far to the west in what is today the state of Oklahoma. The relocation process was tedious and harsh, yet when the survivors of the forced removal found themselves at their new home, conditions were often more trying than the exodus from Florida had been. Tribes already on the government-sponsored reservations were by no means welcoming to the new arrivals, denying them access to promised plots of land and the basic necessities of life on the plains of the Indian Territory. Eventually, many frustrated Seminoles left the reservations to emigrate once again, this time across the Rio Grande to Mexico. A number of the so-called Seminole Negroes joined them on that journey of more than five hundred miles to the south.

In 1850, the Mexican government, eager to populate its northern borderland, gave the new arrivals a generous grant of seventy thousand acres on which to establish farms. In return, the Indians and their black cohorts were expected to help defend the Mexican boundary with the United States from the fierce raids perpetrated by warlike tribesmen from across the Rio Grande. Over the next twenty years, many of the Seminoles grew tired of their meager existence in Mexico and returned to the Indian Territory, where many of their families remained. The Seminole Negroes, however, decided to stay south of the Rio Grande, having had enough of their earlier confinement on the reservation. More than three hundred of them stayed on the Mexican side of the river.

In 1870, the commanding officer at Fort Duncan, Texas, located just across the river from the Black Seminole community, learned that most members of the group had finally come to tire of the constant, politically inspired violence in Mexico and now wanted to rejoin their families in the Indian Territory. The officer offered to provide safe transportation back to the reservations, along with adequate provisions, until their return could be arranged. Shortly, he considerably enhanced the offer to include money, some land, and the necessary equipment to farm land near the fort until the final but complicated details of their return to the territory could be worked out. In accepting this suspiciously generous proposal, which was in fact apparently never signed or officially approved by U.S. officials, some of the Black Seminoles were compelled to serve as scouts for the army. The absence of that army in the west during the American Civil War had permitted a great resurgence of hostile Indian depredations along the Rio Grande, resulting in an urgent need for more military manpower.

Thus, the Black Seminole Scout fighting unit came into existence, albeit unofficially. Its members had an innate ability to track quarry and live off the land. Each had learned by association with various nomadic tribes the ways of the Indians, and every man possessed an almost uncanny ability to handle all manner of weapons while enduring long periods of deprivation in the field. These unique characteristics made the Black Seminole Scouts arguably the most formidable force ever to be encountered by the marauding Indian bands roaming the Texas-Mexico border. While their families maintained small farms provided by an undermanned army grateful to have gained such invaluable combat support, the Scouts went on countless patrols to seek their Indian enemy. The new black enlistees accomplished in short order what their white counterparts had proved unable to do for years.

With the appointment of Lt. John Lapham Bullis as their commander, the Scouts' success in time reached new levels. Bullis, described as being slightly under medium height, wiry, with a small mustache and a face often burned red by the sun, proved to be the organizing force that would make the Black Seminole Scouts unsurpassed in accomplishing their deadly mission of tracking and destroying hostile Indians. The Scouts he led into frequent battles called him either "Whirlwind" or "Thunderbolt," while a famous artist and writer found his fearlessness to be worthy of comment in one of his magazine articles. Frederick Remington speculated that Bullis must be required to pay very high life insurance premiums due to his "total lack of fear on the desert wastes of the Rio Grande."

Ranging at first out of Fort Clark at present-day Bracketville, Bullis and his Scouts pursued their prey by day and night with total disregard for either the international boundary or the official Mexican protests about the increasing frequency of its breaching. The Scouts, not previously known to show appreciable loyalty to any white man, found in Bullis a leader they could trust. The relationship was said to be more akin to that between a tribal war chief and his braves than to that of an army officer and his enlisted men. Bullis could match any of his Scouts in endurance on the trail and could stay in the saddle for seemingly endless hours, sustained by only water from his canteen and the contents of a single can of food. It was said he would open his tin can at high noon and, as the only meal of the day, devour its contents, be they sliced peaches or corned beef.

For the eight years under Bullis's command, the Scouts operated virtually independently of any other military orders. He and his men accompanied Col. Ranald Slidell Mackenzie on his famous invasion deep into Mexico to overtake a band of marauding Indians at the village of Remolino. The men also were with Mackenzie at the pivotal battle of Palo Duro Canyon near present-day Amarillo, which effectively put an end to most of the warlike Indian activity on the Texas plains. For the most part, however, Bullis and his troops served as an early version of modern-day special operations forces. They usually found the track of their quarry and simply destroyed them without seeking official permission of any superior officer. It is estimated the Scouts pursued hostile Indians well into Mexico on at least twenty different occasions. The soldiers' devotion to John Bullis was also without question. On one occasion the lieutenant became unhorsed in a heated battle with a large band of Comanche warriors. Three of his Scouts had galloped away in the face of the superior force, thinking Bullis was riding just behind them. When they realized this was not the case, they reined about, plucked their commander from the mass of the enemy, and rode off untouched, leaving behind a number of dead braves in the process. For their heroism, the three black Scouts received the Medal of Honor, the nation's highest military award. Another Scout earned the same medal for his valor in action in the Red River War in the Texas Panhandle.

Sadly, the Scouts eventually became the victims of their own success. As the Indian threat diminished, so did the army's need for them. No longer required as warriors, the Scouts soon became the target of civilian violence. White citizens' distrust of the black troopers next led to demands that the properties given them by the government be surrendered. Although the evidence was never substantiated, it has been suggested that the creation of the subpost for the Scouts at Meyers Canyon in far West Texas was the direct result of often strident civilian demands for their relocation to some remote spot. It is unlikely that a more isolated site for a military encampment could be found, although some strategic reason for placing a camp on the eastern edge of what is now Terrell County may actually have existed.

Located some nine miles northeast of present-day Dryden, the setting of the encampment was less than twenty-five miles from the banks of the Rio Grande. When banditry and smuggling began to replace Indian raids along the river, the need for such highly qualified trackers was once again in demand, although in a more limited fashion. They also played a role in patrolling the border when Indian leaders Geronimo and Victorio began raiding white settlements. At Meyers Canyon, a natural spring provided a rare supply of good water nearly year-round. There was also a rough roadway from the site to Camp Peña Colorado, a onetime Scout location near today's Marathon, as well as ample construction material to build a simple camp serving the fairly primitive needs of Bullis's hardy Scouts.

During their roughly two-year stay at Camp Meyers, the Scouts erected perhaps seventeen buildings, including fifteen one-room adobe huts and two relatively sizable limestone buildings likely used as dining and cooking facilities. The presence of both square and round tent bases in the immediate area indicates that some of the men still preferred canvas walls to those made of stone. A dam built at the spring retained water, and the men also constructed a cistern to catch and hold the rare raindrops that might fall in usually arid West Texas. Some have speculated that John Bullis himself built the stone dam, a possibility enhanced by a cornerstone beside it that reads "Errícted [*sic*] by J. Bullis." Although he was an army officer, Lieutenant Bullis had no record of any formal education, so perhaps he can be forgiven his spelling misstep if indeed he did write the words on the stone.

Some ten feet from the spring, the Scouts found Indian pictographs. The inclusion in this primitive artwork of indications of contact with early Spanish explorers suggests the pictographs were created sometime after the mid-sixteenth century. The relatively reliable source of good water, combined with the presence of the ancient rock art, likely led Bullis to assume the site was not only a traditional camping site for nomadic tribes but perhaps a sacred location to them as well. If so, he reasoned that a military encampment at the site would serve to diminish Native American travel along the trail to Mexico.

While the Scouts guarded the spring in the canyon, other Black Seminoles without any direct military affiliation made a concerted effort to escape the white persecution that followed the gradual removal of Indians from West Texas. A desire to join their extended families already living on reservations in Indian Territory seemed heightened by the demonstrable suspicion and obvious loathing of the black families shown by the ever-increasing tide of white emigrants to the region. Also at issue was the fact that the Seminoles (the original Indian Seminoles from Florida) living on the reservation had grown as intolerant of the Black Seminoles as had the white settlers. The government proved to be every bit as bigoted in the matter, refusing to either force the admission of the Black Seminoles back to the reservation or make the Scout units a permanent part of the army. The government also refused to give the Black Seminoles a grant of land to make their squatters' village on Las Moras Creek near Fort Clark legal. Despite the sincere pleadings of many army officers, including Bullis and General Philip H. Sheridan, the government remained intransigent.

When the final order arrived at Fort Clark that their village was to be destroyed and its occupants turned away with no place to go, the last bitter chapter of the Black Seminoles' long struggle came to a close. Although army soldiers burned most of the ninety-three homes in their village in June 1914, a few of the elderly and infirm were allowed to remain in their shacks until, as the army orders put it, they either died or left voluntarily. The balance, nearly three hundred in number, including women and children, stayed to fend for themselves in nearby Brackettville. Some of their descendants still reside in the vicinity, having somehow survived the rigors of forced acculturation. Only the cemetery holding the ashes of their ancestors, including those of the Medal of Honor awardees, remains at the Black Seminole village site along Las Moras Creek.

John Bullis fared much better than his Scouts. Upon leaving command of the unit in 1881, he remained in the army, in which he had served since before the Civil War. Upon leaving Texas, he was presented with two commemorative swords in recognition of his leadership while in command of the Scouts. One came from the citizens of Kinney County, home of Fort Clark. The other silver and gold sword, bearing the inscription "For protecting our homes, our homes are open to him," was a gift from "the citizens of West Texas." Promoted to major in 1890, Bullis went on to fight in the Spanish-American War. His service in Cuba apparently earned him the admiration of Col. Theodore Roosevelt, who promoted him to brigadier general a short time later. He retired from the army in 1904.

Bullis frequently returned to the West Texas region, where he had first gained fame. After his retirement, he lived for a time at Camp Meyers and began acquiring extensive acreage in that region. He soon became a major landholder in Terrell County and elsewhere, eventually leasing thousands of his acres to the big cattle ranches that developed after the threat of Indian depredation had totally disappeared. In time, Bullis also became a partner in a Big Bend area mining corporation founded by William R. (Pecos Bill) Shafter, his fellow officer. Records show that General Bullis continued to visit his properties and business concerns in the region until 1910. The general died in San Antonio on May 26, 1911, and is buried in that city.

The site of Camp Meyers is still visible. The two limestone buildings are partially intact, as are a few other scattered ruins. An effort by Sul Ross State University's Center for Big Bend Studies to reconstruct one of the limestone structures was under way in late 2012. When completed and properly interpreted, it should become a fitting monument to Bullis and particularly to his Black Seminole Scouts, the early day frontier fighters now largely forgotten by the government they served so long ago.

LOCATION: On private property northeast of Dryden, Terrell County.

ACCESS: No public access except with owner's permission.

SOURCES

Britten, Thomas A. "The Dismissal of the Seminole Negro Scouts." *Fort Concho and the South Plains Journal* 24(2) (1992): 54–77.

Downie, Alice Evans, ed. *Terrell County Texas: Its Past, Its People.* San Angelo: Anchor, 1978.

Mulroy, Kevin. *Freedom on the Border: The Seminole Maroons in Florida, the Indian Territory, Coahuila and Texas.* Lubbock: Texas Tech University Press, 1993.

Porter, Kenneth Wiggins. "The Seminole Negro Scouts, 1870–1881." *Southwestern Historical Quarterly* 55 (January 1957): 358–77.

San Angelo Standard Times. January 6, 1968.

San Antonio Sunday Express-News. April 8, 1990.

Texas Historical Commission. National Register of Historic Places files, Austin, Texas.

Wallace, Edward S. "General John Lapham Bullis, Thunderbolt of the Texas Frontier, I." *Southwestern Historical Quarterly* 54(4) (April 1951): 452–61.

15 FORT D. A. RUSSELL 1911–1945

The glory days of military activity were over. Marfa would never be the same again. — *Cecilia Thompson, 1986*

Louie was thirty-one years old when he was shot and killed at Fort D. A. Russell on December 14, 1932. Although some other horses had been known to live to be older, the U.S. Army's veterinarians found Louie no longer fit to serve as a cavalry mount. Although regulations clearly stated that such condemned animals were to be hauled away to the nearest slaughterhouse, Louie, much beloved by the troopers at the fort, was, as the official report put it, "painlessly dispatched." For several years at the fort, the old warhorse had been allowed to participate in reviews with an empty saddle on his back. After Gen. Douglas MacArthur, the army's controversial chief of staff, had determined that the long tradition of the service's Horse Cavalry had run its course, the 1st U.S. Cavalry Regiment, located at Fort D. A. Russell, was permitted to have this one last sentimental mounted review before it shipped out to Fort Knox, Kentucky, to begin its transition to mechanization. All of the horses in the review, except Louie, were to be sent to slaughterhouses or to pastures at other cavalry stations in Texas and elsewhere to await their fate. In a post review ceremony witnessed with sadness by soldiers and civilians alike, the euthanized horse was laid to rest in a deep grave on the now-deserted review parade ground. The burial symbolically represented not only the end of a good horse but also the conclusion of more than two colorful decades of cavalry life on the West Texas post. In many respects, it also symbolized the fading away of the Old Army altogether, but that was not to be recognized for another decade.

The Horse Cavalry arrived in Marfa, future site of Fort D. A.

Russell, on the January 29, 1911. One hundred officers and men of Troops E and H of the army's 3rd Cavalry Regiment had arrived on the train from Fort Clark, located near Brackettville, Texas. Finding no camp to occupy, the men pitched tents near the tracks on the southern edge of the little West Texas village, awaiting the arrival of other units and the construction of a more suitable encampment elsewhere in the vicinity. The civilian population of Marfa at the time was slightly more than one thousand. The 1883 arrival of the Galveston, Harrisburg, and San Antonio Railroad, which later became the Southern Pacific line, marked the beginning of the village. It was the coming of the railroad that guaranteed Marfa's future. Ranchers in the area were thus provided with a relatively economical method of transporting livestock to markets, and local stores then had a way to bring wholesale goods to their shelves for resale to the public.

The railroad also made Marfa a likely location for a military outpost, located as it was between San Antonio's Fort Sam Houston on the east and Fort Bliss at El Paso some 250 miles to the west. Even though travel and shipping by rail was far more expeditious than by stagecoach and wagon, it still required twenty-three hours to travel the three hundred miles from San Antonio to Marfa. In a short time, all of the army units ordered to Marfa had arrived. The combined military complement at the fort amounted to 770 officers and men. Considering that the entire United States Army in 1911 consisted of 4,585 officers and 79,421 enlisted men, the relative size of Marfa's garrison reflected the importance the army placed on its new outpost. The troops soon bivouacked at what would be the army's home at Marfa for more than a quarter of a century. Designated a temporary installation, the new tent encampment just south of town was at first called Camp Albert and later Camp Marfa.

The army's mission at its new West Texas camp evolved rapidly because of the Mexican Revolution. Mexican armed forces, ostensibly in support of one or another of the many factions involved in that conflict, held little regard for the integrity of the U.S. and Mexican international boundary formed by the Rio Grande. A year old in 1911, the upheaval that erupted on the Mexican side of the river had already spilled across to the American side. Citizens in the Big Bend country of Texas, which lay roughly one hundred miles south of Marfa, were particularly concerned, with good reason, that the violence could not be contained by the often shallow waters of the Rio Grande. As a result, the army chose Marfa, with its east-to-west rail line in place, to be the center for its armed patrols, which would range south to the river, hopefully to deter any revolutionary-inspired activity that endangered American citizens as well as the nation's sovereignty. It soon became clear that the patrols would be dealing with more than armed insurgents. Seeking treasure and livestock, Mexican bandits seized an opportunity to take advantage of the chaos created by the revolution to prey upon remote ranches. Gunrunning and cattle rustling often defied the sanctity of the international border. Stolen Mexican cattle were frequently herded across the Rio Grande to be sold to ranches located deep within the Big Bend area. Money paid by ranchers to the rustlers next found its way into the coffers of El Paso gun shops. In one twelve-month period, one such shop sold forty thousand Springfield rifles, millions of rounds of ammunition, and even machine guns to Mexican buyers, who used the proceeds of their stolen cattle transactions to finance the purchases.

The frequently ineffectual patrol units consisted of one noncommissioned officer and two enlisted men. On average, the units would cover more than six hundred miles while on patrol in a month's time. An individual patrol unit would traverse nearly two hundred miles as it made its way through the particularly harsh and unforgiving borderland along the river. Frequently, the rustlers and bandits merely waited on the Mexican side until the army patrol rode out of sight and earshot before making their illegal crossing. The fact that the Mexicans usually knew the terrain far better than the newcomers in army uniforms further hampered the patrols. When the situation only worsened as the violence of the revolution amplified and expanded, it became necessary for the army to broaden its reach as well. As a result, it established a series of outposts at Texas villages scattered along the Rio Grande. Small garrisons soon located at villages such as Candelaria, Ruidosa, Lajitas, and Glenn Spring, where a somewhat more sizable force was placed to protect a successful wax-making facility that flourished there. In all, the army established fourteen subposts, with Camp Marfa serving as the headquarters and supply center for the entire riverside network.

In January 1914, Pancho Villa, the colorful revolutionary with presidential ambitions of his own, attacked and soundly defeated the well-armed but poorly led Mexican federal garrison at Ojinaga, located opposite Presidio, Texas, and less than seventy miles from Marfa. Rather than surrender to the notoriously violent Villa, the entire federal force of two thousand soldiers and thousands of other refugees crossed the Rio Grande to seek sanctuary in the United States. Troops from Marfa were quickly dispatched to shepherd the Mexicans across the desert and on to Marfa to await their fate. Along the way to the camp, the size of the group of defectors increased. On arriving at Marfa, the number of displaced persons and defeated soldiers was estimated at five to seven thousand. The procession approaching the camp stretched over twelve miles as it made its way over particularly harsh terrain. Once the forced migration reached its destination, a temporary detention camp held the defectors under guard until trains arrived to take them to El Paso and further detentions prior to being escorted across the International Bridge to Juarez.

General Villa was soon heard from again. His raid on Columbus, New Mexico, in March 1916, quickly followed by another raid by suspected Villistas on Glenn Spring, finally served to awaken the U.S. high command to the seriousness of the entire Mexican situation. Activated by Pres. Woodrow Wilson to deal with the emergency, as many as 150 thousand National Guardsmen arrived in Texas to protect the border. In the meantime, Maj. Gen. John J. Pershing's futile Punitive Expedition launched in pursuit of the wily Villa. Mexico and the United States were soon on the brink of war. When an actual conflict in Europe involved the United States in 1917, rumors of a German-motivated invasion by Mexican forces made the border area even more likely to erupt in violence. With most of the guardsmen, who had been federalized to protect the border, now gone to France to fight in World War I, Camp Marfa's mission took on renewed significance. The patrols continued but on an amplified schedule. Aircraft from San Antonio aided in the daily reconnaissance, with flight operations conducted from the newly established Royce Field, located east of Marfa. The land patrols were conducted largely by units such as the 4th Texas Infantry and the 1st Texas Cavalry Squadron. Two battalions of the Pennsylvania National Guard remained at Camp Marfa during World War I. Eventually, the 34th U.S. Infantry and the 5th U.S. Cavalry arrived at what had become an important major military site.

The end of World War I proved to be a significant turning point in the history of Marfa's military encampment. The successful conclusion of the war in Europe apparently occurred more quickly than War Department planners had predicted. As a result, unused and uncommitted quantities of federal money filled the army's coffers. With no war to fight, the service's senior officials set about investing those funds in improving and expanding its military installations all across the country. Camp Marfa was an immediate and direct beneficiary of that highly unusual largesse. As the money started flowing from Washington, construction crews embarked on a massive project to transform the camp into a permanent installation. Workers discarded tents in favor of new, more substantial buildings of adobe and concrete. In all, more than three hundred new buildings went up. Included was nearly every kind of club, depot, gymnasium, and quarters traditionally found on most permanent army installations. Some were quite elegant, particularly the commanding officer's quarters, erected, naturally enough, on the highest point of land within the cantonment. Consisting of five bedrooms and four baths, the home became the center for official social functions for years. An administration headquarters was rivaled only by the new officers' club in its appointments and modern conveniences. Construction of a hospital and comfortable barracks for enlisted men got under way on what soon came to be known as the Marfa Command Center. It was the heart of the U.S. Army's vast operating area that stretched from Fort Bliss to Fort Clark, focused on seemingly endless problems along the Rio Grande.

In many respects, Camp Marfa was the last, large cavalry post to be built in the United States. In recognition of its importance, the army declared it a permanent installation in January 1929 and renamed it Fort D. A. Russell. Some confusion resulted from the change in names, however, since the army already had a post in Wyoming known as Fort D. A. Russell. The decision to change the older fort's name to Fort Francis E. Warren came from the army's chief of staff, General John J. Pershing, by then famous as the commander of the victorious U.S. Army in France during World War I. The general's late father-in-law, a U.S. Senator who had masterminded the highly unusual acceleration of rank for his daughter's husband, became the posthumous namesake of Fort Warren, courtesy of his grateful son-in-law. The newly named installation attained increasing importance. One of its more noteworthy functions between the two world wars was to serve as the site of massive field maneuvers involving thousands of troopers and their mounts. Local ranchers permitted the army men and their international counterparts access to nearly four hundred thousand acres of West Texas land. There, cavalry tactic demonstrations took place during the day, while lavish entertainment followed in tents on the field in the evenings. Receptions, dinners, and even field dances were frequently held. Officers from Russia, Japan, and other countries participated in all of the cavalry and social activities at the fort during the early 1930s.

The fort and the town grew closer together socially as the years passed. Dances and dinners staged at the post were reciprocated by similar civilian events in town. The proximity to the Mexican border tended to nullify the legal effects of the Volstead Act, which had imposed prohibition on the nation. Liquor flowed across the river just as easily and as illegally as guns had only a few years earlier. Duty, if it can be termed that, for officers at the fort proved to be leisurely at best. Aside from a short schedule from 9:00 until 11:30 on weekday mornings, officers were free to pursue other, more pleasurable activities for the rest of the day. Riding, hunting, and playing golf or cards were among the pastimes enjoyed by officers of all grades.

Although heat and dust made assignment to Fort D. A. Russell slightly less than desirable, the absence of any rigorous responsibilities made it otherwise quite acceptable. Even officers with families seemed to have enjoyed serving on the Marfa base, in part because the army took steps to make the installation totally independent of its host town. The fort had its own reliable water and electrical resources, as well as paved streets, unlike most of the ones in Marfa, and the social amenities, often shared with the townspeople, were undeniably the best in the entire Big Bend region.

Just as quickly as the fort attained its luxurious prominence, however, stunning proof that nothing is every truly permanent in the army arrived at the Marfa headquarters in 1932. Due to the dire effect of the Great Depression, the government sent orders to close the fort, no doubt influenced by General MacArthur's insistence that the cavalry's mission was no longer relevant.

Two years later, however, the army returned to reopen the facility, this time in the form of the 77th Field Artillery with a complement of seven hundred officers and men. Soon the mechanized 1st Cavalry returned to the fort to join the artillerymen in various maneuvers and exercises on its twenty-four-hundred-acre training grounds.

At the outset of World War II in late 1941, more than one thousand officers and men were stationed at the fort. During the war years, other mechanized cavalry units saw service at the facility. They were later replaced by two chemical-warfare battalions that remained until war's end. German prisoners of war had their own encampment at the fort not far from the homes of the army officers. They performed labor on the base as well as in town, in return for which they received scrip redeemable at their own post exchange for cigarettes, sundries, and even beer. Two of the prisoners, Hans Press and R. Hamper, received permission to decorate the walls of the officers' club with oil murals. The result of their work was a colorful depiction of life in West Texas, with cowboys, herds of cattle, and distant mesas dominating the scenes.

When the war ended in 1945, Fort D. A. Russell permanently closed. Unlike with most military installations abandoned after the war, however, the army's earlier campaign to expand and improve the facility caused many of the old but well-constructed buildings to be of further use. The high quality of its residential prop-

These gateposts marked the entrance to Fort D. A. Russell. Although many old buildings remain on the century-old military post, no descriptive historical signage is to be found. *The Alexander Collection.*

erties was such that civilians purchased many of the houses for their homes. Although most of the larger buildings were allowed to remain vacant, some found utilization that even the most foresighted army planner would likely never have imagined.

In 1979, artist Donald Judd began remodeling and rehabilitating several large buildings, once used as truck and gun sheds by the army, to transform them into art exhibition spaces. Judd, who often worked in large media, realized the wide open space available within each building, coupled with the bright Texas sun streaming through the banks of windows, served as an ideal housing for his works. Judd's Chinati Foundation now owns and maintains these and other buildings, annually attracting large numbers of visitors to the old military installation.

Unfortunately, there is little to tell these visitors about the story of the vital military post that once flourished all around them. Even though the Fort D. A. Russell Historic District delineates all but eight of the installation's original 424 acres, no information panels on the site tell visitors what the various vacant buildings once housed. No site-identification signs are to be seen, and no handout materials describing the fort are available at the Chinati Foundation Visitor Center. That center, for example, is located in what was formerly the post's exchange building during World War II, but no information regarding that fact is offered to the visiting public. Many of the army's old residences are still occupied by local citizens, although the buildings have been materially altered and remodeled. Only the former commanding officer's spacious quarters seem to reflect any of its onetime attractiveness.

Walls within the officers' club retain actual artifacts of the fort's colorful past. Somehow, through seventy years of sporadic occupation and despite neglect and occasional vandalism, the murals of Herr Press and Herr Hamper have remained intact. The German prisoners' views on life in West Texas in the 1940s are now forever preserved in their murals. Fanciful and colorful, these paintings are virtually all that remains, almost miraculously unchanged, to bear witness that Fort D. A. Russell was once far more than the collection of largely unidentified structures still standing on the Marfa Plateau.

LOCATION: On the southwestern edge of Marfa.

ACCESS: Much of the site is owned by the Chinati Foundation; tours are available. Some private residences and many other buildings are still standing. Building 98, formerly the officers' club, is now used as an art gallery and event center.

SOURCES

Alexander, Thomas E. *The Stars Were Big and Bright: The United States Army Air Forces and Texas during World War II*, vol. 2. Austin: Eakin, 2001.

Bennett, Lee. "Fort D. A. Russell." Unpublished paper, Marfa, TX, 1996. *Big Bend Sentinel,* May 22, 1942.

Davenport, B. T. *Soldiering at Marfa, Texas, 1911–1945.* Kearney, NE: Morris, 1997.

Grube, Susanne. "A Brief History of Camp Marfa and Fort D. A. Russell." *Chinati Foundation Newsletter,* n.d.

Krammer, Arnold. *Nazi Prisoners of War in Texas.* New York: Stern and Day, 1979.

Taylor, Lonn. "Fort D. A. Russell, Marfa." *Chinati Foundation Newsletter* 16 (2011): 1–16.

Texas Historical Commission. National Register of Historic Places files, Austin, Texas.

Thompson, Cecilia. *History of Marfa and Presidio County, Texas 1535–1945,* vol. 2. Austin: Nortex, 1986.

Tillapaugh, J. "The Construction of Fort D. A. Russell." *Journal of Big Bend Studies* 8 (1996): 167–98.

16 PENN FIELD
1918

Thy son has not died but he liveth
A life free from sorrow and sin
And our Father who all blessing giveth
Allows anguish to draw us to him.
— Ada Caroline Read Penn on the death of her son, Eugene Doak Penn

---

In 1916, as rumors spread that the United States would soon be drawn into the war then raging in Europe, despite the insistence to the contrary by Pres. Woodrow Wilson, there were those preparing for the eventuality. Among them was Robert Ernest Vinson, who had recently resigned his post as the head of Austin Presbyterian Theological Seminary to accept the presidency of the University of Texas. Asking the board of regents for financial support to develop a series of military courses on the campus, he received an appropriation of fifteen hundred dollars, which went toward the establishment of an aviation school on the campus. The School of Military Aeronautics actually began on the campus of the Presbyterian Seminary and soon moved to Brackenridge Hall, commonly known as B Hall, an 1890 men's dormitory located east of the main building (not to be confused with the present Brackenridge Dormitory or Old Main currently on the campus). Over time, the training school would move to what had been the Asylum for the Blind, which George Custer utilized as his headquarters in the years following the Civil War. In the 1920s, it transferred to the University of Texas and became known as the Little Campus.

Not long after training got under way at the university, the situation worsened in Europe, and on April 6, 1917, the U.S. Congress issued a formal declaration of war, joining the Entente powers of

Britain, France, Russia, and Italy. The nation, however, was too ill prepared in terms of both matériel and trained personnel to be immediately effective. As a result, the War Department quickly initiated an emergency training plan to enable U.S. forces to get to the European fronts as soon as possible. Particularly critical was the state of formal military aviation instruction, which had been in existence only since 1909, when Wilbur Wright personally taught two lieutenants of the U.S. Army Signal Corps the fundamentals. Eight years later the army had only three certified air training fields in the nation and only a few dozen flight officers. The War Department thus had to rely on the more experienced and war-tested members of the Royal Flying Corps, which had facilities at the ready in Canada and in Fort Worth, Texas.

The federal government, as well as the American people, showed a great deal of resolve and focus as the nation rushed to war with unprecedented speed. As construction on air training centers accelerated, enrollment in ground schools, such as the one at the university, filled to capacity. Among those enrolling quickly were the residents of B Hall, all of whom would eventually enter the war effort. By 1918, more than a dozen airfields had become operational, including some with names now well known, such as Brooks and Kelly fields in San Antonio, Ellington in Houston, Langley in Virginia, Love in Dallas, and Wilbur Wright Field in Ohio. Additional bases in Texas included Call Field at Wichita Falls and Rich Field in Waco. Additionally, work was under way by the summer of 1918 on an airfield just a couple of miles south of the capitol in Austin, only a short distance south of St. Edward's University.

Graduating at the end of the spring semester that year from the University of Texas was a young man named Edward Doak Penn. A native of Taylor, he was the son of Robert Lee Penn, who served briefly as the Williamson County judge at the turn of the twentieth century. When Gov. Joseph D. Sayers later appointed him to head the 26th District Court, he moved to Austin. The Penns moved into an existing home on sizable acreage along the city's near north side at 3112 West Avenue, not far from the university. After a few years, however, Robert Penn left the bench to open a law firm, which quickly became one of the most prestigious in Austin. As both his family and his stature grew, Penn expanded his home considerably. Tragically, though, at the height of his promising career, "a stroke of apoplexy" took his life when he was in his forties. He left behind his wife, Ada Caroline Read Penn, and nine children.

Exhibiting much of his father's determination and zeal for public service, Edward Penn yearned to join the war effort, so much so that immediately upon completing his course work at the university, he opted to forego his graduation ceremony and instead enlist in the army. It was during his officer training at Leon Springs, near San Antonio, in fact, that he received his diploma. Penn would return to Austin for his ground training but then ship out soon after to France and then to Campo Ovesto (Camp Ovest), near Foggia, Italy. There, on May 20, 1918, while continuing his aviation training, his propeller broke, sending him plunging to his death from an altitude of twelve hundred yards. The army returned Penn's body to Austin for a service at his home, in which Dr. Vinson and J. E. Pearce of the university's anthropology department both delivered eulogies. Burial took place in Oakwood Cemetery, where a modest gray granite tombstone now marks his gravesite, and flags flew at half-staff on the campus. Within weeks, the Austin Chamber of Commerce, one of the local liaisons for the airfield under construction south of town, petitioned the War Department to rename the site in honor of the young airman, who was the first from Austin to die in the war, and in June it became known as Penn Landing Field.

Funding for Penn Field came from a number of local sources, most significantly a loan of approximately $750,000 to the University of Texas brokered by George W. Littlefield, president of the American National Bank. Providing additional support were the chamber of commerce, headed by Walter E. Long, and a special citizens committee. At Long's request, most of the buildings at the airfield had brick walls in order to make them more viable after the war for future site development by either the university or private business.

A local newspaper article on July 31, 1918, revealed the extent of work at Penn Field. President Vinson reported on plans for the expansion of the university's radio school, as well as other military-based operations, including training for auto mechanics and both artillery and aerial observers. As the paper reported on the latter, "This has now been realized, and negotiations are under way for the University to take over St. Edward's College and convert it into an air and artillery radio operators' school, capable of handling 1000 men at a time." It further elaborated that Vinson would travel the following day to St. Louis to meet with Catholic officials from Notre Dame, who had oversight of the Austin church school, to transfer it to the state school "for the duration of the war." Although St. Edward's lacked the facilities to handle the projected influx of trainees, Vinson did not anticipate any permanent buildings there, only the use of tents or temporary barracks.

Of particular interest in the newspaper report are the financial and administrative structures for Penn Field. Although the university expected to be reimbursed for its expenses by the federal government, the site was technically leased to the chamber, which then subleased it for administrative purposes to Kelly Field in San Antonio. To keep development costs low, the chamber relied on preparatory fieldwork by local citizens. "The ground was prepared for the government free of charge," the article reported:

> Committees of Austin business men worked on the field during April and May, putting it in shape when it was first designated as a landing field. Citizens of Austin went out themselves and cleared the land of brush. The county and city furnished graders and steam rollers and rolled eighty acres of the field as smooth as a floor. Boys from the Deaf and Dumb and the city schools gathered 300 wagonloads of rock from off the land. The field is kept mowed and is in perfect condition. The erection of hangars is all that is needed to make it an ideal flying field.

The commander of the School of Military Aeronautics at Penn Field was Maj. Barton Kyle Yount, an Ohio native who later served with distinction in World War II as the commander of the Air Forces Training Command. In August 1918, as work on the initial phase of Penn Field neared completion, he hosted a number of dignitaries, including Maj. Gen. W. A. Holbrook, commandant of the army's Southern Department, who formally inspected the site. Holbrook and members of his staff flew into Penn Field and, after visiting

Planes lined up at Penn Field, ca. 1918. ***Courtesy of the Austin History Center.***

with Gov. William P. Hobby, toured the military training facility and the university-run training schools. Within two months, however, significant changes in the operations occurred. As the *Dallas Morning News* reported, Harry Landa (shown in the article as Lands), a successful miller and business leader in New Braunfels, joined with others to sell the Penn Field tract of approximately 316 acres to the State of Texas, on behalf of the University of Texas, for $40,000. Plans were still ongoing to expand the radio school. The following month, though, on November 11, the war formally came to a close with the surrender of Germany. Even though the airfield was not yet complete and represented a sizable investment by a number of entities, its future was quickly in doubt.

By early 1919, efforts were under way to demobilize many of the wartime airfields, including several in Texas. The future of Penn Field, though, remained open to speculation. As the *Dallas Morning News* reported, it appeared the radio school and the field might survive, but that failed to materialize, and during the summer the university advertised the sale of the property. The high bidders were

Sam Sparks of Austin and D. J. Woodward of San Antonio, who acquired the tract for a bid of $107,000. They immediately set about converting the facilities for industrial purposes and soon opened the Woodward Truck Body Company, which provided wooden truck body components for Ford Motors and other clients. All was going well with the new endeavor until May 5, 1922, when a series of tornados raked the capital city. One of the twisters formed on the near east side below the Travis Heights neighborhood and moved west-southwest directly across St. Edward's and the former Penn Field site. Devastation at both sites was extensive and resulted in the death of a worker, Ben Roberts, at the truck body plant. Even though the paper reported total destruction at Penn Field, many of the buildings in fact proved salvageable or at least restorable. Nonetheless, the owners chose to sell the land, and new owners W. T. Caswell, E. H. Perry, and Dave C. Reed converted the facilities into a furniture plant. Named the Woodward Furniture Factory, although D. J. Woodward was not involved, it remained a successful operation through the 1930s.

Over time other uses were made of the former military buildings, but many of the remaining structures eventually fell into a state of disuse and disrepair. In recent years, however, developers have extensively reworked the site as a complex of offices and commercial operations. Elements of the original facilities remain, and a large, unique water feature utilizes airplane parts, all of which lend an air of history and authenticity to the complex. Given other development in the immediate area, though, it is difficult to discern any dimensions of the field itself.

Not long after the Great War, officials at the University of Texas chose to convert B Hall into classroom and office space. Beloved by its former residents, it was the center of legal maneuverings to ensure its continued viability, but in early 1952, citing the building's lack of structural integrity, the school leadership opted to raze the historic building. Over time, the storied structure faded from memory, but in 2010, workers on an East Mall project encountered its buried remains, including a decorative stone floor and other features. Thanks to the efforts of the University of Texas Heritage Society, however, the wartime story of B Hall has been revived and

Although an office park is now located on the site of Penn Field, there are visual reminders of and references to the World War I installation. *Photo by Dan K. Utley.*

will be a central part of commemorative plans for the early building. Regardless, with their jobs complete, workers filled in the excavation, allowing the archeological story to perhaps remain for some future group to uncover once again.

The Penn home at 3112 West Avenue, a landmark in what is now known as the Heritage Neighborhood, serves as a visible reminder of the Penn family's many contributions to the quality of life in Austin and has a unique and significant story of its own. Not long after the death of Judge Penn, Ada Penn embarked on a career that would bring her great acclaim and, more importantly, help her provide much-needed financial support for her large family. Taking advantage of the sizable land estate she inherited, she taught herself the architectural design, real estate, and construction trades and subdivided the land for a neighborhood called Penn Place, which she personally developed. In effect, she got to design her surroundings in the manner that she envisioned. It was her ultimate goal to send all of her children to college, and according to family lore she would allow them to choose any institution of higher learning, "as long as it was the University of Texas." Ada Penn lived a long and productive life at the family home and passed away in 1955 at the age of eighty-seven.

LOCATION AND ACCESS: The site of Penn Field, on the east side of South Congress in Austin, just south of Woodward Avenue, is a commercial development open to the public. B Hall remains largely an archeological site under the grounds of the University of Texas and is therefore not accessible. The Penn family home on West Avenue is a private residence and not open to the public.

SOURCES

Austin History Center. Vertical files. Austin, Texas.

Austin Statesman, Austin, Texas, July 31, 1918.

Bartlett Tribune and News, Bartlett, Texas, May 24, 1918.

Boyer, Anne Olivia. "Reminiscences of the Heritage Neighborhood." Heritage Neighborhood Association website, heritageaustin.org/about/history, accessed July 2013.

Dallas Morning News, May 28, 1918; June 8, 1918; August 17, 1918; October 17, 1918; March 8, 1919; June 27, 1919; September 16, 1920.

Freehill, Lynn. "UT's Most Storied Building Uncovered." *Alcalde* (blog), *Texas Excess,* July 15, 2010.

Kroll, Harry David, ed. *Kelly Field in the Great World War.* San Antonio: Press of San Antonio Printing Company, 1919.

"List of Training Section Air Service Airfields." Wikipedia, en.wikipedia.org/wiki/List_of_Training_Section_Air_service_airfields, accessed July 2013.

Long, Walter E. "B Hall of Texas." *Southwestern Historical Quarterly* 62(4) (April 1959): 413–41.

Penn Field and Penn Family files. Austin History Center, Austin, Texas.

Tyler, Ron, ed. *The New Handbook of Texas,* 6 vols. Austin: Texas State Historical Association, 1996.

17 JOHNSON'S RANCH AIRPORT
1929–1943

There was just nothing else quite like Johnson's Ranch.
— Lt. Col. Howard E. Rinehart, US Air Force (Ret.)

Two notable incursions into United States territory by armed Mexican forces in the early twentieth century clearly demonstrated that the international boundary separating the two nations was porous at best. Following Pancho Villa's raid on Columbus, New Mexico, in 1916 and an almost immediate Mexican attack on Glenn Spring, Texas, the fear of similar raids long continued to grip the portion of Texas that lay along the Rio Grande in the rugged landscape of the Big Bend mountains. In early 1929, a brief political insurrection launched in Mexico by Gen. José Gonzalo Escobar reignited fearful anticipation of possible new violence along the border. Although the so-called Escobar Rebellion shortly played itself out with no verifiable incursions into Texas by any Mexican forces, it once again caused paranoiac apprehension in the residents of the Big Bend. There is likely no better example of how effectively that easily-aroused panic served to create unusual situations than in the legend of Johnson's Ranch. Its transformation from a family-operated agricultural enterprise and trading post into the only known civilian-owned and -operated, yet very much official, U.S. Army Air Corps station was directly due to the fear of Mexican incursions into Texas.

The thousand-acre ranch was on the southern edge of what later became Big Bend National Park. The ranch house and its attendant trading post were situated directly adjacent to the Rio Grande in such a way that the often snake-like wandering of the stream placed Mexico on three sides of the Johnson property. Only its northern edge directly touched other American soil. Elmo Johnson and his wife, Ada, purchased the already established ranch in 1927, apparently unconcerned by its proximity to Mexico, located literally a stone's throw across the Rio Grande. The place was about 150 miles south of Alpine and could be reached only by traveling along dirt roadways that were little more than double-tracked cattle trails. The Johnsons' nearest American neighbor lived sixteen miles upriver at the village of Castolon.

Johnson's motive for acquiring a place so remote was, in his words, to "do a little pioneering." Before he became a rancher and trading post operator, the thirty-eight-year-old had worked as a hand on his father-in-law's ranch for a time. Tiring of rural life at least temporarily, Johnson then moved to Dallas to work for the financial services firm of Dun and Bradstreet. From Dallas, he moved to San Antonio to enter the real estate business. Although that career proved to be short lived and unsuccessful, the Johnsons eventually had the wherewithal to acquire the ranch on the Rio Grande. Johnson's trying years in larger cities and experience in various unsuccessful white-collar undertakings perhaps prompted him to seek both success and solitude in a location that was, and still is, about as remote as one can find in the entire United States. On the ranch he raised livestock, primarily goats and cattle, as well as horses and mules to provide transportation through the rugged landscape of the Big Bend. On his property he also grew cotton, sugar cane, onions, watermelons, strawberries, and, of course, pinto beans, with which to augment his frequent goat-meat feasts.

Although the ranching and farming activities provided sustenance for the two pioneers, the trading post was a more reliable source of income. In return for wolf pelts and other furs he received from the Mexican hunters who lived across the river, Johnson would trade the many essentials for living that the local Mexican families otherwise found hard to obtain. The most wanted item was ammunition for the hunters' rifles, but staples such as flour, sugar, and rice were available for consumption by ranchers and farmers living on both sides of the river. Tobacco was another popular trade item, along with coffee, sardines, and some basic apparel.

Had it not been for a colorful part-time Big Bend resident named Wilfred Dudley Smithers, better known as "W. D.," the Johnsons likely would never have gone into the army airfield business. Smithers was born in Mexico in 1895 but had come to the United States with his family in 1905. An early interest in photography eventually led him to a career as a photographer for a San Antonio newspaper, but only after a stint as mule team teamster and cavalryman in the U.S. Army. During his years in military service, Smithers made friends with officers in the Army Air Corps. Against all regulations, they often permitted him to expand his photographic experience by taking in-flight pictures from army airplanes. His favorite subject was the Big Bend region of Texas, where he once served.

In time, W. D. discovered Johnson's Ranch, perched on the edge of the Big Bend with an unobstructed view of the river, which all but surrounded it. Smithers and the Johnsons became good friends, even to the extent that the photographer moved into the ranch house to stay for several years. He also built a darkroom on the property so he could instantly see the fruits of his daily camera work. Smithers's relationship with the Johnsons, coupled with his close association with a number of San Antonio–based army flying officers, served to launch Elmo and Ada on their new career. When a group of Mexicans crossed the river to steal some of Johnson's livestock, Smithers perhaps hastily assumed they were renegade soldiers fleeing from the ruins of General Escobar's failed revolution. Concerned for his friends' safety in the wake of this minor incursion, Smithers urged Johnson to offer some land to the U.S. Army to establish an air facility, which might deter further such raids. Johnson, having nothing to lose, agreed, and Smithers, having everything to gain, wasted no time in convincing his army friends in San Antonio to accept Johnson's kind offer. The army moved with remarkable speed in getting one of their pilots in the air and on his way to the ranch to inspect the site only hours after the meeting with Smithers. The inspecting pilot, Thad V. Foster of the 8th Air Corps, landed in a rough pasture at the ranch on April 24, 1929, bringing his De Havilland DH-4 to a full stop in the late afternoon. Foster liked what he found and eventually grew to like both of the

Johnsons even more. He was particularly fond of Ada's excellent goat tacos.

Foster returned to San Antonio bursting with enthusiasm after receiving Johnson's agreement to lease ten of his acres to the army for one dollar per year for as many years as the service desired. Foster's recommendation to accept the offer met with immediate approval. Fortunately for all concerned in this speedy transaction, the army's intelligence officers had long considered placing some kind of observation outpost deep in the Big Bend area. Johnson's Ranch gave them a suitable place as deep in the Big Bend and as close to Mexico as any U.S. installation could possibly be. Within hours of Foster's return, an army truck carrying fundamental airstrip supplies such as tires, gasoline, and a windsock had made its way to the ranch from the army's auxiliary field at Dryden, about 110 miles to the northeast. The driver of the truck was Sgt. John McCabe, and his excited passenger was none other than W. D. Smithers himself, likely overjoyed that his mission had been so swiftly accomplished. By the time the truck arrived, Johnson had already marked the location of the first of four landing strips to be provided on the ranch.

The first airplane to land on the newly created field at Johnson's Ranch was, as might be expected, piloted by Lt. Thad V. Foster. Upon landing, he entered his name in a leather-bound registry that was to remain on the spacious patio of the Johnsons' ranch house for nearly fifteen years. That rare book is now in the Archives of the Big Bend at Sul Ross State University, in Alpine, Texas.

Not surprisingly, the most frequently entered name in the book is that of Lieutenant Foster, who was apparently somewhat typical of Air Corps pilots in the years between the two world wars. He was a daredevil to the extent of flying his clumsy aircraft at dangerously low altitudes over the Rio Grande, its wingtips mere feet from the river's towering canyon walls. As if that were not violation enough of Air Corps regulations, Foster also often took female civilians with him on his official flights. In addition, the barnstorming lieutenant thought nothing of entering the names of his lady passengers alongside his in the registry. Various women from several Texas cities had their presence at Johnson's Ranch knowingly or otherwise preserved for posterity in the register thanks to Lieutenant Foster. Other names appearing in the book include those of future chairman of the Joint Chiefs of Staff, Air Force Gen. Nathan B. Twining, who signed in as a captain in 1932, and Brig. Gen. Jonathan Wainwright, the army's commander at Fort Clark at the time and the future hero of Bataan. Rumor persists in the region that the famous aviator Amelia Earhart also landed at the field but for some reason did not sign the register. Similar rumors contend that John Dillinger was once a passenger on a plane that touched down on the field, though under what circumstances has not been revealed.

The army designated the field as an official station in its Southwestern Airways Section. Since the new field was more than one hundred miles from any established military airway, it could not be deemed to be either an auxiliary or an emergency airfield, but as Johnson's Ranch Airport, it was nevertheless regarded as an official U.S. Army installation. Its uniqueness lay in the fact that no government funds were ever allocated for its upkeep, the army had no direct supervisory authority over it whatsoever, and no significant government equipment was ever sent there. Elmo Johnson, former Dun and Bradstreet employer turned rancher, remained in total command of the facility. Eventually the army did send a surplus radio to the site, along with a young soldier to operate it, and Johnson built an adobe hut to serve as the radio shack.

The army was clearly pleased with its new, very low-cost operation. It provided a strategic outpost from which to report any potentially dangerous massing of Mexican forces on the U.S. side of the river, possibly preparing to mount a raid on the Johnsons' place or on some other ranch located within striking distance along the Texas side of the Rio Grande. Elmo Johnson himself was considered by the army to be an intelligence resource. As friend of and provider to many Mexicans, he was in a good position to hear any hints that a bandit raid might be in the offing.

The paranoia stemming from decades of border violations by Mexicans pursuing various objectives continued to grip the residents of the Big Bend even as the army's planes flew into Johnson's Ranch. That latent fear, even though largely groundless by the early 1930s, still produced a flow of often frantic correspondence from the region to elected officials in both Austin and Washington, DC. The political pressure created by the letters and telegrams resulted in the Army Air Corps having an increased presence in the Big Bend. As a result, despite countless rumors that indicated just the opposite, no significant organized river raids occurred during flight operations at Johnson's Ranch. The army speculated that the sheer presence of its aircraft, flying into and out of the ranch and frequently strafing and bombing the river for both fun and practice, was the major reason for the lack of Mexican incursions. The validity of that claim will likely never be affirmed.

What can be affirmed is that the army's fliers frequently elected to fly the 325 air miles from San Antonio down to Johnson's Ranch to spend some prime off-duty time. If by flying into the site they might also be keeping any bad men from Mexico at bay, so much the better. Each pilot acquired the benefits of logging official time in making the trip and also had an opportunity to practice landing at and taking off from a less than well-developed strip. Too, they could use their newly learned navigational skills to find the ranch. If a nighttime landing was called for, Johnson would make the task a bit easier by lighting some lanterns at the approach to the main landing strip. In 1943, the ranch could offer pilots four runways, one of which was more than forty-two hundred feet long and nearly a thousand feet wide, which was longer and wider than the main runway at Austin's municipal airport at the time.

While the fliers were doubtless pleased to believe their flight activity actually kept at least a part of the Mexican border safe from bandits, they were likely even more content to lounge about on the Johnsons' cool patio, resting after a hard day of hunting deer or an easy day of swimming, usually without swimwear of any kind, in the river. The highlight of the day was dining at Mrs. Johnson's table. The couple never asked the men for any money to pay for their meals, so they often brought store-bought commodities with them on their flight from San Antonio to augment Ada's simple homegrown fare.

Word rapidly spread throughout the Air Corps of the good times waiting to be savored at the Johnsons' place. The register shows that planes from virtually every major U.S. Army airfield in Texas landed at the field. In addition, entries include flights from faraway fields such as Langley in Virginia, Mather in California, Maxwell in Alabama, and even the Air Corps headquarters at Bolling Field, at the nation's capital. Sometimes the entries would indicate that an officer and his wife made the trip, indicating that the nonregulation transportation of civilians on military planes was not limited to junior-grade officers such as Thad Foster.

As word spread, the number of flights to the ranch increased, doubling one year and tripling the next. The lure of the magnificent scenery of the Big Bend, the opportunity to hone flying skills, go hunting or fishing, and then relax, perhaps with an illegal beverage or two, seemed compelling enough to attract hundreds of army pilots. The practice that no rank was observed at the site was particularly welcome news to junior officers. Discipline was so relaxed that it was not uncommon to see an enlisted mechanic sharing a venison roast with a colonel who had flown in World War I. The only commanding officer at the ranch was the owner himself, the civilian Elmo Johnson.

Periodically, strong rumors swirled throughout the region about a large-scale raid being planned by a Mexican bandit leader. Taking no chances that the rumor might be spurious, the Air Corps would send fairly sizable formations of aircraft to Johnson's ranch from San Antonio. The pilots, eager to get away from Kelly or Randolph fields, volunteered to fly to the site. For whatever reason, be it relative stability in Mexico or the daunting exhibition of force staged by the airborne visitors to the ranch, raiding in the region all but ceased in the late 1930s. The few reported incidents involved mainly petty rustling or just the theft of food by Mexicans hungry enough to ignore the demonstrated might of U.S. airpower. It is likely that the added knowledge that U.S. aircraft were far more effective than U.S. Cavalry horses helped discourage raids from Mexico. The planes had clearly demonstrated their ability to travel the course of the river in a very short time. Further, the altitudes at which they flew provided a far wider visual perspective than that formerly attained from the back of a slow-moving horse.

World events taking place in the late 1930s diverted the army's attention from the border. In any event, the creation of the U.S. Border Patrol served to shift the responsibility of protecting the citizens of the Big Bend region from the army, permitting the Air Corps to focus on preparing for a much larger conflict, widely believed likely soon to come. As a result, the pilots who had often come to Johnson's Ranch no longer had either the time or the official permission to casually fly to the ranch and play on the Rio Grande. They now had new and far more challenging responsibilities.

The last airplane to land at the ranch came and left on November 25, 1943. By that time, the rapidly dwindling number of visitors made it apparent to the Johnsons that their ranch's time as a destination for army pilots had run its course. An unhappy Johnson had also been experiencing tax issues with the county even though he deeded to it the ten acres he had previously leased to the army. To make matters even more complex, the plans to make the entire Big Bend region into a huge national park soon became reality. Ada Johnson had been a strong advocate for the proposal, but she and her husband later became disillusioned when the National Park Service indicated no interest in permitting their ranch to be transformed into a tourist attraction deep within the soon-to-be-created park. Like many other property owners whose land the government hoped to include within the national park acreage, the Johnsons had no option other than to sell their property. They received a total of $12,599.83 for their 996.3-acre ranch. The government determined that the improvements on it were worth $12,007, but the vast acreage was appraised at only $492.43, or 49 cents per acre. In addition to the four long, graded runways, the property also contained seven buildings.

The combination of the creation of the Big Bend National Park and the coming of World War II brought an end to the Johnson's Ranch story. Elmo and Ada left the now federal property in late 1943 and moved to Sonora, Texas. Ada died there on July 3, 1945, leaving behind her husband, who, having filed for bankruptcy, lived on his brother's ranch. Elmo Johnson died on Christmas Eve, 1974.

National Park Service bulldozers leveled most of the old Johnson Ranch buildings soon after acquisition in keeping with its preservation concept of minimizing if not obliterating anything created by the hand of man. As a result, few historic structures survived

An aerial view of the long-abandoned landing field at Johnson's Ranch indicates the extent of its pre–World War II facilities. ***Courtesy of the W. D. Smithers Collection, Archives of the Big Bend, Bryan Wildenthal Memorial Library, Sul Ross State University, Alpine, Texas.***

this early frenzy of demolition. For some reason, the ranch house initially escaped destruction by the National Park Service, only to be reduced to rubble by local residents, who carted off any even remotely usable material. Today, only a pile of rocks marks the site of Johnson's Ranch, along with a faint impression of one of the runways:

> The irony of the Johnson's Ranch story is that it was born of the raw fear of Mexican bandits or renegades crossing the river to raid, and then nourished by the freedom from military structure that it offered. It was doomed by the success of the army's show of force staged by the carefree fliers who came to the river to enjoy the pleasures offered at the ranch. Its eventual mindless final destruction by the National Park Service was really

only the final *coup de grace* to a carefree between-the-wars way of military life that abruptly ended at Pearl Harbor, Hawaii, on December 7, 1941.

LOCATION: On the Rio Grande in Big Bend National Park, southeast of Castolon Historic District.

ACCESS: Public property, but a four-wheel-drive, high-clearance vehicle is required. Check with park headquarters to determine seasonal accessibility.

SOURCES

Archives of the Big Bend. Bryan Wildenthal Library, Sul Ross State University, Alpine, Texas.

Gomez, Arthur R. *A Most Singular Country: A History of Occupation in the Big Bend Country.* Provo, UT: Brigham Young University Press, 1990.

Horgan, Paul. *Great River: The Rio Grande in North American History,* 2 vols. New York: Holt, 1954.

Ragsdale, Kenneth Baxter. *Wings over the Mexican Border: Pioneer Military Aviation in the Big Bend.* Austin: University of Texas Press, 1984.

Willeford, Glenn. "A History of Johnson's Ranch and Trading Post on the Rio Grande." Master's thesis, Sul Ross State University, 1993.

18 ARLEDGE FIELD 1941–1944

I made them a proposal. I told them I didn't have any money but was sure I could get the support of Congress in the next appropriations bill. Would each of them be willing to go out and set up at his private school the facilities to house, feed, and train flying cadets for the Army Air Corps? — Gen. Henry Harley "Hap" Arnold

---

The municipal airport for Stamford, Texas, in Jones County, is located in a rural area four miles east of the city. Its quiet and somewhat remote setting away from nearby farm-to-market road traffic is in stark contrast to the busy role it played during World War II. At that time it was the site of a civilian flying school established to provide basic aircraft training for cadets who would, upon graduation, move on to more advanced flight training elsewhere. During the war, planes were in the air almost continually so that each cadet could receive his required sixty hours of training in as short a time as possible. Initially that was twelve weeks, but as the war progressed and the demand for pilots increased dramatically, the training period decreased to first ten and then nine weeks. The story of the training at Stamford and at similar civilian schools across the country is one that is largely unknown, but one that played a significant role in the early days of the nation's war preparedness.

In 1938, as rumors of impending war started to spread through Europe and the Far East, the United States military command began cautiously conducting readiness assessments for a foreign conflict that might, for the second time in the twentieth century, involve the nation. The consensus was that the United States was far from ready to be a viable participant in any immediate military action, and so the planning steadily intensified. In his assessment of the U.S. Army Air Corps he commanded, Gen. Henry Harley "Hap" Arnold had to deal with not only inadequate numbers of modern aircraft but also the reality that, before any planes could become wartime operational, expanded air training and aircraft maintenance programs were essential. This reality proved to be even more critical when the lag time for building air bases and related facilities from scratch in the eventuality of war was factored in. The United States, Arnold believed, could not afford to wait.

As Arnold and his advisors in the air corps worked on a wide range of preparedness contingencies, the general developed a plan that would allow his training command to focus its combat mission with greater purpose. At the time, flight crews underwent essentially four stages of combat training. As W. F. Craven and J. L. Cate point out in their seminal study, *The Army Air Forces in World War II,* a cadet would learn the basics of flight using a relatively low-power, stable trainer and then advance to more complex aircraft before moving on to combat-type aircraft, and finally to the actual type of plane used in battle-setting missions. In surveying the needs for detailed training at each level of the process, Arnold came to believe he could rely on civilian trainers at the basic level, thus freeing his limited personnel for the more advanced instruction. Thus, in 1938, acting largely on his own and initially without congressional approval, the general pitched his idea to representatives of three of the nation's leading flying schools. Essentially asking them to commit to the necessary infrastructure and the concomitant liability, but with technical assistance and materials provided by the federal government, he received a favorable response. With that, Arnold quickly moved his planning forward, calling on members of his staff to determine which existing schools would be best and also the most ready for the assignment. With his homework done, he then had to present the plan to Congress for authorization and funding, utilizing the political muscle of the private schools and their supporters to keep the pressure on and arguing for ultimate cost savings to the military. In the spring of 1939, Congress passed Public Law 18 (eventually a part of the National Defense Act of 1940), which gave the secretary of war the leeway to work with private entities for basic army air corps training when existing facilities proved limited and also allowed the government to loan planes for that purpose.

Shortly after the formal authorization, the small West Texas town of Stamford sought to secure one of the new facilities, hoping to use the federal government to construct what city leaders anticipated would become a municipal airport at the war's end. The competition was fierce, especially in Texas, where the climate and open terrain in parts of the state were conducive to new fields outside the congested air spaces of existing urban facilities. In making its proposal, Stamford relied on the leadership of Roy Wade Arledge, a prominent businessman, chamber of commerce leader, and rancher who had also been a pilot since the 1920s. Arledge headed the city's aviation committee, which included C. M. Francis and R. G. Bowdry. After an extensive survey of suitable land, the committee recommended the city purchase four hundred acres from local gin operator W. B. Harrison and his wife, Leanora. The land had earlier been part of the extensive SMS ranching operations of Swedish-born Swante Magnus Swenson, a noted Texas business magnate. The conveyance took place a week before Christmas in 1940, and on the following day the city council leased the property to the Lou Foote Flying Service, of Grand Prairie, for the operation of a civilian flying school to train army pilots. In return for the five-year lease, the private company assumed the responsibility of constructing a number of buildings, including a hangar and barracks, as well as space for classroom and administrative functions. Work got under way immediately on what would become known as Arledge Field, named for the man who helped broker the deal. Across the state, similar air training facilities, both existing and new, geared up for service at places such as Bruce Field, Ballinger; Curtis Field, Brady; Corsicana Field, Corsicana; Garner Field, Uvalde; Hicks Field, Fort Worth; Love Field, Dallas; Cuero Municipal Airport, Cuero; and Howard Hughes Airport, Houston. With operations in other states as well, the wisdom of Arnold's plan was soon evident; the number of pilots who had undergone basic training in aviation had increased far beyond what would have been possible with only existing army installations. As the nation moved closer to war, this proved to be profoundly significant.

Frank Luther "Lou" Foote, a native of Los Angeles, California, had an extensive record of flight training as a result of his longtime operations in the Dallas area, where he was often in the news because of his business success and personal eccentricities. In August 1934, for example, the *Dallas Morning News* reported that "James A. Boze, self-styled rainmaker, Miss Gertrude Jeffries, a passenger in his chartered airplane, and Pilot Lou Foote were burned Wednesday when a bomb exploded in the plane and set it afire." The accident occurred in the air above Waxahachie "as Boze prepared to drop the bomb into a cloud to prove his theory that explosions would induce rain." Although burned in the mishap, Foote managed to safely land his "blazing craft" in a farmer's field. Boze died of his injuries, though, and as mourners later gathered for his funeral, Foote flew overhead, dipping his plane in an aerial salute to the would-be rainmaker. The following year, a *Morning News* article noted, "A lone pilot [Foote] droned backward and forward over Dallas between midnight Friday and daylight Saturday circling the city in huge spirals. In the rear cockpit was the body of an 11-year-old dog," the mourning pilot's beloved and recently deceased Irish setter, Duke, who had often accompanied him on flights.

Not much is known of Foote's personal involvement with Arledge Field, but the early public indications were of a successful venture. Cadets arrived, and regular flights began in March 1941, and on May 17 and 18 of that year, a crowd estimated at ten thousand gathered at the rural installation for a formal dedication, which included the presentation of a U.S. flag by the Veterans of Foreign Wars and a speech by Maj. Stanton M. Smith of Brooks Field, San Antonio, calling for national unity if war should come. Little did those there at the time know, but that would occur before year's end. It was a day filled with meaningful events and interesting demonstrations of appreciation by the local community. As a newspaper account of the event recorded, "Buck Rowe of Dallas, visiting civilian flier, was presented a pair of cowboy boots by the Stamford Chamber of Commerce and wore them during the festivities, but limped to his plane, boots in hand, for [his] farewell takeoff." Only a couple of weeks after the site's dedication, the first class of nineteen cadets graduated and then reported to Randolph Field, northeast of San Antonio, for the next phase of training.

Only a few months after the dedication, news arrived that the size of the flying classes at Arledge would be expanded, resulting in the need for several new buildings, including hangars. Over time, a hospital, a recreation building, and a parachute tower would also be added. Despite such promise, the connection with the Foote Flying Service soon came to an end only days after the attack on Pearl Harbor, Hawaii, signaled the nation's entry into the global war. Whether the change in civilian administration was the result of overcommitment, a lack of capital, the need for new direction, or some other reason, Lt. James B. Knapp, military commander at Arledge, announced that the civilian element of the facility had transferred to the Coleman Flying Service of Coleman, Texas. Activities, he was careful to note, were to continue "without interruption." That seemed to be the situation both at the field and in town, where residents continued to support the Arledge personnel with great enthusiasm and purpose. In May 1942, the townspeople rehabilitated the 1909 Carnegie Library, moving books upstairs and repairing and reconfiguring the ground floor for use as recreation space—including an auditorium, kitchenette, writing room, and game rooms—for the cadets.

Following his association with Arledge Field, Lou Foote focused on his successful flight operations near Dallas, continuing to support the war effort through civilian training schools for both the army and the navy. In August 1942, however, tragedy struck a unit of his business on South Beckley Road below Oak Cliff when a plane fire quickly spread to nearby buildings and equipment, ultimately resulting in the loss of two hangars and fourteen planes. Persevering, Foote continued to be a leading force in Dallas aviation. Only a few years before the Arledge contract, he had married the noted aviator Jean LaRene, one of the first women in the United States to receive a commercial pilot's license. She was also an air racer and air endurance competitor, once flying over Oklahoma for more than eight days before engine trouble forced her to land. Jean Foote died in 1960, and three years later Lou Foote wed another pilot, Virginia Stone, at a ceremony in Washington, DC. The wedding announcement in the Dallas newspaper described Foote as a rancher who had previously owned airports in California, New Mexico, and Texas. It concluded by noting the couple planned to reside at Hidden Valley Ranch in Lockhart, in Central Texas. In 1992, Lou Foote died in Marble Falls at the age of ninety-five.

As the need for trained pilots escalated into 1942 and 1943, civilian operations at Arledge Field continued as initially planned, with an additional tract of 212 acres acquired in 1942 to provide space for expanded programming. In general, the private-public partnership worked well, with civilian ground and flight instructors attached to the War Training Service and an army presence and disciplinary structure maintained through the officer corps of the 308th Army Air Forces Training Detachment. Initially, training planes at Arledge were Stearman PT-17s—two-seat, open-cockpit, fabric-covered biplanes powered by 220-horsepower radial engines. Over time, the Fairchild PT-19A became the preferred plane at the field since it represented significant advancements in technology and was therefore better suited to future transition training. The low-wing Fairchilds had lower horsepower but quicker speeds and more responsive handling, thus relating more directly to the combat planes then in service. One drawback of the planes, though, was the plywood cladding, which deteriorated quickly in the dry, hot climate of West Texas. Both the Stearmans and the Fairchilds were painted in blue and yellow. Retired U.S. Air Force Lt. Col. Dwade R. King, the Jones County Historical Commission chair who prepared the historical marker application for Arledge Field, noted that because neither plane had electrical systems, they relied on Gosport tubes for communication rather than radios. "On the instructor's end," he wrote, "was a sort of funnel attached to a tube running back to the rear cockpit, where the tube forked and the two ends [were] placed on little aluminum tubes attached to the earflaps of the student's leather helmet." If communication proved too difficult, the instructor might hold the Gosport outside the plane, where the fierce wind and engine roar were sure to get the most reluctant cadet's attention.

Although safety was of the highest concern for everyone based at Arledge Field, the young pilots had their share of accidents and even deaths. Newspaper accounts of such incidents recorded not only the names of those involved but also something about the national scope of the command. In August 1942, the *Dallas Morning News* reported that instructor J. J. Gault, age twenty-six, of Buda, Hays County, had died in a crash south of Stamford along with cadet Robert M. Warner, twenty-seven, of Ceres, California. The article concluded with this somber note: "Last Sept. 5, an instructor and cadet were burned to death in the field's first accident, and a cadet was killed in a crash during July." Another article in August 1943 noted a crash five miles east of the field that took the lives of Abilene instructor Delmon Dee Rice, twenty-one, and trainee James Melvin Godfrey, twenty-three, of Murray, Utah. Similar incidents no doubt continued to occur throughout the wartime existence of the field.

As military historians Craven and Cate have noted, "The peak of primary flight training was reached in May 1943, when there were fifty-six schools in operation. The peak graduation figure was attained in November 1943, when 11,411 aviation cadets were sent on to basic flying training schools. Retrenchment set in immediately thereafter," they added, "and only ten schools survived the year 1944." Only two remained in 1945, and one of those was for the celebrated Tuskegee airmen. As the war mission changed in the mid-1940s, the army began to phase out the civilian schools based on a number of factors, including location, performance record, financial stability, and weather. The army inactivated the Arledge operations in September 1944 and declared it surplus property after the close of war in 1945. For a time, the government stored surplus planes there until they could be sold or otherwise removed. Among them were a wide variety of aircraft, including B-17s, a B-24, a P-39, and numerous trainers.

In April 1947, the military phase of the field came to an end when the War Assets Administration sold the site and remaining equipment to the City of Stamford, which, as originally planned when the aviation committee first began its deliberations, transformed it into a municipal airport. With time, the community's memories of the former training field began to fade as many of the individu-

One of the remaining wartime buildings at the site of Arledge Field.
Courtesy of the Texas Historical Commission; photo by William A. McWhorter.

als associated with the operation passed away or moved away from the area. Renewed attention came in 2005, though, in conjunction with the placement of an interpretive marker funded through the Texas in World War II initiative of the Texas Historical Commission. At the dedication ceremony, a crowd once again gathered by the central flagpole, this time to remember and to honor those who had served there.

LOCATION AND ACCESS: Arledge Field is four miles east of Stamford via State Highway 6, FM 704, and a local airport road. It is an active airport, so access to structures is limited.

SOURCES

Arnold, Henry Harley. *Global Mission.* New York: Harper, 1949.
Craven, W. F., and J. L. Cate, eds. *The Army Air Forces in World*

War II. Vol. 6, *Men and Planes.* Washington, DC: Office of Air Force History, 1983. www.afhso.af.mil/shared/media/document/AFD-101105-019.pdf, accessed January 6, 2015.

Dallas Morning News, August 30, 1934; September 1, 1934; September 4, 1934; June 2, 1935; January 9, 1941; May 31, 1941; May 13, 1941; May 19, 1941; September 7, 1941; December 20, 1942; April 5, 1942; May 3, 1942; June 11, 1942; May 31, 1960; September 3, 1942; September 26, 1942; September 30, 1943; June 16, 1963.

Murdock, Scott D. "W.W. II Army Air Forces Contract Flying Schools." www.airforcebase.net/aaf/schools.html, accessed August 2013.

Pisano, Dominick. *To Fill the Skies with Pilots: The Civilian Pilot Training Program, 1939–1946.* Champaign: University of Illinois Press, 1993.

Texas Historical Commission. Marker files, Austin.

19 CAMP BARKELEY
1941–1945

When I awoke that first morning in camp [Camp Barkeley], the only white space was on my pillow. Everything else, including my face, was covered with red dust. — Lt. Bob Tiffany, 358th Infantry Regiment, 90th Infantry Division, Barkeley, Texas

---

It is doubtful that many of the 1.5 million men who served at Abilene's Camp Barkeley during World War II considered it to be a glorious army post in any way. Sprawling across nearly seventy-six thousand acres some ten miles south of town, the so-called tent camp was hastily constructed in sixty days. As a result, the first cadre of occupants found few amenities awaiting them in the rough cactus- and mesquite-filled hills of West Texas. Basic utilities such as running water, sewers, gas lines, and paved roadways were slow in coming. Weather conditions that created either vast seas of mud or blinding clouds of red dust made the normally rigorous training regimen unusually difficult. Yet despite all the hardships encountered on the base and the social problems created in town, the city of Abilene took instant pride in the patriotic knowledge that it, too, had a full-fledged army base to call its own.

Procuring the base had not come easily. By early fall 1940, the city leaders of Abilene, population twenty-seven thousand, were well aware of the possibility of the United States' involvement in the war, already raging in both Europe and Asia. They were, of course, by no means alone in recognizing this dire possibility. Representatives of other neighboring towns such as Brownwood, Lubbock, and San Angelo had long been traveling to the nation's capital, where they worked with their representatives and senators in a lobbying effort to bring major military bases to their respective towns. In anticipation of the conflict almost certain to come, other cities all across the state of Texas, as well as throughout the nation, were being successful in persuading the U.S. Army to establish new forts and camps in their immediate vicinity. Although no war had been declared, a patriotic fervor seized the country, and although the desire to host a big army facility was sincere, the lobbying effort had a less altruistic subtheme. What came to be called the Great Depression had stubbornly gripped the United States for nearly a decade, and although the crippling effect of the economic catastrophe seemed slow to reach Texas, it had finally arrived in full force by the late 1930s. As terrible as the approaching war was likely to be, it also held the golden promise of a tidal wave of government dollars to fuel America's preparedness and defense requirements.

In Abilene, an agricultural and petroleum center, the Great Depression created financial havoc. With no eastern markets financially able to purchase its cattle, wheat, and crude oil, the city, along with all of Texas, was eager if not desperate to find a new and reliable source of income. Immediately before the war the U.S. government had become a limitless fountain of immense recovery dollars in the form of military installations. Under the direction of its newly formed military committee, the Abilene Chamber of Commerce mounted a major campaign to ensure the city would get at least its fair share of the federal money that was part and parcel of the promise of a new military installation. First came the construction-phase monies flowing from the influx of carpenters, equipment operators, concrete haulers, and the like. This would then be followed by the direct benefits from the large military payroll dispensed on a regular basis. The larger the installation, the bigger the payroll and the greater the benefit, or so reasoned the chamber's leadership. Its efforts at first appeared less than successful. Even though War Department officials seemed interested in Abilene as a future military site, they were quick to point out that other neighboring cities had already convinced them to award installations more or less immediately. As a result, Brownwood became the site of a new Camp Bowie, and San Angelo welcomed an air base, which in time became known as Goodfellow Army Airfield.

Realizing that something more compelling had to be added to

their plea, the city rightly determined that the offer of a sizable piece of Texas real estate made free and clear for the army's purposes might clinch the deal. The added incentive of virtually no cost to the government gave the Abilene proposal what it required to be accepted. On November 15, 1940, a full year before the war actually involved the United States, the city announced that an option it had acquired on 2,289 acres south of town had been accepted by the War Department as a potential site for an army training base. On November 26, jubilant headlines proclaimed that the city had officially struck a deal with the government. Abilene agreed to buy the optioned land and then lease it to the army for one dollar a year. The army in turn agreed to construct a "temporary tent city" training camp on the site. The only catch to these happy arrangements was that cash-strapped Abilene did not have the $125 thousand needed to purchase the land. The government, suddenly convinced that the Abilene site was a top-priority acquisition, sternly demanded the money be raised in one week's time, or the whole deal would be nullified. With the powerful support of the *Abilene Reporter-News* and arm twisting by chamber of commerce officials, a fund-raising campaign exceeded its goal in less than the given time. Local citizens had responded wholeheartedly, mainly through personal donations that averaged between five and fifteen dollars, and managed to raise $144,081 in just six days. Clearly pleased with the civic response, the army promptly announced that it would lease, with no further contribution from the town's citizenry, nearly seventy-three thousand additional acres adjacent to the original site to provide for maneuver areas, firing ranges, and other purposes. That leasing process concluded on December 7, 1940.

Construction at the site began at once and continued on an around-the-clock schedule. An estimated eight thousand workers flocked to the site and into what limited rental accommodations were to be found in the area. Although the initial building phase was more or less completed on February 26, 1941, the construction consisted mainly of tents, unpaved roadways, and little else. The government paid the contractors more than seven million dollars for their two months of work.

The search for a name for the new post began as soon as the construction work took place. Before long, the announcement came that Abilene's base would be called Camp Barkeley in honor of an eighteen-year-old native Texan awarded the Medal of Honor for his actions at the end of World War I. The fact that the honoree's name was actually "Barkley" instead of "Barkeley" was not discovered until after the official naming announcement. The incorrect spelling was conveniently attributed to "clerical error," in the traditional army manner. More than forty years later came the revelation that Private David Barkley had been the first Hispanic soldier in army history to be given the Medal of Honor. During World War I and earlier conflicts, it was reported, neither Hispanic nor black soldiers were regularly issued weapons. As a result, they were obviously not allowed to participate in combat. Eager to fight, Barkley had not mentioned his ethnicity but died in combat less than three days before the end of World War I. In addition to his coveted U.S. medal, Barkley also posthumously received the French Croix de Guerre and the Italian Croce al merito. An elementary school in his hometown of San Antonio was later named in his honor.

The initial unit to be assigned to the still unfinished camp was the 45th Infantry Division, known as the Thunderbird Division. Some twenty thousand strong, the unit trained at the camp for nearly a year before moving out to fight in Sicily, Italy, France, and Germany. Although the army designated Barkeley as a tent cantonment for twenty thousand men, it soon had a population of more than thirty thousand as even more new troops arrived. By the end of the war, the camp was home to as many as seventy thousand at its peak. The population on the base was usually twice that of Abilene itself and sometimes nearly three times larger. The average payroll totaled well over one million dollars per month and frequently went much higher, depending on the troop size at the camp. The overall economic impact of the camp was at one time estimated to be more than $22 million per year.

Although Abilene's economic plight swiftly ended with the opening of the huge camp, other problems soon arose. Restricted to the base for six weeks following their arrival, the young men of the U.S. Army were more than eager to sample the night life of Abilene just as soon as their initial restrictions were lifted. The first group of thirteen hundred soldiers to endure the restriction rushed into town in mid-March 1941. To their collective dismay, the men found a bone-dry community where no legal alcohol could be obtained. They also discovered a straight-laced Bible belt city that tolerated no waywardness. The two movie theaters provided little in the way of entertainment, and even they were not open on Sundays. The citizens of the town were hospitable to the newcomers although reportedly wary of their supposedly more worldly customs. Some soldiers were fortunate enough to receive invitations to private homes for Sunday dinners and the like, but many were forced to loiter around the darkened downtown streets hoping something exciting might somehow happen. It soon did. Having taken no heed of the army's early requests that steps be taken to minimize if not restrict the vice of prostitution, frequently associated with military men and their money, the city's leaders were soon appalled by the numbers of unescorted females who began appearing on the town's streets at night and even during the daytime. Further, a startling increase in the number of apparently inebriated young men in uniform was suddenly noticed around town. As one veteran of service at Camp Barkeley put it, "There were more bootleggers in Abilene than I have ever seen in my whole life." It was clear something had to be done, so the army and the city put in place a plan that at least limited the prostitutes' more obvious plying of their ancient trade. By some eyewitness accounts, however, that trade more or less moved into the shadows of what was deemed the shabbier side of town, closer to the camp.

The chamber of commerce, having created this two-headed creature of economic boom and social disruption, swung into action. In time, there were four United Service Organization (USO) venues operating in Abilene to provide suitable dancing partners and entertainment. The Bluebonnet Brigade was formed for officers and enlisted men seeking wholesome companionship. Membership was open to older high school and college girls and was granted only after each young woman had been interviewed in depth. Despite the fact that sponsors turned down more than 15 percent of the applicants, more than eleven hundred young ladies became members and were encouraged to come to the USOs to visit and dance with the military men, but only on a closely chaperoned basis. At one dance staged at the camp, nearly three thousand officers showed up to dance with the two hundred Brigade girls bused from town for the event.

Yet another major problem confronted both army and city officials. The shortage of housing, a situation that plagued every military town during the war, seemed particularly acute in Abilene. Few apartments were available, and decent rental houses often went to local civilians. The parallel shortages of both construction materials and construction workers made the building of new housing a casualty of the war. With thousands of officers and their families continuing to arrive in town, the situation became just short of intolerable. Landlords with living space to rent ignored federal wartime rent ceilings and demanded exorbitant fees. Profit-seeking landowners put aside their proudly demonstrated patriotism to pack large families into small spaces without regard to their comfort or safety. Eleven families, for example, simultaneously occupied one three-bedroom house on the edge of town.

Enterprising residents erected tiny wooden shacks in their backyards. A home on Palm Street had five such one-room huts available for nine dollars a week. This was at a time when a good steak dinner in the best restaurant in town cost less than a dollar. At one time, three thousand such shacks, housing six thousand families, were located throughout the town. One woman placed a cot in her living room and charged soldiers in town for the weekend a dollar and a half per night to sleep on it. One report told of a family of six who lived in a wagon bed on the edge of town. Unable to pay a sudden increase in rent for their tiny living space, they took in a renter to defray the cost of living in the wagon.

Despite such hardships and evidence of greed, Abilene in general flourished for the first time since the onset of the Great Depression. Inflation became a problem as legitimate wartime shortages competed with widespread price gouging on most essentials. Sales at stores and restaurants, however, increased in double-digit increments as the soldiers and their families brought a new economic energy to the entire community.

As Abilene worked its way through its wartime crisis to eventual success, Camp Barkeley began to evolve from a rustic tent city to a full-fledged military installation. In time, more permanent quarters, including hutments, which were half-tent and half-building, and barracks with indoor bathroom facilities replaced the early tents with their two-mile-long row of primitive latrines located a half mile away. Workers transformed unpaved roads into a network of hard-surfaced streets and cross streets that stretched more than a hundred miles. Twenty-five miles of waterlines were eventually put in place, along with nineteen miles of sewer pipe, thirty-three miles of electrical wires, and fifty-one miles of gas lines. With the addition of natural gas to the installation, the smoke and soot from earlier wood and coal stoves disappeared. The extensive pavement eliminated at least some of the red dust that frequently still darkens Abilene skies. One earlier new arrival at the camp said that he found the site by simply driving south from town toward the dust cloud that constantly hovered over the continually used drill field.

The improved camp had a bakery, four theaters, two service clubs, fifteen chapels, an officers' club, and three swimming pools. In addition, thirty-five post exchanges offered a vast array of goods at considerably lower prices than those at civilian stores in town. According to sales records, however, the lower military pricing did not materially affect the sales volume of the local stores. Restaurants, grocery stores, drugstores, gasoline stations, and the movie theaters in town enjoyed greatly improved sales and profit levels during the war years. Military families living off the base, including those whose only shelter was a tiny wooden shack, kept the Abilene stores humming with heavy traffic. Although the pay that each soldier earned was not large, the aggregate dollar amount paid out each month far exceeded any amount ever injected into the community before the war.

As Abilene basked in the economic good fortune the camp generated, the war in both Europe and the South Pacific raged on. With U.S. forces now fully involved, the disquieting attrition rate put new emphasis on the training program at Camp Barkeley. When the 45th left the base, the 90th Infantry Division arrived to begin training. Previously known as the T-O Division, signifying the Texas and Oklahoma makeup of its personnel during World War I, the 1942 version of the division had taken on a new name. The "T-O" then stood for "Tough 'Ombres," a more appropriate fighting appellation to be sure. Following the 90th's departure, the camp next became home to the 11th Armored Division, known as the Thunderbolts. When that division completed the camp's training regimen, it was replaced by the 12th Armored Division, the Hellcats. It would be the veterans of the 12th who would honor their time at Camp Barkeley by funding a postwar museum, which is still operating in downtown Abilene.

Among the more famous soldiers who endured the rigors of Camp Barkeley was Bill Mauldin, whose later cartoons created for *Yank, the Army Weekly* provided World War II soldiers with a humorous viewpoint on the dire realities of war. Lew Ayres, the Hollywood actor who first portrayed Doctor Kildare in many films, proclaimed himself to be a conscientious objector when the war started. He soon found himself in Abilene learning to become a medical corpsman. Camp Barkeley was a good place for the actor to learn his new, less glamorous role. Its medical replacement training center, its Medical Administrative Corps Officer Candidate School, and particularly its twenty-three-hundred-bed hospital gave future Corpsman Ayres a good opportunity to serve his country without firing a shot in anger. Another well-known army officer later was the direct beneficiary of the skills of the medical men who trained at Camp Barkeley. Future U.S. senator and presidential nominee Robert Dole served for a time at the camp before being assigned to the 105th Mountain Division. Grievously wounded in combat, Lieutenant Dole was awarded two Purple Heart medals and a Bronze Star for his service.

Even before the war ended in September 1945, it became apparent that Camp Barkeley's mission would soon be fulfilled. With Germany out of the war and Japan apparently soon to be, the need to keep training new soldiers had all but disappeared. As a result, the army deactivated the huge cantonment on April 3, 1945, and soon declared it to be surplus. Discharges came to many of the permanent personnel while others transferred to other posts to be separated from the service as soon as records could be properly

The site of Camp Barkeley's gatehouse is one of the very few visual remains of the huge World War II army posts south of Abilene.
The Alexander Collection; photo by Dan K. Utley.

processed. The more than eight hundred German prisoners of war who had been detained at the camp were soon on their way back to their homeland.

The editors of *Life* magazine considered the closing of Camp Barkeley to be big enough news to warrant the dispatching of a reporter to cover the story. In an article that appeared in the May 7, 1945, issue, soon after the camp's deactivation, the writer described a city on the brink of economic despair. One Chinese restaurant, the Canton Café, declared its business had dropped off by almost 90 percent since the camp's closing. Three other restaurants had already gone out of business during the first week after the camp closed. Nearly two thousand rooms were suddenly available for rent in town.

A rare high-altitude view of Camp Barkeley at its prime during World War II. No vertical remnants of the huge installation are extant. ***The Alexander Collection.***

On a brighter note, *Life* reported that wealthy ranch families and former prewar out-of-town customers had rushed back to Abilene to catch up on delayed purchasing now that all of the soldiers had departed. Although many young women told the magazine's writer that their social life had all but vanished along with the well-paid soldiers, others, now newly married, awaited the return of their grooms, soon to be discharged from the service. Many ex-soldiers would return to Abilene to live in the city with the hometown girls they had married while at the camp. According to Taylor County records, 511 marriage licenses were issued in 1940. By 1944, that number had jumped to 1,534, with each intervening year showing similar increases. As one wifeless soldier returning home to Abilene after serving overseas put it, "They cleaned out all the old maids in town."

If any military glory was ever associated with Camp Barkeley, it has now faded to the point of invisibility. The slab where military policemen guarded its entrance gate can still be seen, along with an occasional pile of rubble and tangled metal. Faint roadways can be glimpsed through the forests of gnarled mesquite trees, which have returned to reclaim the land their ancestors once dominated. A Texas Historical Commission marker indicates the site of the camp.

Several buildings removed from the camp can still be found in Abilene. The American Red Cross Building, a Boy Scout troop building, and Elmdale Church, off Farm Road 18 east of town, are among the more readily found architectural artifacts of Camp Barkeley's existence.

Without doubt, the single greatest asset of Camp Barkeley's heritage lies on Abilene's far west side, on property adjacent to the camp's old site. In the process of acquiring land for its wartime use in 1940, the army also claimed additional acreage to provide for a pilot training center to augment Barkeley's overall mission. That site eventually became Abilene Army Airfield, also known for a time as Tye Army Airfield. Today, the site is Dyess Air Force Base, a key factor in Abilene's economic strength. Because of Camp Barkeley, Abilene became a successful military city, and, directly because of that previous achievement, it continues as such more than seventy years later.

LOCATION: The main gate was ten miles south of Abilene on US Highway 287. A Texas Historical Marker is present at the site.
ACCESS: Private property. Some construction debris is visible off FM 1235 between Buffalo Gap and View.

SOURCES

Abilene Public Library, Camp Barkeley vertical files.
Abilene Reporter-News, March 29, 1943; May 8, 1945; March 15, 1981; June 1, 1981; June 21, 1981; November 18, 1981; September 27, 2001.

Compere, John. "Camp Barkeley: Our First Military Installation." Buffalo Gap, TX: Buffalo Gap Round-Up, August 2011, 1.

McCombs, Holland. "The Army Pulls Out of Abilene." *Life,* May 7, 1945, 23.

Shilcutt, Tracy M. "Soldiers Were Everywhere: Camp Barkeley and Abilene, Texas, 1940–1945." *Sound Historian: Journal of the Texas Oral History Association* 12 (2009): 31.

Tiffany, Bob. "Camp Barkeley—My Home." Unpublished paper, ca. 2005, 7.

20 BIG SPRING ARMY AIRFIELD 1942–1946

Who ever [sic] decided on the construction of the buildings at Big Spring AAFB must have been an extreme pessimist and believed that we would loose [sic] the war in a hurry or an extreme optimist and believed we would get it over with, right off.
— Bill Steagald, Big Spring, Texas

Prior to World War II and the construction of Big Spring Army Airfield, the city's economic existence had been based almost exclusively on the railroad, agriculture, and, most significantly in the recent past, the petroleum business. During the war years, however, and for nearly three decades thereafter, aviation arguably became the most reliable pillar of the area's fiscal well-being. The first aircraft to visit Big Spring landed on pastureland north of the city in 1911, just thirty years after the railroad had constructed its rather primitive depot alongside its newly laid track. By the end of World War I, local interest in the increasingly popular pastime of flying caused former army pilots to make the town something of a regular stop for their barnstorming aerial circuses.

One such military aviator, on a surveying mission to identify potential sites for future army landing fields, selected a location just west of Big Spring for possible development. Concurring with the airman's unofficial recommendation, in 1928 the town's leaders purchased a 275-acre site as the future location for Big Spring Municipal Airport. A hangar, terminal, and runways were soon under construction, and on March 1, 1929, the first commercial flight landed at the new facility. Transcontinental airmail service began making stops at the airport early in 1932, with Capt. Eddie Rickenbacker of World War I fame on hand for the initial event. Within a few years, Big Spring's strategic location, between Fort Worth and

El Paso, ensured that its airport became a regular stopover point for several major airlines. In early 1941, perhaps remembering that the airport had been built on a site originally chosen by an army aviator, Big Spring's Chamber of Commerce officials launched a well-orchestrated political campaign to convince the War Department that the twelve-year-old facility would be an ideal site for an army flight-training base. Following the Japanese attack on Pearl Harbor, the city's efforts swiftly came to fruition.

The wartime-generated demand for flight-crew personnel caused the army to acquire or build training facilities all across Texas, with its largest school for bombardiers being located just forty miles west of Big Spring at Midland. When it soon became apparent that what was being hailed as the "world's largest bombardier school" could not graduate its cadets fast enough to compensate for both the deadly attrition of combat and the ever-increasing need for flight-crew members, other schools were speedily opened in relative proximity to the big mother base at Midland. Because of its location, its existing facilities, and the persuasive selling techniques of its civic leaders, Big Spring's airport was among those chosen to become a bombardier-training school. As the *Big Spring Herald* proudly proclaimed in a lead story on April 22, 1942, the refitting of the airport would require some five million dollars, to say nothing of extensive cooperation between civilian and military authorities. Estimates predicted that the construction phase of the army field would generate an increase of at least 40 percent in the area's population while the school district would likely experience at least a 30 percent growth in enrollment. The city built new water lines to carry the projected million gallons that would be required daily by the completed base, and planning began as well for miles of roads and highways soon slated for construction, expansion, and upgrading. While the cost to the city was certain to be sizable, as the newspaper assumed, the prospect of more than five million dollars in annual military payroll somehow seemed to make any startup expense more than worthwhile.

Just days after the announcement of the plan to open the expanded bombardier school, new construction on the field was in full sway. When the army officially declared it operational just four

A refurbished World War II hangar at Big Spring houses the Hangar 25 Air Museum. Exhibits within tell the story of this onetime bombardier training base and later fighter-training facility. ***The Alexander Collection.***

months later, a small city had been created on what had only recently been a municipal airport of fewer than three hundred acres. New construction included three sixty-two-hundred-foot-long runways and two huge hangars, as well as barracks, classrooms, a gymnasium, a chapel, an auditorium, and miles of streets and sidewalks. The entire installation sprawled across nearly thirteen hundred acres.

As noted in the official history of the 812th Bombardier Training Squadron, which was made up primarily of the initial cadre at the new base, "There was clear evidence that the carpenters had not done much more than build." The barracks were filled with rubbish, the latrines lacked many important things, including mirrors, shelves, and, as the squadron historian noted with heavy irony, "even water." The men of the cadre unit soon acquired enough brooms and shovels to make their accommodations at least livable. Other personnel found hammers, nails, and lumber to start building partitions and shelving that had apparently been overlooked in the original government building specifications. Not content to wait until the army air force provided for their recreational needs, the men of the 812th continued to build and enhance their barracks and immediate area when not training the bombardier candidates. The airmen built a dayroom for their leisure hours, complete with writing desks, ping-pong tables, and magazine racks. Money from the squadron fund helped purchase lamps, chairs, and a radio. Eventually, two pool tables were added to the dayroom, much to the delight of many of the off-duty personnel. In a further effort to make their existence more pleasant, the men bought grass seed to sow across the sunbaked caliche, which seldom, if ever, experienced much in the way of rainfall. Apparently, the seemingly futile undertaking was at least in part successful, as the unit history records that the seed that "did not blow away, [but] sprouted and grew, thereby enhancing the appearance of the area."

Shortly after the apparently less than enchanted but clearly highly resourceful cadre arrived, the first class of 130 bombardier candidates began its training on the base, then still under construction, in late 1942. The course of instruction lasted twenty-four weeks and included ground school, an introduction to the secret Norden bombsight, and actual in-flight practice bombing experience. The flying training utilized Beechcraft AT-11s on an around-the-clock basis, with hundred-pound practice bombs dropped on area target ranges both day and night. The prime target used by all bombardier schools was a wooden shack, located at the center of a series of concentric circles marked with lime. The shack was lighted for night practice, with the power coming from generators located about a half mile from the structure. If and when a cadet managed to score a direct hit, crews from the base were dispatched the next day to repair both the shack and its electrical system. The AT-11s had 35 mm cameras on board, and the base photography lab received daily deliveries of film upon the completion of missions, in turn providing developed photos overnight so that instructors could use the prints to evaluate their pupils. Aside from a few unscrupulous opportunists seeking money for alleged damage done by poorly aimed bombs, the citizens of Howard County and Big Spring warmly welcomed the young men and women assigned to the base, located just west of town. At any one time during the field's wartime operational peak, more than three thousand military personnel were stationed there. Some lived off the base with their families in town, where the population had soared to nearly seventeen thousand, up from only twelve thousand in a very short time. Soldiers from the airfield made the less than three-mile trip into town quite often, but particularly on weekends. As it was against army regulations for military personnel to wear civilian clothes off base, they were easily recognized in their olive drab or khaki uniforms as they flocked to Big Spring's four movie houses and drugstore soda fountains. Airfield authorities declared a few saloons such as the Blue Bonnet off limits, but the men from the base generally felt welcomed in all places of business.

A USO facility opened in downtown Big Spring, providing a well-chaperoned rendezvous spot for local girls and lonely soldiers. According to both oral histories and newspaper articles of the war years, many marriages eventually grew from the dances and social hours held at the USO building, and some of the soldiers and their dates found the lush green lawn of the courthouse to be a comfortable spot for a tête-à-tête. Military police routinely cleared the lawn each night at 11:00 p.m. If a soldier met an interesting girl at the USO or the drugstore, he might well find himself invited to her family's home. After meeting her parents and having supper with them, the duo might go to the movies, making sure to be at her home no later than 11:00 p.m. If the next day happened to be Sunday, the soldier would likely attend church with the girl and her family and then enjoy dinner with them before returning to the airfield. A thoughtful airman might carry some of his food ration stamps along with him to the family dinners to leave behind, a technique that was often particularly effective in gaining the favor of the girl's mother.

Traveling shows frequently performed at the field. In 1943, Bob Hope came to Big Spring to entertain the troops as he did at many other military installations during the war. He was accompanied by his popular cast, which included singer Frances Langford, sidekick Jerry Colonna, and the usual bevy of beautiful Hollywood starlets. Occasionally, base officials would invite local high school boys to come out for an orientation visit. As the invitations were extended to senior class boys only, the purpose behind the airfield tour was rather transparent. A photograph of a group of the young men on the base appears in the Big Spring High School annual of 1945 with the biting caption "Draft Bait."

In its three and a half years of existence, the field developed a high level of training intensity and proficiency. One contemporary bulletin issued by air base headquarters stated that trainees logged a thousand hours of in-air instruction each month and that more than 4.5 million pounds of bombs were dropped on practice targets. "In just over one year," the bulletin declared, "a distance of 18,000,000 miles had been flown, with but one fatality." When the bombardier training school closed, the final tally showed that four hundred thousand hours had been flown, for a combined distance of sixty million miles. Unfortunately, four fatal accidents also occurred. In total, more than six thousand bombardiers received their wings from the Big Spring facility during the course of World War II.

As the war drew to a close and graduation ceremonies occurred less frequently, it soon became apparent the Big Spring base and its bombardier-training mission would no longer be of use to the government. Despite an effort by the chamber of commerce and the region's elected officials, the base finally closed in early 1946, some five months after the war had ended. Although the closing had a definite economic impact on Big Spring and all of Howard County, opinions differ as to just how severe it was. Joe Pickle, editor of the *Big Spring Herald* when the base closed, recalls that the "economic repercussions [of the closing] were not too pronounced." According to Pickle, the pause in economic growth was only momentary, and renewed activity in oil exploration and production soon erased any financial difficulties for the region. However, A. J. Prager, who operated Prager's Men's and Boys' Wear when the base shuttered, recalls things differently. "There's no way you can take that much money out of Big Spring's economy," he said, "and not have it hurt each and every one of us, particularly the businessman." Population figures for the time indicate that the region was not immediately severely affected by the closing of the base. In fact, Big Spring reached an all-time-high census count of more than thirty thousand in 1960, reflecting a robust increase from its previous high of seventeen thousand just after the base closed. The military facility itself reverted to municipal ownership, and Big Spring Airport once again occupied the site. The expanded runways and large hangars built by the army were soon put to good use by commercial and general aviation interests.

Unlike many World War II air installations, however, the old bombardier school site was destined to again hear the sound of military aircraft. On October 1, 1951, the government reactivated the Big Spring Air Force Base and designated it a pilot-training center. On May 18, 1952, the field was renamed Webb Air Force Base in honor of Lt. James L. Webb, a Big Spring pilot who lost his life in a plane crash in 1949.

As most of the World War II–era buildings had been destroyed or moved off the site, the Defense Department spent more than three million dollars to provide the old base with all that it would need for its new jet pilot–training mission. The first class of trainees arrived in April 1952 and graduated sixty days later. Eventually, the course of instruction would include all phases of pilot training and last for nearly a year. In the air force base's twenty-six-year history, some fourteen thousand student pilots received their silver wings at Big Spring.

Even though the United States was involved in intensive air wars in Asia during Webb's existence from the early 1970s on, rumors of its impending closure were almost constantly in circulation. The *Big Spring Herald* confirmed in its issue of March 10, 1976, that military officials had marked the base for closure. Even though the city had deeded the airport property to the federal government in an effort to keep base-generated dollars flowing into the local economy, it became evident that Webb would soon be closed. In a last-ditch effort to stave off the inevitable, J. D. Nelson of the Big Spring Chamber of Commerce urged citizens to write directly to Pres. Gerald Ford. Pointing out that Webb AFB, with its facilities worth $128 million, generated a payroll of $33 million and thousands of jobs, Nelson asked that at least one thousand letters protesting the proposed closing be hand-carried to the chamber's offices "no later than noon, Friday." Despite the correspondence to President Ford and the vow of Texas Senator John Tower to fight the closing "to the last bloody ditch," Webb Air Force Base ceased all operations on September 2, 1977. The property reverted to the city of Big Spring for use as an industrial park and, once again, a municipal airport. In time, federal officials approved a major prison for the property, and, in a fitting Texas-like gesture, producing oil wells also went up on the site where AT-11s and T-38s had once roared.

Toward the end of the twentieth century, a group of local citizens set about preserving something of the combined heritage of Big Spring's Bombardier School and Webb Air Force Base. Forming an organization called the Hangar 25 Air Museum, the resourceful group has completely refurbished a once-derelict hangar on the field to its original condition, complete with shining, glass-paneled doors and a rare wooden ceiling. In answer to the organization's call, memorabilia from the old air-base days are returning to be housed in the venerable hangar, seemingly new once again. Support for the project, both financial and material, has come not only from those who once served there but also from the still proud and patriotic citizens of the region, who remember what the once-mighty base meant to them and to their nation a long half century ago. Precious little physically remains to reflect the memory of the three decades of military aviation that once flourished on this sun-baked stretch of West Texas caliche—precious little except a reborn and hauntingly beautiful old airplane hangar, a fitting symbol of a glorious time gone forever but clearly not forgotten by the people of Big Spring.

LOCATION: Adjacent to the southwestern edge of town.
ACCESS: On public land and, except for the prison, open to public access. The Hangar 25 Air Museum is open Tuesday through Friday from 10 to 4 and Saturday from 10 to 2.

SOURCES

Big Spring Herald, April 22, 1942; January 9, 1945; September 16, 1946; March 10, 1976.
El Rodeo. Yearbook of Big Spring High School, Class of 1945.

History of the 812th Bombardier Training Squadron. Big Spring Army Airfield Headquarters, n.d.

Lubbock Avalanche Journal, August 1, 1999.

Midland Reporter-Telegraph, July 7, 1991; July 18, 1991.

Steagald, Bill. "The Big Spring Army Air Force Base or Big Spring Bombardier School: Some Recollections." Privately published, n.d.

Texas Almanac and State Industrial Guide, 1943–1944. Dallas: A. H. Belo Corporation, 1943.

U.S. Army Air Forces Directory of Airports, vol. 3. Washington, DC: War Department, 1944.

21 PAMPA ARMY AIRFIELD
1942–1945

I have always been proud to have been a pioneer at Pampa [Army Airfield] in those memorable years. We never forgot the friendliness and hospitality we encountered from everyone in Pampa.
— Vernon Baumgart, Lt. Col. U.S. Army (Ret.) (Cadet Class 43-B)

Unlike most Texas cities that hosted army airfields during World War II, Pampa apparently did not aggressively pursue a military installation until after the war had actually commenced. The first published evidence of any organized effort to obtain a base appeared in the March 14, 1942, edition of the *Pampa News.* An article noted that a committee of local citizens, headed by Mayor Fred Thompson, was on its way to Washington, DC, to discuss with unspecified governmental authorities ways in which the Pampa area's low-cost natural gas could be employed in the war effort. The mayor and his committee sought to convince federal government officials that a major war-production facility would find the area's cheap fuel and other natural resources a sufficient reason to come to the Panhandle. It is easy to speculate that the mayor's committee, or some other unidentified but powerful civic-minded group, had in fact long been engaged in extensive behind-the-scenes lobbying efforts on behalf of the city's desire to attract a war-related entity. Any suspicion of a long-standing lobbying campaign might well be confirmed by an announcement that appeared just two months after the appearance of the article about the mayoral visit to Washington in March. Dated May 15, 1942, a report with three-inch headlines trumpeted the news that Pampa was to receive a major army air installation within a very short period of time. The newspaper carried copies of telegrams from Washington, DC, confirming the welcome announcement. On May 17, another report confirmed that advance construction officials would soon arrive in Pampa to survey the site of what was eventually to become a massive twin-engine flight school.

The War Department had acquired more than twenty-five hundred acres of land twelve miles east of Pampa near the tiny community of Heaton as the site for the base. Reportedly, the principal factors taken into consideration by the government officials in placing the flight school near Pampa were the city's excellent location, housing facilities, water supply, schools, and churches. Conspicuously absent was any mention of Mayor Thompson's highly touted inexpensive natural gas. Construction costs were estimated to be in excess of five million dollars, with the overall project to be supervised by the U.S. Army Corps of Engineers. On May 22, 1942, the first group of engineers arrived in the city. The first contract let for work on the new base was for a test well that they hoped would supply the seven hundred thousand gallons of water per day that the War Department specified as the requirement for a base of the magnitude of the one it was planning to construct. The City of Pampa pledged to cover the costs of drilling the tester and any subsequent water wells. A $15,000 bond issue campaign opened on July 5, 1942, and one week later leaders announced that the bond issue had been approved by an overwhelming margin. The easy passage of the bond package, according to the *Pampa News,* "reflected Pampans' earnestness to cooperate in every way possible in the development of the new air base."

With water wells successfully drilled, other contracts were soon let. The firm of Poole Brothers in Shawnee, Oklahoma, was the successful bidder on many of the site-preparation contracts, which included excavating, fence building, and pipe installation. Officials estimated that 540 thousand yards of dirt would be excavated to construct the runways and aprons, while twenty-six thousand feet of pipe and more than eight miles of fence would be required. The dollar amount of the initial contracts was not disclosed. The construction continued at top speed, and contractors issued urgent pleas for more workers. Desperately needed were general mechanics helpers, who could expect to earn $150 per month; sheet metal workers, who would be paid $1,500 to $1,800 dollars a year; and blacksmiths, electricians, and draftsmen, whose compensation packages were not noted.

As the buildings neared completion, and before the paint dried, military personnel began filtering in to occupy them. Once in operation, the base would be home to an average of four thousand personnel at any given time.

On November 22, 1942, officials held a ceremony to feature the first landing on the base's principal concrete runway, which, on completion, measured sixty-five hundred feet in length. Lieutenant Colonel Daniel S. Campbell, newly appointed commander of the base, circled the runway just long enough for a sizable crowd to gather to witness his landing of the first aircraft. An army pilot for more than ten years, the thirty-two-year-old lieutenant colonel most likely anticipated his moment of glory with relish. Unfortunately, something of the drama of the event was lost when the civilian pilot of a plane based in Chickasha, Oklahoma, was directed to Pampa because of inclement weather at his original destination. Probably unaware that he was ruining Lieutenant Colonel Campbell's grand entry, the Oklahoma pilot landed his plane on the new runway just three minutes before the base commander's plane touched down to the cheers of the only slightly disappointed onlookers.

Celebration of the first Christmas at the new airfield occurred in grand style and afforded a welcome break in the schedule. To help ensure that enough kitchen workers were on hand to prepare the planned gala feast, squadron officers devised a clever trap. All personnel who did not believe in Santa Claus were asked to sign a sheet of paper posted in the dayrooms. Those whose signatures appeared on the sheet were then advised they had voluntarily assigned themselves to Christmas Day KP duty. The behind-the-scenes duty in the airfield's kitchens on Christmas 1942 must have been daunting, to say the least. The menu included fresh shrimp cocktail, roast turkey, baked Virginia ham, candied Louisiana yams, whipped Idaho potatoes, and a tossed salad with French dressing. Also offered were fresh broccoli, creamed onions, buttered peas, and carrot strips. To conclude the feast, the participants enjoyed Wisconsin cheese sticks, assorted nuts, old-fashioned fruit cakes, homemade pumpkin pie, and a variety of ice creams. It was all washed down with gallons of coffee, hot chocolate, milk, and tea and topped off with complimentary cigars and cigarettes.

The only significant problem encountered by military personnel in town was a shortage of housing for those airmen with families. Jamie Gough, who later retired from the United States Air Force as a major general, recalled that the only lodging he could find for his family was a former funeral home. There were, the general wrote, "discarded caskets in the basement plus a long, slanting metal counter and sink in the kitchen." Harold H. Noah, an enlisted radio mechanic, lived in the back of Wilson's Drug Store with his wife and two children. His wife's lasting impression of her days in Pampa was her astonishment at the size of the Texas roaches that shared their quarters.

The first class of cadets arrived in Pampa some three days later than expected. Heavy traffic on the nation's railways was cited as the cause of the seventy-two-hour delay. When the train carrying them finally arrived at 2:00 a.m. on a Saturday morning, it was met by a somewhat bedraggled but excited group of cadets' wives who had arrived in Pampa well ahead of their husbands. The women had met every arriving train for three days, and when the long-awaited cadet section finally "snorted into" town, as the *Pampa News* reported, the wives "bounced into the arms of their husbands with whoops of delight as they marched from their section of the train." Despite this much-anticipated reunion, all of the cadets soon marched to waiting buses, which transported them directly to the airfield. After consuming coffee, sandwiches, and soup, the men went to bed in preparation for the first day of training, which began later that same morning.

This first cadet class to arrive at the Pampa airfield graduated on February 16, 1943, receiving its commissions and wings from Brig. Gen. Isaiah Davies, commanding general of the 34th Flying Training Wing. Just four days later, Class 43-D arrived and began its training in advanced flying instruction. The second cadet class consisted of young men from forty-two states, the District of Columbia, and Puerto Rico.

On February 28, 1943, army officials announced plans to hold an open house on March 7 at the less-than-one-year-old air base. According to Col. Daniel S. Campbell, the purpose of the event was to thank Pampans for their cooperation and hospitality. In a letter that appeared in the newspaper, Campbell wrote, "Pampa people, and those of the entire Panhandle, have time and again demonstrated their willingness and desires to make us feel at home and to cooperate with us in every way." More than forty years later, as a retired air force major general, Campbell continued to regard his welcome in Pampa as one of the warmest he received throughout his long military career.

In addition to the *Pampa News,* which had served the community since 1926 and reported airfield happenings with great thoroughness, another community newspaper began publishing later in the war. Named the *Pampa Flyer,* it debuted on November 1, 1944, as the voice of the Pampa Army Airfield. Like many base publications, the small newspaper carried mainly items about sporting events, inoffensive gossip concerning enlisted personnel, and, without fail, a presentation of inane jokes that would have embarrassed even the most tasteless vaudeville comedian.

When the first contingent of the Women's Army Corps (WAC) arrived on the base in late 1944, the *Pampa Flyer* dutifully reported that Dorothy Braud, who hailed from Lake Jackson, Texas, was a sheet-metal worker, while Alice M. Doyle, from Edenborn, Pennsylvania, was a welder. Mary S. Sutkins, of Rochester, New York, served as a control-tower operator, and Lena E. Vertucci as a surgical technician. While still on the subject of the WAC, the base paper saw fit to announce that the army had decided it was providing too much food to its female soldiers. Rather than continue with the 3,750 calories per day that each WAC received, new regulations ordered that only 3,100 calories per day would be served until the end of the war. It is a wonder that existing photographs of Pampa WACs on parade show that the women were, for the most part, far trimmer than their recommended daily intake of calories might suggest.

Among the subjects seldom covered by the reporters of the *Pampa Flyer* were aircraft accidents. The pages of the civilian-published *Pampa News,* however, presented tragic proof of the dangers of flight training. The first fatal crash occurred on January 27, 1943, when two aircraft collided on a taxiway at an auxiliary field. Killed was Cadet William H. Kidd, age twenty-one, who was scheduled to graduate in three weeks. A midair collision claimed the life of instructor William A. Gibbons on May 10, 1943. Three other aviators parachuted to safety while debris from the two destroyed aircraft fell to earth among oil derricks located two miles north of Pampa. Five weeks later, another midair crash proved fatal for four more fliers. On December 15, 1943, two cadets died when their plane crashed just after taking off from the field. They were both scheduled to graduate within weeks. Another midair collision took the lives of three fliers on January 5, 1944. Following that tragedy were three more fatal crashes within a month's time. In total, ten aviators from the airfield died during the four-week period. Despite what seems to have been a high incidence of fatal accidents, the pace of training did not begin to slacken until much later in the war. Until then, all activities on the base continued at what must have been an almost fevered pace.

In a strikingly nonmilitary occurrence, the army sought to reap an agricultural windfall from the vast acres it owned surrounding the airfield. The entire area had been planted in wheat long before the government acquired the acreage and built the base, and the crop continued to flourish on the land not covered by the airfield's concrete. In a rare example of federal practicality, military leaders decided to permit civilian operators to bid on a contract to harvest the wheat. Not fully versed on commodity pricing, the army anticipated it would earn at least four thousand dollars from its agrarian endeavor. As it soon developed, the estimate was overly optimistic by nearly fifteen hundred dollars as a result of lower-than-anticipated prices and yields. The harvest consisted of more than three thousand bushels.

Among those assigned to the base during the war were William P. Clements Jr., a future governor of Texas, and George McGovern, a future presidential candidate, U.S. senator, and ambassador, as well as movie star Jack Palance. Both McGovern and Palance saw combat action in the multiengine aircraft they learned to fly in Texas.

The names of some of the men who trained at Pampa were enshrined in the airfield's Hall of Fame, which opened on November 2, 1944. If a pilot had been killed, wounded, or declared missing in action, his photograph and combat record received a place of honor in the exhibit. Prisoners of war, as well as those cited or decorated for valor, were also included. Seventy-seven Pampa Hall of Fame honorees received the Distinguished Flying Cross, two received the Distinguished Service Cross, and three were awarded the Silver Star. Additionally, forty-one men received the Purple Heart. In all, 507 Pampa graduates were honored in the Hall of Fame when it opened, including ninety two killed in action, sixty-two who were missing, and eighty-one known to be prisoners of war.

The airfield continued to train pilots for combat on a regular schedule until early May 1945, immediately following the surrender of Nazi Germany. A letter from Lt. Gen. Barton K. Yount notified base personnel that the aviation cadet program was to be "drastically cut back." Those personnel awaiting aircrew training were notified that they were being diverted into other branches of the army, including the infantry. Probably sensing that this diversion might be unsettling to those who had enlisted to become pilots, the general made reference to their likely "keen disappointment" while assuring them "that each man still had a big job to do in battles yet to be fought." Though probably well intentioned, General Yount's words probably did little to assuage the disappointment of the former aviation cadets.

In a public announcement on July 30, 1945, base commander Col. James A. DeMarco made not the slightest hint of any plans to close the airfield. Speaking on behalf of all of his personnel, the colonel invited residents of Pampa and other nearby communities to attend what he promised would be one of "the greatest Army Air Forces celebrations ever held" at the base. The event, staged to mark the thirty-eighth anniversary of "the world's largest Air Force," had been in the planning phase for months. Nearly thirty of the field's B-25 bombers were scheduled to fly over the crowd at a low altitude, with P-38 fighters to follow close behind. A formal military review and parade were to take place in the early afternoon, with martial music provided by the band from Lubbock Army Airfield. No mention was made about why Pampa Field's own highly vaunted band was not slated to perform. Following a full day of flying, parading, and athletic events, the celebration ended with a dance in the recreation center.

Despite such highly successful festivities, it became increasingly apparent that the base would soon be deemed unnecessary. On September 6, 1945, following the surrender of Japan, the announcement that Pampans had long feared finally came from base headquarters, stating the airfield would be deactivated no later than September 30. Although the base commander had stated only a week earlier that he was not aware of any impending closure, personnel on the base were not surprised at the news. Finally, on September 23, under a banner headline only slightly smaller than the one that announced the coming of the base, the *Pampa News* declared that by the end of the week only a skeleton crew would remain on the base. The aircraft were already on their way to a base at Enid, Oklahoma, and the few cadets still in training had been transferred there or to Houston and Bryan, Texas, and Kearns, Utah. It was also announced, in error as it developed, that the government would sell the base buildings.

After the base finally closed, the tremendous wartime growth that had occurred in the region's numerous petroleum-related industries cushioned to some degree the economic impact on its host city. At nearly twenty-five thousand during the war years and in the following decade, the town's population had doubled. The cyclical nature of the oil business took its toll on the community over the ensuing years, however, and by 1990 the population had decreased to roughly twenty thousand.

Pampa's airfield fell into disrepair virtually overnight. Despite the earlier announcement to the contrary, the buildings were for the most part razed or moved away to be used elsewhere. The post chapel, moved twelve miles into Pampa, continues in use for Church of Christ Sunday services. Workers air-hammered the main runway's concrete surface into dust and removed the base material, which was reused to build some eighteen miles of Texas Highway 152.

Although the hangar survived World War II on the Pampa airbase, it later became a sheltering barn for cattle on the feedlot that occupied the site after the war. *The Alexander Collection.*

In 1952, the City of Pampa, which had acquired the entire airfield property from the federal government at no cost, sold it for $2.60 per acre to a feedlot operation. A daily average of fifteen thousand head of cattle soon occupied the land, making exploration of the old base a somewhat challenging and at best a brief undertaking. The taxiways made excellent paved livestock alleys, while the few remaining concrete foundations provided substantial flooring for pens and water troughs. The field's long-idle compass rose remained intact, understandably of no interest to the cattle, which apparently did not particularly care to know what direction they were facing as they contentedly chewed their cud.

To many veterans, memories of Pampa are for the most part good ones, and the comradeship of old flying buddies is important. Life in the present tense is fine, of course, they seem to say, but reliving the unforgettable flying experiences of seventy years ago can be sweet indeed. To many of them, it was the greatest adventure of their lives.

LOCATION: Twelve miles east of Pampa on State Highway 152.
ACCESS: Now a feedlot, privately owned and with no public access.

SOURCES

Pampa Flyer, November 1, 1944; December 22, 1944; December 27, 1944; December 29, 1944.

Pampa News, March 14, 1942; May 15, 1942; May 17, 1942; May 23, 1942; July 9, 1942; July 23, 1942; September 11, 1942; November 3, 1942; November 29, 1942; December 15, 1942; December 24, 1942; February 23, 1943; February 28, 1943; May 13, 1943; June 20, 1943; December 1, 1943; January 6, 1944; July 25, 1944; November 28, 1944; May 7, 1945; July 31, 1945; September 6, 1945; September 13, 1945; September 23, 1945.

22 PORT ARANSAS AND COASTAL DEFENSES 1942–1944

If you cannot cover your windows like you're supposed to, then turn off your house lights and just go to bed. — *Blackout order, Port Aransas, Texas, January 28, 1942*

It is somewhat unfortunate that most visitors to Mustang Island and its only town, Port Aransas, do not come to study their diverse military history. Fishing, boating, and sundry pleasant seaside pursuits are understandably more widely popular than the ferreting out of some gem of military history. The island, however, has seen enough military activity to make it a rewarding destination for those who would study the historical backwaters of many wars. The gulf barrier island was first occupied by settlers in 1855, seven years after the Mexican War. It was that conflict that brought nearly half of the entire U.S. Army in 1845 to the then tiny village of Corpus Christi, just across the bay. Mustang, as well as St. Joseph Island, located immediately north of present-day Port Aransas, were the landing sites of many of the men of Gen. Zachary Taylor's army of occupation. From the islands, shallow draft vessels transported the troops across Corpus Christi Bay to Taylor's sprawling bay-front encampment. A young lieutenant named Ulysses S. Grant managed to fall overboard while in transit to the Corpus Christi camp but was pulled from the water and thus saved for greater service to the Union Army some sixteen years later. General Taylor placed an artillery unit at the tip of Mustang Island to protect the entrance to Aransas Pass, the channel that separates Mustang from St. Joseph Island. Although the pass was then normally too shallow to allow passage by large ships, it is today the main sea route into Corpus Christi Bay.

With the coming of the Civil War in 1861, soldiers and sailors from both sides saw action in the Gulf of Mexico. Aransas Pass provided access to the Texas mainland and served as a vital link in the exportation of cotton, the state's major crop at the time. Clashes between Union cutters and Confederate blockade runners occurred frequently. Union troops actually occupied Mustang Island briefly during the war. Corpus Christi Bay was also the scene of battle action, including an attempted Union invasion of the city by troops ferried into the bay via Aransas Pass.

A present-day promotional brochure adds a bit of colorful if wholly false detail to the role Port Aransas played in the Civil War. According to one entry, Zachary Taylor "marched the beach in search of enemy soldiers during the war." Taylor, the Mexican War hero who later became president of the United States, died while in office on Tuesday, July 9, 1850, a full decade before the Civil War began. By the time the war ended, the then unnamed Mustang Island village that would become Port Aransas had a population of fifty people, according to local sources. Other references later claimed the town had the very same number of inhabitants in 1925. By 1931, the village size had reportedly grown to more than three hundred.

The building of rock jetties at the mouth of Aransas Pass in 1885 led to the dredging and permanent deepening of the waterway to allow the passage of much larger ships into Corpus Christi Bay, directly from the Gulf of Mexico at Port Aransas. As a result, Corpus Christi was successfully positioned to become a major seaport and petroleum-refinery location.

In Port Aransas, early day livestock raising and meatpacking industries eventually gave way to recreational fishing as the principal economic activity. The seasonal presence of massive schools of tarpon attracted anglers from across the nation. A number of schools of the large fish were said to be more than twelve miles long. The tarpon often grow to be up to nine feet in length and sometimes weigh nearly three hundred pounds. They present a challenge to sport fishermen who attempt to catch them with angling skill and a lightweight test line. One such angler was William Howard Taft, former president of the United States and chief justice of the U.S. Supreme Court at the time of his visit to Port Aransas. In 1937, another president, Franklin D. Roosevelt, successfully fished for tarpon just off the coast. He autographed a large scale from one of the fish he caught and gave it to the Tarpon Inn in the village. According to one report, in 1943 a collector once offered to pay $2,000 for the scale bearing Roosevelt's signature. The offer was refused, and the scale can still be seen in the lobby of the venerable Tarpon Inn.

Built in 1886, the old inn predates the establishment of the first Port Aransas post office. The inn took its name, in fact, from not only the fish that attracted so many anglers to its doors but also from Port Aransas's earlier name: Tarpon, Texas. Some accounts state that Roosevelt actually stayed in the hotel during his 1937 visit, but no records can be found to confirm the claim. It is known for certain, however, that the famous California evangelist Aimee Semple McPherson was a guest at the inn, as was the famed animal trainer Clyde Beatty. With Beatty during his stay were Lucky and Reba, two of his circus-act lions, and their two small cubs.

The pursuit of tarpon and the casual way of life for which Port Aransas was already famous came to an immediate halt on December 7, 1941. The beginning of World War II gave rise at once to rumors of German U-boat activity in the Gulf of Mexico. The rumors were confirmed when the German submarines began taking a deadly toll on Allied ships carrying petroleum products from Corpus Christi and Houston's refineries across the gulf. To provide a network of reconnaissance patrols on the gulf coast, the U.S. Coast Guard recruited many fishing guides in Port Aransas to serve as volunteer lookouts on the water. Some craft were actually commandeered by the Coast Guard to establish a more military-like fleet of patrol boats.

The Coast Guard was familiar with Port Aransas, and in some ways the village had actually developed around the service's duty station, established there on June 18, 1878. The State of Texas purchased the one-and-a-half-acre plot for the Coast Guard's "lifesaving station" for $750. The modern-day station, as well as the one in use during World War II, is still located on the original site. The property is directly across the street from the Tarpon Inn, built nine years after the first station. With the Coast Guard and its fleet of gulf-watching small craft, the citizens were relatively confident they were making a difference during World War II, particularly since so many of the town's young men had already volunteered to serve in the nation's armed forces.

When the war was not quite eight weeks under way, an event occurred in the Gulf of Mexico that transformed the lazy fishing resort of Port Aransas into a small-scale military town in short order. On January 28, 1942, a U.S. Navy patrol aircraft reported sighting what appeared to be a German U-boat cruising on the surface of the gulf a short distance off the entrance to Aransas Pass. The result of that sighting galvanized military authorities into a rapid reaction. The sheer prospect of the havoc that the torpedoes and even the deck guns of an enemy submarine could bring to bear on the tank farms and refineries along the inland waterways and at Corpus Christi caused the War Department to act with remarkable speed, even by wartime reckoning.

Although the initial sighting was never confirmed, the army immediately decided to send a coast artillery battery to Port Aransas without delay. On the very afternoon of the navy aircraft's reported submarine sighting, the commanding officer at Third Army headquarters, at San Antonio's Fort Sam Houston, ordered the only two available weapons at his disposal to be immediately transported to Port Aransas, some 150 miles to the south. The guns, 105 mm howitzers, arrived at the mouth of Aransas Pass within hours of leaving Fort Sam. By 6:30 that evening, the entire region had been placed under a mandatory blackout order, with roads closed to all except military vehicles. The two weapons that arrived at Port Aransas were not designed to function as coastal defense artillery but rather as field pieces with the limited capability of firing at relatively fixed targets on the battlefield. As such, they were unlikely to be of any significant worth in striking a distant moving target traveling over water at a fairly impressive speed. Inadequate though the hastily dispatched weapons were, they were all the Third Army could provide on such short notice. More important, they arrived quickly at Port Aransas, where almost any kind of weapon might be urgently needed to at least deter the progress of the reported enemy submarine.

After reaching Port Aransas from the mainland on a commandeered ferryboat at the end of the overland trip from San Antonio, the army convoy turned left at the ferry landing, drove past the darkened Tarpon Inn, and made its way onto the beach. The artillerymen quickly set up their two weapons next to the south jetty at the entrance to Aransas Pass. Once they had loaded the guns, the soldiers set up their tents on the sand and spent much of the cold January night peering out toward the pitch-black sea, waiting for a submarine to reappear. Having no field searchlights to train on any incoming U-boat, the weary soldiers could likely not have seen the craft had it somehow managed to creep silently up the narrow waterway immediately in front of their hastily erected gun emplacements. The field artillery unit from Fort Sam remained camped on the beach for nearly two months with their all-but-useless 105s pointing out to sea, waiting in vain for something resembling a German submarine to suddenly rise up out of the waters. The gun crews did reportedly fire a few practice volleys seaward, if only to see how far the projectiles could travel before creating a small geyser of water out in the gulf. The howitzers stayed on the beach until April 11, 1942, when Battery E of the 50th Coast Artillery Regiment arrived to assume responsibility for the defense of Aransas Pass. The two guns the new unit brought were 155 mm artillery pieces widely used as coastal defense weapons by many other countries. They could fire a six-inch shell up to ten miles and could rotate rapidly over a fixed track to keep firing at a target without being manually hoisted and moved, as had been the case with the departed 105s.

Upon arrival at the gulf shore, the unit's commander ordered that the big guns be transported up into the high dunes that lay approximately a half mile off the beach. Still close enough to the jetty mouth to be effective should an enemy sub manage to enter the pass, the elevated gun position greatly increased the weapons' chance of striking a craft operating on the surface even several miles out at sea. To stabilize the guns in the sandy dunes, two circular concrete pads had to be poured. Embedded in each pad was a round metal track that would permit the guns to smoothly traverse while firing at a moving target. As the concrete pads were under construction, the heavy weapons were temporarily mounted on tall wooden platforms close to where the field artillery pieces had originally stood on the soft sand next to the jetty.

Military officials halted construction on the new gun emplacements in late August of 1942 when a major hurricane made its way toward Port Aransas. The complete battery, including the guns themselves, were hurriedly pulled from the beach and transported to safety off storm-vulnerable Mustang Island. Because of the immensity of the storm, the army determined to leave the approach to the pass virtually unguarded until the hurricane season ended, usually in late November. The 155s were actually returned before then but remained temporarily positioned on the beach without the ability to traverse effectively should the need arise. Another battery, part of the 20th Coast Artillery Regiment, soon replaced the original unit. The dune-top emplacement was eventually completed and augmented by a string of powerful searchlights designed to illuminate any enemy craft that might dare approach the mouth of the pass.

Totally completed only after the threat of yet another hurricane subsided, the emplacement featured the two big guns, each mounted on a nearly thirty-nine-foot-diameter concrete pad. There were five powder magazines, a battery commander's observation post, and, at first, troop accommodations consisting of sixty six-man huts with latrines. A fourteen-hundred-square-foot recreation hall and a repair shed had also been constructed. Two additional sixty-inch searchlights on eight-foot towers were built directly on the beach in such a way as to brightly illuminate any vessel approaching the entrance to the pass. Although the big guns of the coast artillery were never to fire in anger, they often lobbed practice shells out to sea. Not only were the sounds of the guns nearly deafening in the town center, less than a mile away, but the vibrations created by the explosions also proved disturbing, particularly at night.

Social vibrations as well as those caused by artillery echoed through Port Aransas during the more than two-year period the gunners and their support troops were in the dunes. With the town's population variously reported as being between two hundred and five hundred when the war started, it is safe to assume

The Gulf Coast dunes at Port Aransas conceal the remains of a World War II coast artillery outpost created to guard the ship channel against Nazi U-boat incursions. ***The Alexander Collection; photo by Jordan Alexander Leggett.***

the permanent population declined as men left to join the armed services. With the arrival of up to 360 officers and men to operate the shore battery, it is possible that at times the number of people in uniform outnumbered the town's civilian population. The arrival of the newcomers created a flurry of social activity not unlike that which occurred in other suddenly military towns and cities. While the ratio of lonely soldiers to available females could have only been extremely high, no serious repercussions were recorded beyond the customary—usually alcohol-related—minor incidents. The navy also came to the town early in the war to add to the social mix. It maintained a control post at the pass that inspected any suspicious vessels arriving from the gulf.

In July 1944, the War Department determined no enemy activity was likely to take place in the waters off the jetties at Port Aransas. Indeed, an examination of German naval records after the war showed that in fact no U-boat had ever operated anywhere near the location of the original January 1942 sighting. Perhaps the entire big-gun battery on the shore had been unnecessary after all, or maybe general knowledge that the guns were up there in the dunes kept the Germans well out to sea and safely out of range. The truth will likely never be known.

What is known is that little remains of the World War II gun emplacement. All of the wooden quarters and command buildings have long since been dismantled. The large concrete pads remain, however, with their mobility tracks still in place. The steep trail that leads up to the site once had signs posted warning of snakes. Those signs are no longer present, suggesting the reptiles have perhaps somehow been persuaded to leave the area now that plans are being discussed to make the old emplacements something of a visitor destination.

An excellent model of how the battery looked during the war can be found at the Port Aransas Museum. The model depicts the gun mounts and how the whole site appeared during the years of futile operation in the dunes. As no photographs of the actual installation are known to exist due to the army's strict wartime rules, which prohibited any camera-toting civilians from walking around any of its sites, the museum's model is the only known, fully dimensional illustration of the Port Aransas gun emplacement in World War II.

LOCATION: Port Aransas on the Gulf Coast near the south jetty of Aransas Pass and the University of Texas Marine Science Center.

ACCESS: Via the sand dune off the Cotter Avenue beach access road and open to the public. The Port Aransas Museum has a model of the gun emplacement. Open Thursday through Sunday, 1:00 p.m. to 5:00 p.m.

SOURCES

Ford, J. G. *The Coast during War and Strife.* Port Aransas: Port Aransas Preservation and Historical Association, 2001.

Port Aransas Visitors' Guide. *Port Aransas South Jetty* (Winter) (2011–2012).
Texas Historical Commission. Vertical files, Austin.
U.S. Coast Guard Station, Port Aransas. Vertical files.
Writers' Round Table. *Port Aransas.* San Antonio: Naylor, 1950.

23 ATLAS ICBMS 1961–1965

Today's airmen are much like the army troopers of the West Texas frontier: The main ingredients are still courage, dedication, patriotism, and strong fiber, no matter how much the weapons have changed. — Texas Gov. John Connally, speaking at Dyess Air Force Base, February 1964

In the summer of 2013, a group of individuals gathered near the town of Lawn, in Taylor County, to learn the fundamentals of oral history as part of a workshop sponsored by the Texas Historical Commission (THC). The gathering itself was not unusual, although it was the first under a new initiative by the state agency designed to promote the preservation of memories from the Cold War era. Indeed, the THC had in the previous nine years conducted an extensive series of similarly focused military oral history workshops all across the state as part of a special Texas in World War II initiative. What was unique about the Lawn workshop, however, was its location—several feet underground in the former launch control center of what had been, in the 1960s, an armed and active Atlas Intercontinental Ballistic Missile (ICBM) facility. Sites such as the one near Lawn were once at the forefront of a national military policy known unofficially as massive retaliation. In effect, the ICBMs were designed to provide a swift, accurate, and overwhelmingly powerful response to any threat from an enemy nation, most likely the Soviet Union. Such was the intense nature of superpower angst between the East and the West in the second decade following World War II. In effect, the true outcome of that war remained somewhat uncertain as nations that had previously united against common enemies now found themselves vying with the highest of stakes to determine their own perceptions of security and peace.

In 2014, when the Texas Historical Commission initiated a series of oral-history workshops for its Cold War in Texas initiative, it appropriately chose to conduct one of the first ones underground in the launch control center of the former Atlas ICBM site near Lawn. *Courtesy of the Texas Historical Commission.*

While some might argue that the roots of the Cold War reached back into the era of international colonialism, they became most clearly defined in 1945, toward the end of World War II, as the leaders of the Union of Soviet Socialist Republics (USSR), Great Britain, and the United States gathered at the Yalta Conference and then the Potsdam Conference to determine the parameters of a postwar world. With liberation in Europe came new questions related to spheres of influence, and by the time the war against Japan formally came to a close in August 1945, the East-West rift that would mark the reality of a Cold War could neither be denied nor adequately addressed, given the immediate concerns of reconstruction in all of the participating nations. Exacerbating the rift was the manner in which the war ended, with the introduction of weapons whose scale of fury and devastation almost defied human comprehension. A key question by those who authorized their use was whether or not the dreadful new technology could be successfully contained for a common good. It was that uncertainty and uneasiness that marked the decades to come.

Slightly more than six months after the war ended, Britain's wartime prime minister, Winston Churchill, gave public voice to the emerging crisis when, escorted by Pres. Harry S. Truman, he delivered an important speech before a crowd gathered at Westminster College, a liberal arts school located in the small, central Missouri town of Fulton. Titled "The Sinews of Peace," the speech is now more commonly known as "The Iron Curtain Speech." In it, Churchill carefully set the contemporaneous context by noting, "I can therefore allow my mind, with the experience of a lifetime, to play over the problems which beset us on the morrow of our absolute victory in arms and to try to make sure with what strength I have that what has been gained with so much sacrifice and suffering shall be preserved for the future glory and safety of mankind." Conceding the world's restlessness over the vulnerability of atomic technology, he then spoke the line that came to identify the sharp edge of the emerging rift: "From Stettin in the Baltic to Trieste in the Atlantic, an iron curtain has descended across the Continent."

What ensued in relatively quick succession throughout the latter 1940s and the decades that followed were the landmark international crises that set the tone of the era, whereby the capitalist nations of the West sought to contain the spread of communism. In 1947, under the umbrella of the Truman Doctrine, which vowed support of the struggle for democracy wherever it occurred, the United States began to intervene in places such as Greece, Turkey, Berlin, and, perhaps most notably as an early hot spot of the Cold War, Korea. Soon after came a pattern of crises in places such as Vietnam, Hungary, and China and with issues such as the Red Scare, led by Joseph McCarthy, and the emergence of new international coalitions, including the North Atlantic Treaty Organization (NATO).

In the midst of the continuing Cold War came two announcements that threatened to lead to war or at the least to an imbalance in the prevailing postwar power structure. The first came in September 1949, when the USSR successfully exploded an atomic bomb, ending forever the hope of restricting the technology so long protected by the United States and its closest allies. Eight years later, on October 4, 1957, came news that truly devastated American leaders—the Soviets' launch of an orbital satellite known as Sputnik. While U.S. military and political leaders had long accepted the inevitability of both advancements, they occurred far earlier than anticipated. News of the Sputnik launch, in particular, proved difficult to accept because the event meant the Soviets had quickly developed rocket technology that could deliver payloads thousands of miles downrange, in effect directly threatening the United States. It also served to bolster earlier, internal U.S. military reports that showed that, although the nation was likely ahead in rocket development, it had significant "missile gaps." Sputnik thus served as an important wakeup call for a military program that had languished somewhat in recent years due to political and economic considerations, as well as a reliance on more conventional bomb-delivery systems. At the time, that meant a primary reliance on long-range bombers such as the B-52, a decision that meant, in the early years of the Eisenhower administration, a strategy that favored smaller atomic weapons, which could be delivered relatively easily, over larger weapons, which would necessitate sizable missiles. With the advent of the Soviet technology, the game plan changed, and the superpowers of the East and West focused on an exponential increase in a space race.

The international events unfolding in the late 1950s coincided with the successful testing and initial deployment of what would become, for a brief time at least, the workhorse of the United States' ICBM arsenal—the Atlas missile. Eisenhower's elevation of ICBM research to the highest level in 1955 greatly accelerated planning that had been ongoing, albeit inconsistently, since the 1940s. As Sheila McCarthy, Roy McCullough, and James Gorski (representing the Tri-Services Cultural Resources Research Center) noted in a 1996 Historic American Engineering Record (HAER) assessment of an Atlas F missile site near Winters, in Runnels County, "The establishment and rapid expansion of the United States ICBM force was the product of a complex, yet very rapid, program of research and development that witnessed a number of innovations in both the technological and the organizational spheres." These innovations included structural design, propellants, and guidance systems. Earlier, changes in command structure, reinforced over time, resulted in the placement of long-range missiles under the purview of the newly established U.S. Air Force (USAF) and its Strategic Air Command (SAC). As a result of these changes and the program's increased visibility and viability in overall strategic military planning, work on the Atlas system moved quickly toward approval and activation.

The first operational model of the Atlas missile was the D series, which represented steady, phased improvements through the years on earlier models. Following a number of test flights that began in 1957, SAC commander Gen. Thomas S. Power, who early in his career served as a flight instructor at Randolph Field outside San Antonio, called for deployment of an Atlas D, complete with a nuclear warhead in 1959. Thus, the first armed ICBM for the United States went online at Vandenberg Air Force Base in California. And, as McCarthy, McCullogh, and Gorski wrote, "Events proceeded quickly and by the summer of 1962, there were 11 operational missile sites and seven operational missile squadrons." Heightened research and development continued as well, resulting in important design modifications that led to the Atlas E and F series. The Atlas F missiles, representing the culmination of the program, deployed from hardened underground silos with massive, complex, high-capacity elevators that moved them into launch readiness above ground.

With the Atlas system approved for inclusion in the nation's military arsenal, the central issue became one of site locations. Key criteria for choosing the sites included the geology of soils and substrata, the location with regard to primary targets, and what the *Dallas Morning News* reported in a January 27, 1960, article as the ability to "withstand high 'overpressures' that might result from exploding enemy nuclear weapons." In effect, the sites would, by the nature of military action, become targets in the arms race. Also important as a consideration for the silo sites was accessibility to nearby SAC bases, which would serve as support, command, and supply centers for the isolated sites. Eventually, the air force selected six bases, each of which would be ringed by complexes of twelve silos. Those bases were Altus in Oklahoma; Dyess in Texas; Lincoln in Nebraska; Plattsburg in New York; Schilling in Kansas; and Walker in New Mexico. Planning for the complex centered on Dyess Air Force Base began in 1959. With feasibility and field testing completed by early the next year, and with command authorization initially attached to the 96th Strategic Aerospace Wing at Dyess, requests for proposals went out in April 1960. In May the contract was awarded to H. B. Zachary and Brown & Root. With the project on a fast track, work began on the first silo the following month. Within one year, construction on the entire complex was nearly 90 percent complete.

On November 9, 1962, the *Dallas Morning News* carried a front-page story headlined "ICBM Units Activated at Abilene," in which it noted, "The squadron (of rockets), comprising 12 Atlas 'F' missiles stored in underground silos, was declared operational by the Strategic Air Command." And, it added, reflecting the prevailing and still evolving national military policy of massive retaliation, "The missiles and approximately 1,500 Strategic Air Command bombers are considered by the Defense Department to give America a strategic force which could survive any attack and strike back with enough power to devastate the attacker." The system would, Secretary of Defense Robert S. McNamara concluded, adequately address the "Soviet rocket-rattlers."

The choice of Dyess Air Force Base seemed a logical one, given the site's military significance and demonstrated community support in prior decades. Established in 1942 during World War II, the base initially known as Tye Army Air Field provided vital support for U.S. Army operations at nearby Camp Barkeley. Deactivated along with the camp at the end of the war, however, and later utilized for municipal aviation purposes, the site again became a base in 1952 in association with military buildup during the Korean Conflict. Although work on enlarging the facility began soon after, it continued for several years. Formally rededicated as Abilene Air Force Base in 1956, the site began a new operational life as a SAC facility, utilizing at first the conventional bombers of the time; the first B-52s, which marked a new era in aviation preparedness and delivery, did not arrive until 1964. Late in 1956, the base assumed its present name, Dyess Air Force Base, in honor of William Edwin Dyess, a World War II hero who grew up at Albany in Shackelford County, thirty-five miles northeast of Abilene. A distinguished aviator and commander early in the conflict, he was among the U.S. forces captured at Bataan in the Philippines in April 1942. Subjected to the horrors of the infamous Death March and its aftermath, he eventually escaped his captors and returned to the United States, where his detailed reports of wartime atrocities by the Japanese served to embolden the nation's resolve for victory. Tragically, Lieutenant Colonel Dyess died in December 1943, when the P-38 Lightning he was piloting crashed at Burbank, California. He is buried in the city cemetery at Albany.

Activation of the 578th Strategic Missile Squadron (reconstitution of the 578th Bombardment Squadron, Heavy, of World War II) occurred at Dyess in July 1961, and official completion of the base missile complex came in November. The outlying ring of missile installations, which formed roughly a thirty-five-mile radius around Abilene, included silos near the communities of (clockwise from the northwest) Anson, Corinth, Abilene (near Lake Phantom Hill), Albany, Clyde, Denton Valley, Oplin, Lawn, Bradshaw, Winters, Shep, and Nolan. The 1996 HAER report provided the following detailed general description of the facilities:

> Each launch complex consisted of a Launch Facility, or silo, and a Launch Control Center (LCC). The standard plans called for a silo, constructed of reinforced concrete, varying from 2 feet 6 inches to 9 feet thick, 174 feet deep, and a diameter of 52 feet 2 inches. The silo housed 389 tons of structural steel, suspended from the silo walls from four points. This "crib" assembly housed the missile and supporting equipment, acting as a "shock absorber" in the event of a ground blast. Each silo included two diesel generators, air conditioning units, various mechanical and electrical systems, and a Propellant Loading System.
>
> The Launch Control Center was a two-story structure housing the necessary controls for missile monitoring and missile launch. Like the Launch Facility, the LCC was positioned within a suspended steel framework serving as a shock absorber in the

event of a ground blast. The LCC was an underground facility, constructed of reinforced concrete, located 6.5 feet below ground level.

An additional description of the Lawn facility specifically came from Larry Sanders of Abilene, who purchased the site in 1999 and has since been working toward its preservation, where practical, and its overall rehabilitation. In a December 2007 article in *Texas Co-Op Power,* author Staci Semrad describes a tour she took of the facility with Sanders:

> We descend another stairwell to the launch control center, then down one more flight to a short tunnel connecting the control center to the silo—the now hollow colossal former home of the missile.
>
> We step into a railed stairwell platform and into the darkness, where our voices and the sound of dripping water echo. Sanders points his flashlight to the opposite wall 52 feet away, then up toward the ceiling 45 feet above our heads.
>
> He then points down below us where the stairwell descends 50 feet to a yellow raft floating on the surface of water 90 feet deep.

Then, as Semrad notes, the conversation turned to the graffiti that is prevalent on the silo walls, indications of times when the site was not secured from intruders. "[Sanders] points his flashlight up toward the ceiling to the barren wall, where 75 feet above the water, 'BUD' is painted in red letters. The sight of it with nothing nearby to climb on is chilling. I ask how Bud got up there. 'I don't know and don't know if he ever made it down safely,' Sanders says, pointing back toward the water."

Private ownership of such Atlas sites by Sanders and others is an indication that the program was short lived. In reality, around Dyess at least, the site remained fully operational for less than three years. They were pivotal years in U.S.-Soviet relations, however, for they spanned the Cuban missile crisis of 1963, when all of the Atlas squadrons went on full alert. Despite all of the strategic planning, monumental engineering, governmental funding, technological development, and command realignment it influenced, though, the Atlas missiles were deemed obsolete by 1964 and thus phased out and replaced by the Minuteman and Titan II systems. The air force deactivated the 578th Strategic Missile Squadron in March 1965. In the years that followed, the government declared the various sites across the nation as surplus and began the lengthy process of either razing them or transferring ownership to private or public entities.

As the 2013 oral history workshop and other gatherings at the Lawn facility demonstrated, for the general public, the Atlas sites are still a curiosity. Even though Sanders and other site owners work to rehabilitate the facilities in the hope that they may someday be opened to the public as monumental artifacts of the Cold War era, many of the sites have also been dismantled, filled in, and covered over. Although the Atlas rocket story was a brief one in U.S. military history, lasting nationally only from 1959 to 1965, it had much larger implications. It served, for example, as a technological bridge in the rapid advancement of weapon systems following World War II and, as such, influenced significant experiential planning at a crucial point in the Cold War. It also, many would argue, provided critical backup for U.S. policies of the time, perhaps keeping the East-West tensions from escalating into another global war.

LOCATION: As the sites are located on private property and thus restricted, no specific directions can be provided.

ACCESS: The remaining former Atlas sites in the Dyess complex are in private ownership (or, in the case of the one at Anson, owned by the school district), so access is limited.

SOURCES

Anderson, Marline. "Dyess, William Edwin." In *The New Handbook of Texas,* ed. Ron Tyler. Austin: Texas State Historical Association, 1996, vol. 2, 747.

Dallas Morning News, January 27, 1960; November 9, 1962.

Leatherwood, Art. "Dyess Air Force Base." In *The New Handbook of Texas,* ed. Ron Tyler. Austin: Texas State Historical Association, 1996, vol. 2, 747.

McCarthy, Sheila, Roy McCullogh, and James Gorski. "Historic American Engineering Record, Dyess Air Force Base, Atlas F Missile Site S-8, HAER No. TX-25." U.S. Army Construction Engineering Research Laboratories. Champaign, IL: Tri-Services Cultural Resources Research Center, 1996.

Sanders, Larry. Email correspondence with Dan K. Utley, October 2013.

Semrad, Staci. "Little Nuclear House on the Prairie." *Texas Co-Op Power* (December 2007). http://www.texascooppower.com/texas-stories/people/little-nuclear-house-on-the-prairie, accessed October 2013.

Spires, David N. *On Alert: An Operational History of the United States Air Force Intercontinental Ballistic Missile Program, 1945–2011.* Colorado Springs: United States Air Force, Air Force Space Command, 2012.

Texas Historical Commission. Marker files for Shackelford County.

"Winston Churchill's Iron Curtain Speech." About.com, accessed October 2013.

24 NAVAL STATION INGLESIDE (HOMEPORT) 1985–2010

I just hope this base is not relegated to the archaeologists before its time. — *County Judge Robert Barnes, Nueces County, Texas, September 30, 1988*

In July 1985, the secretary of the navy made an official announcement that brought instant joy to Corpus Christi and other cities on the Texas Coastal Bend. After months of behind-the-scenes lobbying and ill-disguised demonstrations of sheer political pressure, the navy announced it would soon begin construction of a major facility on Corpus Christi Bay at Ingleside. The euphoria created by the announcement was destined to be surpassed only by the heartbreak it would eventually generate. The facility would be one of eight so-called Homeports, each designed to host battleship task forces capable of swinging swiftly into action against any enemy naval aggression that might occur in the Gulf of Mexico. With more than 50 percent of the United States' oil and gas traveling through the Gulf, the presence of a quick-reaction naval force in the vicinity made the navy's announcement seem not only militarily sound but also economically fortuitous. Throughout 1984 and much of 1985, the economy of South Texas had been in the doldrums. Low prices for its petroleum products had combined with the loss of many manufacturing jobs to create a weak and still faltering monetary situation. Texas senators Phil Gramm and Lloyd Bentsen joined other members of the state's legislative delegation in Washington, DC, in pressuring Defense Department officials to provide a military fiscal solution to their state's economic woes. The result was the Homeport. The Homeport proposal seemed at the outset to be the key to ending the Coastal Bend's recession crisis. Specifically, the navy's plan called for a six-ship task force permanently berthed at a facility to be built at Ingleside, some ten miles east of downtown Corpus Christi. The force would consist of a battleship, a training aircraft carrier, a cruiser, a destroyer, and two minesweepers, with the battleship as the primary element.

Chosen to lead the task force was the newly refitted USS *Wisconsin* (BB-64) and sister ship of the more famous USS *Missouri* (BB-63), both Iowa-class battleships. The *Wisconsin,* though less well known, possessed an illustrious combat record that included service in both World War II and the Korean Conflict. Thoroughly reconditioned at a cost of $450 million long after initially being decommissioned, the forty-two-year-old battleship seemed well suited to become the lead ship at what was to be the Homeport at Naval Station Ingleside. Joining her on the Texas Gulf Coast would be the USS *Lexington* (CV-16), known to its enemies as the "Blue Ghost" because of its lack of camouflage. The *Lexington* also had an illustrious history as a U.S. fighting ship of the line but had recently been used as a training craft for fledgling navy pilots at Pensacola, Florida.

A short time after the Homeport announcement, the U.S. Navy conducted an environmental-impact analysis to determine what the coming of the task force and the construction of its new base would mean to both the social and the natural environment of the Coastal Bend. The finished document, titled "The US Navy Gulf Coast Strategic Homeporting Draft Environmental Impact Statement," dated August 1986, was an impressive 788-page book that included thirty pages of notes and bibliography. The study was just short of being excessively comprehensive, suggesting that navy researchers perhaps wanted to ensure that no latter-day environmental or social activists could successfully fault the U.S. Navy for failing to analyze every facet of building a naval facility and operating ships from it. For example, ornithologists studied every species of bird known to dwell within a hundred-mile radius of the proposed naval station to determine how each might react to the noise and bright nighttime lights that would be present. Roadrunners, owls, common moorhens, and pied-billed grebes were among those observed, along with robins, sparrows, and thrushes. Researchers thoroughly observed and recorded their nesting and feeding habits.

Teams of researchers also studied local animals and plants, with the impact on sport fish and wildlife of major concern. They considered potential effects on alligators, snakes, and even the amount of plankton found in Gulf waters, along with the relative seasonal salinity of those waters and the shifting proclivities of the silt and sand that lay beneath the surface and along the shore. They analyzed the potential for disastrous effect on regional vegetation, duly recorded the average weight of every species of fish known to swim in the Gulf, and entered the data in the extensive document. Any adverse conditions that might accrue to the birds, snakes, and grass completed one lengthy section of the book, while another measured the potential social influence of the new base and its future inhabitants on the Gulf-side communities. Water and air pollution, as well as tolerance to increased noise levels, were weighed along with potential crime statistics, the intensity of existing court activity, vehicular traffic patterns, the number of schools and hospitals, and, in general, the civilian population's overall likely reception of thousands of military personnel and their families.

While all of the in-depth reporting about fish, deer, birds, seashells, and human beings themselves might have been at least mildly interesting to those who cared to plow through the thick book, one lengthy section in particular caught the eye of regional community leaders and ignited their passion for the coming of the U.S. Navy to Corpus Christi Bay. That, of course, was all of the economic data the researchers had so painstakingly amassed. Even if economic conditions along the Coastal Bend had already been stellar, the navy's forecast for a future economic boom would have been breathtaking. To the chambers of commerce, the bankers, the politicians, and the countless unemployed workers in the area, the navy's numbers were of such positive magnitude that some publically likened the project to the coming of a deluge of rain after years of drought.

The cost to build the naval base was estimated to be in excess of $220 million and the resulting annual payroll projected to be $170 million. The amount of retail purchases made by navy personnel and their dependents would likely exceed $160 million annually. Local tax coffers would grow by an additional $4 million each year, and the state would realize another $4 million in tax revenue. Nearly nine thousand new and permanent jobs would be created, resulting in the need for an estimated four thousand new homes along the Gulf.

In order to demonstrate their full appreciation to the navy for such economic redevelopment that could soon come their way, the state and local governments made financial pledges in support of the project. The State of Texas appropriated $25 million toward the construction costs directly plus an additional $122 million for roads, parks, schools, and expanded law-enforcement services. Nueces County, the principal local beneficiary, approved the funding of $25 million in construction costs. The City of Corpus Christi pledged another $50 million.

The navy estimated that, once completed, the Homeport would be run by a total of forty-eight-hundred military personnel supported by four hundred civilian employees, with seven thousand dependents joining them when they first arrived in the vicinity. The few downsides of the new base at first received scant attention in the local media. Blinded by the overwhelmingly positive economic news, any mention of increased utility demands and likely new taxes required to expand police and fire departments was relegated to casual conversation at various chamber of commerce and city council meetings. The possibility of coastline erosion, the discharge of gray water into the gulf, air and noise pollution, and other environmental concerns so forthrightly mentioned in the navy's impact study paled in comparison to the prospect of a booming real-estate market and profitable retail activity. If the projected 37,300 daily automobile trips off the base and into the communities prompted any official word of warning, no record of it is to be found.

As might be expected, the Homeport announcement was received with excitement and optimism all along the Coastal Bend. Real-estate agents in Ingleside predicted that residential property values would at least double within a few weeks' time. Local businesses saluted the news by placing American flags in front of their buildings, and patrons of the town's many bars and cocktail lounges toasted the prospect of countless new jobs and new bar customers. One such customer predicted that when the navy men came, "Everybody will lock their daughters up." The owner of a home near the announced site, however, sounded a rare note of displeasure. "I like the water," he said. "I'd rather go out and see the natural habitat than see a big ol' gray navy ship in my front yard."

In nearby Corpus Christi, by far the largest city in the region, plans were put in place to build a USO facility to entertain off-duty sailors. To allay fears about the possibility of misbehavior on the part of the navy men, the chamber of commerce president pointed out that the modern-day U.S. Navy was an all-volunteer force made up of personnel planning on making careers out of their service and therefore not likely to imperil their future by misconduct.

A Homeport steering committee was formed to represent the interests of the various communities most likely to be affected by the new facility. The members were mayors of regional cities such as Corpus Christi, Rockport, Aransas Pass, and Ingleside, as well as commissioners of Nueces, San Patricio, and Aransas counties. Officials hired a coordinator to oversee the public relations and other cooperative activities involved in the project. The steering committee office published a monthly newsletter, providing all of the interested parties with a current overview of the project, as well as navy-supplied information and news about the personnel who would occupy the base upon its completion.

A shadow of doubt fell over the Homeport's future in March 1986 when a number of U.S. congresspersons suggested that the actual cost of the project would far exceed the navy's initial estimate. When Pres. Ronald Reagan signed a $296 billion Defense Authorization Bill in early 1987, however, it included funds for the project. Senator Phil Gramm, the major sponsor for the state's bid to get the Homeport, welcomed the news of presidential approval by declaring that the last major obstacle had thus been cleared. Arguments on the floor of the House of Representatives had earlier raised questions about the need for the facility, and other legislation was proposed to either eliminate the Homeport project altogether or at least reduce the amount of money to be spent on its construction. The Texas delegation in Congress successfully battled against any such action, and with President Reagan's signature on the Defense Funding Bill, Senator Gramm had every reason to be elated.

Back on the Texas Coast, ancillary funding issues began to temper the initial exuberant reaction to the Homeport news. Ingleside School District officials studied the number of school-age children projected to accompany their parents to the town's navy base. The nearly two thousand new students forecast to be flooding the existing classrooms made it essential that additional facilities be built at once. The school board estimated the cost of the expansion at three to four million dollars, not including the money required to hire new teachers and buy new school buses. It also believed that all of the necessary funding to expand the system's facilities would be obtained from the navy itself or through a federal grant. Only as a last resort, they announced, would local school taxes be increased.

A setback to the overall project took place in early January 1986, when the U.S. Navy announced its rejection of all initial sealed bids received from contractors interested in getting the construction contract. One firm, obviously confident that it had submitted the lowest bid, had already established a construction headquarters on the site. Although the firm argued with understandable conviction that the delay caused by the rejection of all bids would postpone the announced groundbreaking event in February, Senator Gramm reiterated his belief that he and other elected officials would be in Ingleside on the date as previously announced to break ground for the Homeport facility.

On February 20, 1988, Senator Gramm kept his promise. Along with fellow Senator Lloyd Bentsen and regional officials, Gramm used a ceremonial steel shovel to break the ground upon which the Homeport would be constructed. To the dismay of many Coastal Bend residents, the navy had ordered that only 2,250 people would be allowed access to the groundbreaking ceremony, but televised broadcasts carried images of the event throughout the region, as well as in Houston and San Antonio.

Newspaper headlines proclaimed, "We are the happiest community in the USA," and photos featured the senators, the secretary of the navy, and a star-filled galaxy of admirals filling their shiny shovels with the gritty sand on the site. Although they had been denied admission to the ceremony itself, thousands of South Texans lined the south bank of the jetty at Port Aransas to watch the USS *Lexington,* one of the future star occupants of the Homeport, make its way slowly up the channel from the Gulf and across Corpus Christi Bay to dock near the groundbreaking event. Nearly one thousand feet in length, the veteran World War II ship was a majestic sight as it made its way across the bay. Texas governor Bill Clements joined Senator Gramm on board the famed carrier before they both flew by helicopter to join the other dignitaries at the ceremony at Ingleside.

It had taken three years for the Homeport project to grow from possibility to the first ceremonial turning of the earth at the site. The project withstood congressional bickering and severe criticism from various governmental agencies to advance to the memorable late-February event. Another six months were to elapse, however, before full-scale construction could actually begin.

As the excitement of the groundbreaking ceremony and the visit of the *Lexington* faded away, news of the formal recommissioning of the USS *Wisconsin,* principal future tenant of the Homeport, soon followed. After a thirty-year hibernation in "mothballs," the forty-two-year-old battleship was commissioned back into active service by John Tower, the former U.S. senator from Texas who had taken a key role in gaining approval for the Homeport's location.

Although various contract disputes and continuing congressional expressions of concern over the whole Homeport concept delayed construction, the first phase of work on the facility was 50 percent complete within a year of breaking ground. With the *Wisconsin* and the *Lexington* scheduled to permanently drop anchor at their new Texas berths in 1991, construction crews found it necessary to work overtime to keep pace with contractors' performance commitments. As work progressed, enthusiasm throughout the region increased daily. A visitor to any of the towns soon to be economically revitalized by the coming of the ships could only be caught up in the Homeport frenzy. Banners welcoming one and all to "Homeport, USA" spanned city streets in Aransas Pass, Port-

During the Homeport's early construction period, many businesses in the local communities made the future facility's name part of their own. Thirty years later, this Aransas Pass firm seems to be the only one still touting the Homeport name. *The Alexander Collection.*

land, and Ingleside proper. Signs touting the services of the Homeport Realty Company, the Homeport Laundry and Dry Cleaning service, and the Homeport Automobile Company served as constant harbingers of the great event soon to take place on the Gulf Coast.

As a dramatic prelude to that occasion, a five-day visit to Corpus Christi by the USS *Wisconsin* in late August 1989 fueled even more enthusiasm. The nearly nine-hundred-foot-long battleship, with its crew of sixteen hundred officers and sailors, docked at the Sun Marine Terminal in the port of Corpus Christi at 8:30 in the morning. Despite the relatively early hour, The *Wisconsin* was greeted by a huge crowd of admirers and an official welcoming party that included the ubiquitous Senator Gramm and the secretary of the navy. After the reception ceremonies, the crew received the liberty to leave the ship and explore their future home. Navy and civilian coordinators organized softball, golf, and volleyball tournaments, with a Tex-Mex breakfast served on Saturday and a party that evening. The visiting sailors, if not too fatigued by the sporting and dining activities, were likely pleased that the party also included a dance featuring local young ladies who had eagerly volunteered to participate. During the ship's stay, the public was invited to inspect the completely reconditioned vessel and to watch a "dry-fire" demonstration of its massive sixteen-inch guns and Cruise missiles. As the *Wisconsin* sailed away, thousands once again took to the Aransas ship channel banks to watch it sail out into the gulf. No one, either on the shore, in uniform on the ship, or at Ingleside working to finish the *Wisconsin*'s projected new home, would have dared to imagine that the ship was never to return.

By mid-November 1989, the overall building of the Homeport facility was reported to be more than 40 percent complete. Work on the wharf and pier neared 70 percent completion with construction still continuing on an expedited schedule. In Washington, at the same time, rumblings about a pending drastic reduction in military construction began circulating through House and Senate cloakrooms. Ironically, it was Senator Gramm's own deficit-reduction bill that had put a searching spotlight on military funding. In late January 1990, the rumblings became the first in a series of economic earthquakes that would eventually prove disastrous to the Homeport. Secretary of Defense Richard Cheney announced a three-month freeze on the awarding of all new military contracts. Construction already under way would be permitted to continue, but no new contracts could be signed. This moratorium meant that Ingleside's Homeport would at least temporarily come to a halt with signed contracts worth $120 million and with work in progress, but the moratorium froze seven other such contracts totaling just over $100 million.

The Pentagon's sudden reticence to build more military facilities stemmed directly from the obvious reduction in national security concerns following the collapse of the United States' long-threatening enemy, the Soviet Union. The immediate by-product of that collapse was a political outcry in the U.S. Congress to halt all military expansion as a prelude to a major reduction in force throughout the nation's uniformed services. In putting the best possible light on the moratorium and its obvious impact on the Homeport, local politicians voiced their opinions that the facility's future remained bright. As if to shore up regional morale, the navy announced that the USS *Lexington* would be revisiting the Corpus Christi area for four days in late April 1990. On March 2, 1990, the secretary of the navy reassured Senator Bentsen that, despite the moratorium, the service still planned to berth both the *Wisconsin* and the *Lexington* at Ingleside. Apparently only partially convinced of the navy's true intentions, the senator reported to the media that the news was "at least comforting."

By the time the moratorium on new contracts was set to expire, the word from Washington concerning the Homeport had turned even darker. The Navy Department announced that the Homeport was now in fact on its list of possible base closures. Congressional hearings posed the logical question of why long-established military bases were slated to be closed while new ones, specifically the Homeport at Ingleside, were being allowed to resume construction. When the moratorium was extended for another six-month period, even those local elected officials known for perpetually wearing rose-colored economic glasses began to speak of the impending catastrophe likely to befall their pet project. Even as the Defense Department continued to send out conflicting reports on the status of the Homeport in mid-1990, developers previously intent on eventually bringing new large-scale civilian projects to the region put a moratorium of their own on any such plans. However, the work already contracted on the Homeport continued without any letup. The project's June 1990 newsletter proudly proclaimed that the entire project was 77 percent complete. By the end of the year, the article boastfully predicted, the Homeport would be 85 percent finished, or in other words, only 15 percent away from being ready to receive its ships. In fact, the navy could actually bring its big vessels into the facility's berths any time it wished to do so, according to the newsletter. The *Lexington* had been briefly moored there a month earlier.

As Defense Department and congressional support for the project waned, protesters began picketing at the main gate, bearing signs reading "No Homeport." Letters to the editors of local newspapers deemed the project to be wasteful and politically motivated. Some even suggested it be given "Homepork" as a new name. Despite all of the negative news, the navy appointed one of its senior officers to be the base's first commander. His initial media interview was laced with barely concealed concern for the future of his new command. The recent announcement by his superior officers that the *Lexington* was to be decommissioned at once and obviously no longer destined to operate out of the Homeport did little to permit the commander to be overly optimistic.

By the end of 1990, just a month after its first commander arrived, all work at the facility came to a halt. Only eighty people were employed in various functions on the project, by then 85 percent complete. Of these, twenty-one were military personnel and the balance civil-service employees. The Homeport, once so full of promise and excitement, had become a ghost base virtually overnight without ever having been officially activated.

In retrospect, historians have pondered how and why the Homeport concept ever came about. It was clear to most military analysts that the navy's "Day of the Battleship" had come to a fiery death at Pearl Harbor on December 7, 1941. No less a naval authority than Fleet Admiral Chester W. Nimitz had often claimed the navy's future lay with aircraft carriers rather than early twentieth-century battlewagons. The creation of a new strategic naval concept based upon decentralized berthing locations for already antiquated nautical weapons of war is difficult to understand.

Even before the collapse of the Soviet Union, prominent federal government authorities began to openly question the wisdom of the Homeport concept, particularly the one planned for Ingleside. Senator John Glenn, a man with considerable experience looking down from space on the North American continent, observed that the navy would be doing the Soviets a great favor by putting a large and expensive facility in Corpus Christi Bay. The simple maneuver of blocking the ship channel at Port Aransas would, the senator noted, "instantly render the entire Ingleside fleet landlocked and ineffective."

After the end of the Homeport dream, the navy did find a short-lived use for the all but completed facility. Ten of the navy's twelve mine-hunter ships operated out of Ingleside until 2005. When the service's interest in the small boats diminished and then disappeared, what had become officially known as Naval Station Ingleside permanently closed. The estimated economic loss to the region was reported to include seven thousand jobs and at least $400 million in trade, salaries, and taxes. The real losers were American taxpayers, as well as the businesses and individuals that had staked their hopes for the future on a concept that was at best antiquated, if not foolish.

Although the Homeport itself proved to have no future, the two big navy ships slated to constitute the Coastal Bend Task Force survived the debacle and escaped the cutting torches of salvage crews. Perhaps in something akin to reconciliation, the USS *Lexington* was given to the City of Corpus Christi to be permanently docked on the north shore of the bay. There, a privately endowed "Blue Ghost" Naval Museum annually attracts large numbers of visitors eager to explore the legendary vintage carrier.

The USS *Wisconsin* remained on active duty until 1992 and served in the Persian Gulf during Operation Desert Storm. Technological advances soon made even the refitted battleship obsolete, and it was once again relegated to the mothball fleet. In 2009, the navy transferred ownership of the vessel, clearing the way for its use as a naval museum similar to the final and successful usage of the *Lexington* at Corpus Christi.

There is no museum in Ingleside to tell the troubled story of the Homeport, which cost nearly $200 million to build but was never home to a single large navy ship. The whole subject is still too sensitive for many local residents to discuss without angrily wondering just how it all had ended so badly.

LOCATION: Ingleside, on Corpus Christi Bay, northeast of Corpus Christi.

ACCESS: Privately owned, no public access. Vestiges of the base can be seen by boat in bay waters. The former main gate is operated by an armed guard.

SOURCES

Corpus Christi Caller-Times, April 12, 1985; April 19, 1985; July 5, 1985; February 6, 1986; March 28, 1987; May 2, 1987; June

24, 1987; October 16, 1987; January 6, 1988; February 6, 1988; February 13, 1988; February 20, 1988; February 21, 1988; September 11, 1988; October 23, 1988; May 18, 1989; August 31, 1989; November 10, 1989; January 25, 1990; March 8, 1990; April 25, 1990; June 15, 1990; September 30, 1990; May 13, 2005; June 1, 2006; July 7, 2006; March 1, 2007; March 14, 2007; November 15, 2007; December 1, 2007; August 11, 2012.

"The Homeport Report." Corpus Christi: Homeport Steering Council, November 1989; February 1990; June 1990; October 1990; December 1990.

"US Navy Gulf Coast Strategic Homeporting Draft Environmental Impact Statement: Corpus Christi/Ingleside, Texas." Department of the Navy, Southern Division, Naval Facilities Engineering Command, 1986. Charleston, S.C.

EPILOGUE THE GOOD WITH THE BAD

Curtis Tunnell, the first state archeologist for Texas and later the longtime executive director of the Texas Historical Commission, traveled to all parts of the state during his celebrated career, giving preservation pep talks to a wide variety of groups. Most often he wrote his speeches well in advance, carefully tailoring them to specific audiences. Sometimes, however, his busy schedule precluded such preparation, and on those occasions he might rely on standard speeches that, when infused with some mention of local projects, worked every time. One he jokingly called "Bad News, Good News." It went basically as follows. Opening with an apology for starting with bad news, he would then cite a number of significant current issues across the state that represented what could be grouped together as failed efforts at preservation—the loss of a particular historic structure (a beloved schoolhouse, a stately home, or a church sanctuary, for example), the wanton vandalism of a rural cemetery, needlessly destroyed records, or insensitive development that encroached on or replaced historic, working-class neighborhoods. The closer he could bring those examples to the site of his speech, the better.

Then, when he sensed he had sufficiently made his point about the vulnerability of history, he would pivot and segue with comments that spoke of hope and not despair. "But, despite such recent developments," he might say, "I bring you good news today. All across this state, people like you are surveying historic districts, recording abandoned cemeteries, placing historical markers, participating in archeological projects, expanding museum collections, and listing sites in the National Register of Historic Places." His good news went on, using specific local examples as best he could, and he would eventually wrap up the talk by thanking those in attendance for their good efforts on behalf of the generations to come. It was always a powerful speech, inspiring those in the audience to do more—or at least to consider doing more—for the common good.

In that same vein, after acknowledging in the chapters of this book the loss, abandonment, or missed opportunities for preserving and interpreting key elements of Texas military history, this epilogue serves as a segue to the good news nonetheless inherent in these and similar stories. Across this state individuals such as Larry Sanders, Jonathan Gerland, Martha Hartzog, Maria Watson Pfeiffer, Glenn Williford, David Keller, Buddy Garza, and countless others are giving generously of their time and extraordinary talents to record, interpret, investigate, commemorate, protect, promote, and preserve the remaining vestiges of our collective military past. Some work on their own, but many also join with like-minded preservationists to form associations, county historical commissions, museums, youth organizations, tourism boards, and public-service groups that in turn educate the public about, as Tunnell clearly understood, the vulnerability of the past. Thanks to their tireless efforts, we have important new perspectives on sites that might otherwise go unnoticed or unappreciated.

Additionally, a number of publicly funded entities set the highest standards of preservation and interpretation in order to fill in historical gaps and, in the process, to serve as models of what can be done when people work together on a common goal. Texas has, for example, the National Park Service, which maintains the Fort Davis National Historic Site, one of the best preserved frontier forts in the country; the Texas Parks and Wildlife Department, which administers a number of unique military sites, including the USS *Texas* and Fort Richardson; and the Texas Historical Commission, overseer of properties such as Fort McKavett, whose cultural landscape retains much of its original integrity, and Sabine Pass, where the cultural horizon has long since disappeared beneath the waters of Sabine Lake. A number of agencies, though, also preserve the materials that help in the interpretation of sites. They include the General Land Office and its extensive archival collection of maps and land records, as well as the Texas State Library and Archives Commission, whose holdings contain diverse items such as battle flags and Confederate pension records. And all across the state are remarkable museums, some large in scope but most of more modest stature, that consistently present artifacts and stories for the exclusive purposes of educating those in the present about our collective past and preserving for those in the future the elements of our evolving heritage.

This is all good news that far outbalances the bad news we associate with lost history, yet much remains to be done. It is our hope that somewhere in the stories collected here will be a spark of recognition that might serve as inspiration for innovative preservation projects, new technological advancements in field investigations, or uniquely creative and analytical research so that the fine layers of similar stories will never fade completely. This is transitional work, easily evaluated by what one generation manages to pass along to the next. It is not the work of military historians or preservationists alone—it is an assignment open to all of us who value the story of our state's rich military past.

INDEX